This book is dedicated
to my wife Mary
and to my family

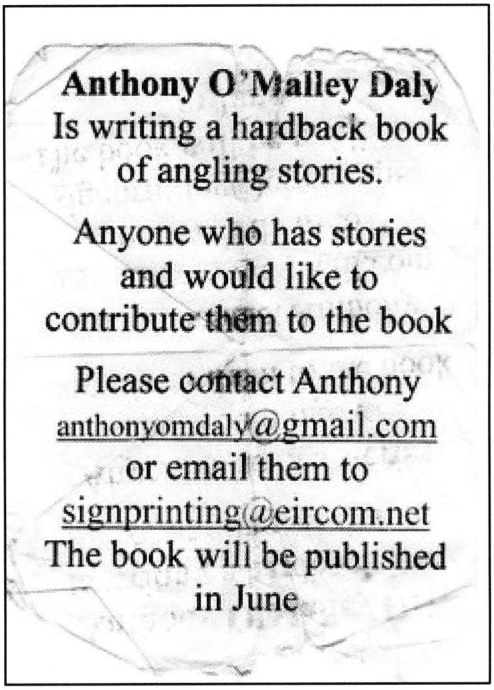

Anthony O'Malley Daly
Is writing a hardback book
of angling stories.

Anyone who has stories
and would like to
contribute them to the book

Please contact Anthony
anthonyomdaly@gmail.com
or email them to
signprinting@eircom.net
The book will be published
in June

Limited Edition

____

No: __________
of 1,000

In a car coming up from the bridge,
Paul Culkin opened the sun roof, stood up,
lifted his hands, and said,
"People of Ballyshannon, I love you!"

– for more on Paul Culkin, see Book Three

Trilogy

by

Anthony O'Malley Daly

Prologue: Mi Amigo
Book 1: My Life – My Way
Book 2: Sixty Years of Angling
Book 3: Injun Joe – Fishing Stories
Epilogue: My Life Today

All profits to be donated to:
The North West Parkinson's Association
The Asthma Society of Ireland

Trilogy

by Anthony O'Malley Daly

Printed by
Browne Printing Ltd.
Port Road
Letterkenny, Co Donegal

Development by
Diamond Sign & Print
Finner Business Park
Ballyshannon, Co Donegal

ISBN
978-0-9574085-0-0

Published by
Mi Amigo Publishing
"Inisfail"
College Street
Ballyshannon
Co Donegal, Ireland

Acknowledgements

I would like to thank the people who have helped me
turn my collections of photos, articles and reminiscences into this book:

Tom Sigafoos, Editing and Book Design
Tara Clancy, Layout
James McGrath, Diamond Sign & Print
John Cassidy, Diamond Sign & Print

With special thanks to the many friends and relatives who have contributed stories to
this book, including:

"Anonymous"
Albert Johnson
Ann McGowan
Austin O'Malley
Billy Grimes
Billy Johnston
Brian Crawford
Charlie O'Doherty
Cillian Meehan
Darren Rooney
Edward Hanna
Eugene Conway
Harry Lloyd
Hugo McGlynn
James G. Daly
Jim Mahon
John Hanna
John McGrath
John Meehan
John Sweeney
Mary B. McEnroy
Michael McGrath
Michael O'Brien
Molly Reynolds
Noel Carr
Paddy Clancy
Ruth Swan
Tara McCauley
Vincent O'Donnell

Prologue

<u>*Mi Amigo - My Friend - Mo Chara*</u>

Mi Amigo - My Friend - Mo Chara was an idea I had and still hold – that I could start a voluntary free organization to help the people of Ballyshannon, Donegal, the province of Ulster, and Ireland combat the various and several ills that have beset society today. Alongside my daughter Orla and my son Patrick in San Francisco, my foundation was given an International outlook.

Orla has an Irish aspect to the principles that I envisage, in that she has an easily recognisable communication with the Irish abroad through her Irish Castle gift shop in down-town Geary Street, San Francisco.

Patrick through his contacts in GAA, political and social connections is ideally situated to promote the goodwill and intentions that are *Mi Amigo - My Friend - Mo Chara.*

RULE: All members must do good deeds to people & animals
MOTTO: Be determined and considerate

Voluntary Free Organisation
Founded by Anthony O'Malley Daly 27th May 2009
'Inisfail' College St, Ballyshannon, Co. Donegal
Tel: (353) 087 0933471
Email: anthonyomdaly@gmail.com

Michael McLoone, Patron
Mi Amigo Charity

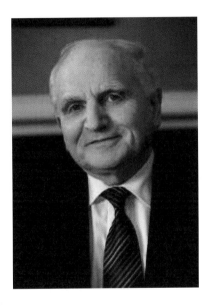

Michael McLoone from Ballyshannon, Patron of the *Mi Amigo* Charity, is a well-known person in the GAA circles. He represented his club, County and Province. He is ranked as one of the all-time greats.

In his career he served as Community Care Manager for the North Western Health Board. He moved to Dublin to become Chief Executive of the Beaumont Hospital, and then returned to Donegal to serve as Manager of the Donegal County Council.

No: _____

Name: _____

Tel No.: _____

Mi Amigo - My Friend - Mo Chara

Voluntary Free Organisation

Founded by: Anthony O'Malley Daly

'Inisfáil' College St, Ballyshannon, Co. Donegal.

27th May 2009

Rule: All members must do good deeds to people & animals.
Motto: Be determined and considerate.

Life

Intercede where truth is being drowned, Rescue the faith,
Pray to God, Even swear a prayer,
Impose good where evil is being promoted,
It is up to you.
Intervene in aid of the underdog and the battered minorities,
When the cause is right and just.
Impede gangsterism, racism, discrimination, bullying and zealots,
Even at the risk of your own comfort. Never look away.
Interfere always by thought, word, deed or omission,
When injustice is dulling the minds of many by false auras.
Lead from the front.
Inspire love of nation, flag and identity.
But, but, but, beware of patriotism,
Lest you lead others into rivers of blood.
Intend from now until your sojourn
down the many roads of your life is ended
To walk tall and stand firm.
Honour your family, respect yourself, enjoy your victories,
Accept your defeats with grace.
Know you have friends-
And when you fall flat, pick yourself up and get back into life.
I love you, you love me.

Anthony O'Malley Daly, Inisfáil, 27th May 2009 - "Mi Amigo"

PRESS RELEASE 2008

New Caring Organisation Started in Ballyshannon
by Veteran Parkinson's Chairman and Charity Fund Raiser

Anthony O'Malley Daly, well known Parkinson's sufferer and charity fund-raiser, and an active pensioner who will be 73 on 15th October, has started a charitable and caring organisation called *Mi Amigo*, which is Spanish for *My Friend*.

Anthony, whose motto is "I have Parkinson's, but Parkinson's does not have me®" also has arthritis and asthma. He said that he was moved by the extent of illnesses that are suffered by people in silence in Donegal and the north west – "...illnesses that were disabling persons until they withdrew into themselves, and sat in the corner."

And he will be attempting to take, and talk, these people back into society. Anthony is particularly thinking of mental sickness, depression and other illnesses such as Parkinson's and Multiple Sclerosis, as well as self-harm, the effects of bullying, and abuse of people from childhood into old age, and into the grave.

He admits that he had a mental depression when he took the decision to walk away from 30 years of working and happiness. After a matter of time he got a job with FÁS as the supervisor on the Eske waters, which included the River Eske and Lough Eske. Working outdoors was new to Anthony, but he loved to work, and he had a crew of 16 working week on and week off.

During that period he received counselling in St. Conal's Hospital, Letterkenny. He says, "I used to laugh at Americans saying, *Do you want to talk about it?*" – but only by talking about his problems did he rid himself of the low esteem and lack of sleep at night, trying to turn back the clock. FÁS employers and his friends finally cured him, and FÁS kept him on as Supervisor for three years after he was due to retire.

"I am not miserable – I just look miserable," is how he dealt with any questions about the black hole he had plunged into. That included being "sent to Coventry" by his work mates.

Anthony O'Malley Daly says he needs volunteers, and friends. And finally he expects *Mi Amigo* to grow from "my friend" into *Mis Amigos*, which means "many friends."

He says, "Any age, young to old, are invited to talk to me and be my friend, until we all have many friends.

"I will play it by ear. We will help each other along the road of life."

Headquarters of *Mi Amigo* is at "Inisfail," College Street, Ballyshannon, Co. Donegal.

Anthony O'Malley Daly was elected Ballyshannon Person of the Year 2007, and one of the Rehab Donegal People of the Year 2010.

14th May 2012

The Desmond Tutu Peace Foundation
PO Box 8428 Roggebaai
8012 Cape Town, South Africa

Dear Sir/Madam

Please find enclosed a cheque for €400.00 dated 14th April 2012 made payable to Archbishop Desmond Tutu as a donation to The Desmond Tutu Peace Foundation. This donation is being made by Mr. Anthony O'Malley Daly of Mi Amigo Charity, College Street, Ballyshannon, Co Donegal, Ireland.

I would be grateful if you could forward a receipt for this donation.

Yours Sincerely

Anthony O'Malley Daly

Mi Amigo has donated a total of €800 to The Desmond Tutu Peace Foundation. We provided €3,900 for relief work in Haiti, and we have funded many other worthy causes.

The Most Reverend Desmond M Tutu, O.M.S.G. D.D. F.K.C.
Anglican Archbishop Emeritus of Cape Town

PO Box 1692, Milnerton, Cape Town 7435
Suite 45, Frazzitta Business Park, cnr Freedom Way & Koeberg Road, Milnerton 7441
Tel: (+27) 021 552 7524
Fax: (+27) 021 552 7529
E-mail: mofia@iiafrica.com

10 January 2012

Mr Anthony O'Malley Daly
c/o College Street
Ballyshannon
Co. Donegal
Ireland

Dear Mr O'Malley Daly

Thank you so very much for the contribution of €400.00 which you have made towards the Mpilo Trust Ministry. Your kindness is appreciated.

I wish you and your family love and blessings this new year.

Archbishop Emeritus Desmond Tutu (Cape Town – South Africa)

To Enjoy This Book:

<u>*Trilogy*</u> *includes a bit of everything – my life story and reminiscences, a selection of my angling columns, and a collection of stories from friends, anglers, and people I've known in the north-west. If you want to focus on one part or another, it's organised this way:*

Book One, <u>*My Life – My Way*</u> *is my autobiography, for the most part.*

Book Two, <u>*Sixty Years of Angling*</u>*, is a collection of my fishing columns from The Donegal Democrat and The Sun Newspaper. If you've won any angling prizes in the past twenty years, your name might be in there.*

Book Three, <u>*Injun Joe*</u>*, is a book of fishing stories and tall tales, all Absolutely True. Some are mine and some were contributed by my family, friends and companions over the years.*

The <u>*Epilogue*</u> *of the book is a collection of newspaper stories about my fund-raising activities for the Parkinson's Association and the Asthma Society. I'm leaving some blank pages at the end so you can paste in the stories about the fund-raisers I haven't done yet.*

Book One

My Life – My Way

My Specimen Fish – 20 lb, 4 oz, caught in Lough Eske in 1985.

When I showed this salmon to my Mother and my Auntie Grace, my Aunt exclaimed, "We'll never eat this!"

Injun Joe – Boat and Boy

I have been fishing for 60 years, boy and man. I have fished in some rare places, at home in Ireland and abroad. I am "Injun Joe." So too is Ed Hanna. So is the boat, *das Boat,* like the name of a Native Indian, or the story of a German Submarine.

I sailed the Briney. I saw the death of ships and mariners!

Injun Joe

Let's Get Started...

I start here, and I hope you all enjoy what I have to say. It covers the very first time I went "Gone Fishing," right up to the time I reached my 76th Birthday, and a "wee bit" beyond.

Profile of the Author

Daly

My name is Anthony O'Malley Daly, born 15th October 1935. I live in "Inisfail," College Street, Ballyshannon – the oldest town in Ireland. Now, if you are settling down to read this book, and you are in good humour, allow me to test your patience, fortitude and tolerance, by telling you that I share my birthday with Eamonn DeValera and Margaret Thatcher, two of the most adored or reviled political personalities of the 20th century. How long their fame or infamy lasts in people's memories will be far longer than mine, but if you put aside your political views and do as I have always done, insist that Angling strips us all to the one "uniform," then you can continue to enjoy this book.

Father

My father, Patrick Daly, was born at the foot of the Nephin mountain in Co. Mayo, near Lahardane on the Crossmolina Road. The house is still standing today, with a capital "D" above the door. My father, one of a family of 6 boys and 1 girl, was a distinguished student at the Royal College of Surgeons, St. Stephens Green in Dublin. His name is 3 times on the panel of honour where he won 2 Gold medals and a silver medal for surgery. My father went on to be the Physician and surgeon in the Sheil and Rock Hospitals for over 30 years.

My father was also the medical officer to the Local Defence Forces (LDF/FCA), and I remember seeing him in his uniform on parade, marching down the Main Street in Ballyshannon.

Blue Shirt

My father was a Blue Shirt, which meant that he supported General Eoin O'Duffy, who was the Garda Commissioner in the thirties. The Blue Shirt movement was very active in the thirties, and when O'Duffy was sacked by De Valera, it sent shock waves throughout Ireland. General O'Duffy then recruited right wing supporters to fight in the Spanish Civil War on the side of Generalissimo Franco, who won. They were *Fascistas*. The defeated Republicans were *Communistas*. It was a bitter war. Locals from Ballyshannon fought on both sides.

My father, Dr Patrick Daly (left), with Dr McNamee

Paddy Casey fought on the side of Franco. He was a porter in the Rock Hospital, and he was a character. He wore a black beret. Paddy was a great friend of my father when he was running the Rock Hospital surgery. He used to meet my father and say to him, "Doctor Daly, we have a full load of operations this morning!" As if he too was a Doctor – Dr. Casey!

My father loved the porters. Johnny Quinn was another porter in the Sheil Hospital, and he was a rare porter, too. When the Health Board installed a paging system called the Tonnoy System in the hospital, Johnny Quinn said, "The Tonnoy System will be the boss now."

Johnny Quinn was a rogue, and a bit of a drinker. When Matron wanted Johnny before, he was often downtown. She had to send the staff looking for him, and he was able to dodge the staff. But with the Tonnoy System, his pager would say, "Johnny Quinn, report to the morgue," no matter where he was. He was no longer able to hide.

When my father died, he was laid out in the Shiel. That gesture was considered to be an honour.

My Mother – Sally or Sal

My Mother was one of family of nine, whose father Austin was from Clare Island. He was a member of the R.I.C. – the Royal Irish Constabulary (and "Paddy married a Peeler's daughter," Uncle Peter used to say to annoy me). My Mother was born in Ballymote, Co Sligo, while my Auntie Grace, my Godmother, was born in Sligo, in one of the small houses beside the Garda station. The houses are still there.

My Mother, Sal or Sally, Sarah Winifred, was considered a beauty, and her walk / elegance was always majestic. "She would not get in that door," is how she was described. She was an O'Malley through and through – with connections to Grace O'Malley, the famed Pirate Queen.

Grace O'Malley

Clare Island was the base for all Grace O'Malley's escapades. She sailed into notoriety when she went to see the Queen of England, Elizabeth 1st, in one of her ships. She sailed up the Thames to dock at London sometime in July of 1593. She gained further fame when she was handed a silk handkerchief to blow her nose by the British monarch, and afterwards she threw the handkerchief into the fire. When she was admonished gently by the Queen, our Queen Granuaile answered, "I only use a 'snot rag' once."

She was indeed "POWERFUL ON LAND AND SEA", as the motto on the O'Malley Coat of Arms says. For Grace, the Pirate Queen, to venture to London, when there was ever the threat of the Spanish attacking. When the plague was ravaging London. You were alive in the morning – you were dead in the evening, and buried immediately. "Throw Out Your Dead" was the cry. And you did just that, no matter how you loved you kin folk. Because if you didn't...

She got on well with the powerful empire Queen. That is the reason I carry the double-barrelled name (of which I am immensely proud), for I was christened so.

Grace O'Malley lived a fabulous life. When she was refused the hospitality of Killiney Castle, she kidnapped one of the noble children and took him back to Clare Island. She agreed to release the child only if the Lord of Killiney Castle would promise to set a place at the table "for A.N. Other" at every meal, "...because you never know when I may return." They still set out a plate "for A.N. Other" to this day.

She got out of jail twice and escaped hanging by the British authorities. She developed new methods of communication, lighting fires on the Irish coast which could be seen in the night sky in Scotland. And Grace was well-educated. Elizabeth I and Queen Granuaile conversed in Latin.

No one knows where Grace O'Malley is buried. The Scots came over to Clare Island and took away many bones to use as fertilizer, so her bones could be in Scotland.

The sea is in our blood. My Uncle Austin ran away to sea. He has returned to Clare Island with his wife Felicity and has built a house on the site of the old school.

My Early Days

My brother Peter is 2 years older than me. We were born in McDaid's house on West Rock, while we lived on Bishop Street. Now, Bishop Street was on the North side of the river, and McDaid's was on the South side of the river. Peter and I had a foot in both camps. McDaid's house was, at that time, a Nursing Home. We lived in the house next to McGinley's Pub. It is occupied today by the Health Board.

I have three sisters. Maeve is two years younger than I and lives in London. She is named for Queen Maeve. Fidelma is a nurse, and she lives in Vancouver. She married John Murchie who is a Tea and Coffee Merchant and an inventor. And last is Grainne, the youngest of us all, named after Grace O'Malley. She is a teacher (now retired) and lives in Canada too.

Asthma

Biking with my brother Peter (left)

I suffered from Asthma as a child, and my outlook was bleak. I was frail. When I was coming down the stairs, I used to have to lie down on each landing to get back enough strength to go down another flight of stairs. At night I slept sitting up, on my hands.

I was an emotional child. I spent my days in the attic, sitting and looking out the window at the side of the gable, pasting my cuttings into books, and dreaming. I had books of cuttings from the papers – racing was Charlie Smirke and Gordon Richards, and the Grand National was Prince Regent. I took my love of Manchester United from Johnny Carey, who captained the 1948 team to FA Cup victory. Then when I was well, I loved Gaelic Football.

Peter and I slept in the attic. We thought the house was haunted, when at irregular times during the "dead of night" we heard sounds that "frightened the life out of us." It took many years before we found out who the "devil" was. In those days, publicans had to bottle their own stout. Frankie McGinley used to bottle his stout after he closed the pub, late at night. He would rush down to his cellar, fill the machine, and commence bottling the stout. No one else in the house got the sound more than Peter and I.

The Iron Cow and Inhalers

The shape of the stout machine was akin to an "iron" cow that you never had to "fodder"or milk, or put out to grass, but you had to have a "style" if you were ever to get the bottles of stout ready for the next day.

Frankie McGinley sat on a stool, took two bottles (one in each hand), stuck the bottle into a "pipe," filled it with stout, and then in one motion, he pulled out the filled bottle, transferred the bottle to another tube where the cork was forced into the neck of the bottle, while at the same time, without "dropping a drop," placing another bottle into the pipe where it was filled. Frankie never got a kick from his "iron cow," but you sure had to move fast and with rhythm.

6

I don't know for how long we (Peter and I) got the "frighteners" from this "Iron Cow," but we moved to "Inisfail" before we got a night's sleep. What a relief.

I developed Asthma during our stay in Bishop Street. From there on I had to sleep sitting on my hands, and only those who suffered the "gasping for breath" will thank God for the invention of the "Inhalers." Remember Franol tablets?

Blackhead Worms and Solitude

When we reached "Inisfail," College Street, I immediately got an orange box, gathered up all the blackhead worms in the district, put them into the orange box, and landed the lot on one of the sheds. I covered the clay with moss. Each morning, I fed my worms with sour milk until they got so tough and hard I could not put them on to a hook.

I was the envy of the town. Everyone wanted my worms. They were so eager for "battle" that I had to put them under armed guard. I got my first brown trout with a blackhead worm. Note: The orange box was ideal for the worms, because they were "ribbed" – meaning there was a gap halfway down the box, which aired the worms, and when I put moss down the side of the box, they were secure. And when it rained, the box did not fill up with water. My worms were the talk of the town.

When I got used to fishing trout and perch, I got two other things – relief from Asthma, and Solitude.

Brother Fidelis

I caught my first trout in the Knather Lake when I was ten or eleven. At that time there was only one other person who fished this clean water one mile East of Ballyshannon. Imagine a lake with wild brown trout (small but stout), and only two people fishing it.

The other person who fished the Knather Lake was a de la Salle Teaching Brother. I disliked him as a teacher, but as an angler, I admired him. He fished a 9ft rod. It seemed like he was always there. When he wasn't teaching – he was out fishing (and at least he was good company).

He was the "Quiet Man." The exception to this was his "Snapper" terrier that came everywhere with him.

My early days in 1946

Brother Fidelis was one of the best anglers I had the pleasure to meet, but I cannot ever forget his Jekyll-and-Hyde image. He is long dead, but he is not forgotten. He

7

left every evening at dusk, made his contented weary way into the door of the de la Salle house, which is now the HSE office next to the car park on College Street.

He was a very quiet man without an ounce of spare weight. He had grey-white hair. He had a terrier dog, which I will tell you about later on. He only spoke when he had to. His name meant Brother Faithful. He taught us Irish, and when we were at Irish, he walked around the class, and if you lost your place, he spotted it straight away. Or if you didn't know where you should be, and you started to follow with your finger – which was in the wrong place, Brother Fidelis swooped, and in a quiet voice would ask you to read a line or carry on where the other boy left off. When, as was usually the case, you failed – you got the hardest slap on the ear. Then he was away again, to swoop on another unfortunate cub.

However, he was a great angler with any bait, but he mostly fished the fly. He never left the lake without a bag full of trout.

When I landed my first trout, it was on the worm. The cork suddenly shot under the water. I struck, and I did not give a half pound brown trout much leeway. He was landed and killed without much play.

I decided to go round and show Brother Fidelis my trout. As I mentioned earlier, he had a terrier dog. When the dog sensed me (or anybody), coming he started to bark. That was his first line of defence, and if barking did not do the trick, he then went to my left leg and tried to climb to have a go on me. I hope you know what I mean, for when I shook him off he started on my right leg. It was only when the terrier (I've forgotten his name) increased his tempo that Brother Fidelis called him off with a few noiseless words. Anyway I made off with my First Trout.

Friday Fish Day

One of my most unforgettable memories...

Friday was always "Fish Day" at the Hanna House in Castle Street, Donegal Town, and if it was fish only on the menu in Castle Street, then it was a similar menu at the Lough House, midway (almost) between Donegal Town and Ballybofey.

It was Friday, and Mama Hanna was over at the Lough House, her ancestral Home. (*I loved David and Maggie Hanna so much that I called them Mama and Dada. To continue:*) Meanwhile, back at the ranch in Castle Street, we were all of us at the "River Wall," taking

David Hanna - "Dada"

8

advantage of a run of salmon and sea trout that had "come off the tide." It had not rained for weeks. Then, literally overnight, it had rained. There was a brown flood. The salmon and trout were moving upstream. John, Patrick (yes, even Patrick), Edward, Jim Thomas, and I were hanging over the river wall, fishing the worm because it was "brown water" that was spilling down the River Eske towards the sea.

The rain had stopped. We would follow the fish until they had entered the lake. We would "arise" on Sunday morning, and if there, and if the level of water had fallen, we would change to the fly. John and Edward had a number of white trout (white or sea trout) landed. I lost a salmon. From what I had seen of him, the sea lice were in strings on him. Fresh as a daisy.

Edward Floats

The "Angelus" rang. Dada came across the Red Bridge and arrived at the house. Kathleen was in the kitchen. Fish on the table, fish in the river. Captain Hamilton arrived. Edward, John, and Jim Thomas were into a great run of sea trout. I reeled up and went in to the kitchen. For the record, I seldom ate trout or salmon, but Mama did cook whiting. I always ate fish of a Friday, when done (cooked) by any of the Hannas. We were all in the kitchen, eating our fish, when someone said, "Where is Edward?"

John answered, "He will be in soon. He would not get off The Wall" – which means he is in a fish, playing the salmon or trout, and the fish is well hooked. (Edward was ten years old at that time.)

The rest of us would strike the fish by raising the rod. In the case of Edward, he gave the fish, one, two, or treble strikes.

Margaret Hanna, nee Glackin

Let me explain – Strike One: Edward raises his rod, and the salmon strikes himself. The fish takes the bait and turns away with the bait in his mouth, and the water is running or flowing, and the rod is raised. For me or John that is more than sufficient, and it is three strikes already:

1) The salmon runs at the bait, or takes the worms, or rises to the fly.

2) The salmon or trout or most game fish turns away with the bait in his mouth, and

3) The angler raises his rod, bending the tip in the salmon.

Edward did all these things, but he pulled the line horizontal to the rod and, as quick as Lightning, jerked his body backwards. That is Edward's Treble Strike, and if you are in a boat, then there is a "sudden speedy jolt." Dare the fish get off, after that.

The door bursts open. Gerry Strewart shouts, "Edward is in the River!" Some one else is shouting, "He is floating under the Red Bridge!" We all desert our fish dinners. It is like the Keystone Cops.

It takes a flash for all of us to reach the street. We are all shouting his name. *"Edward! Where are you??"*

Then we see him. He is floating into the middle of The School Hole, which is a famous pool below the Red Bridge. Such a commotion. Most people are bumping into each other. Some go back, and are galloping like Connamara Ponies across the Diamond.

I am with the gang that took the Diamond route. The car park is full, blocking our view, so we have yet to see him. Then, to our partial relief we all spot the "Bold" Edward, still floating. John orders Jim Thomas, (who is a smoker), Patrick (also a fag puffer), and me – to put the net under the sea trout of 3lbs.

A man is trying to reach Edward, to no avail. That means he can't get him. We see the family on the Red Bridge. John spotted him, and started to roar instructions to him.

I did not say it at the time, but when I caught sight of Edward, he was not struggling or floundering in the water. He was floating, but the noise of the flood left us with no communication to Edward.

Edward Hanna, age 10

Jim Thomas pushed me towards the Court House. "You go that way, and go straight to the quay. We'll go to the other side, and see if there is a boat we can get!"

Edward is slowing down, and is calling for his fishing rod. A man reaches out for Edward, grabs him, and pulls him out. The man is overwhelmed with thanks. He gives his Christian name, and no more. His name is too mundane to repeat. When I asked him where he was from, he said, "I'm the Man from God Knows Where," or words to that effect. We all want to do all kinds of everything for him, but he shakes all our hands. He gives Edward a five pound note, sterling.

The guards put a wet Edward into the patrol car. He is satisfied. Wants his dinner. Later, Edward tells us what happened. He got stuck in a salmon. When he was struggling to pull the salmon up the wall, he was leaning over. He was afraid he would lose the fish. He got up on the wall. Lost his footing as the salmon got free. Fell in.

To Anthony – How do we say "Thank You" for a lifetime of fishing and friendship?

Best wishes from your family and friends at Hanna Hats.

Hanna Hats
Tirconaill Street
Donegal Town
Co Donegal, Ireland.
Tel: +353 (0)74 9721084
Email: info@hannahats.com

BECOME OUR FRIEND ON FACEBOOK:
http://www.facebook.com/#!/hanna.hats

Military Years

I tried to join the Royal Air Force at 17. I actually went to Aldergrove Airport, but was returned to Ballyshannon because I was too young. At the second attempt I was accepted. Looking back on my actions, I was not afraid, even though I was very young.

I was in the British Forces for 5 years, and had to be told to write home after nearly two years. It happened like this – I was going on patrol when I was stopped at the main gate outside Famagusta, Cyprus, in 1955. The OC (Officer Commanding) made me write Home to my Mother.

I spent nearly three years in Cyprus. Then I was sent into Egypt when the French and the British, under Sir Anthony Eden, invaded the Suez Canal. President Eisenhower and John Foster Dulles turned on the Brits and the French and told them to vacate the Suez Canal, which they did "Post Haste." That was surely the end. Later, in my service to Elizabeth the Second, I was sent to Australia, as part of "Task Force Antler" for five Atomic Bomb Tests at Maralinga.

Proud in uniform, in my first days of training

264 Signals Unit

I was sent to Cyprus as a Radio Operator 1954. We did a special job. I was listening in on Russian radio frequencies. We had our camp outside Famagusta, next to the Green Howards Army Regiment. Then we had our work place, about two miles away, and after a roundabout.

We landed in Cyprus, April 1954, and quickly set up our camp. The new camp we squatted in was right beside the road, about four miles from Famagusta. We put up our tents. Most had been already fully set in lines of cement squares. The rest of our big tents were *in situ* before we went to sleep on the first night in Cyprus. Yes, the 264 Signals Unit had arrived, into a peaceful nation.

Dysentery

We were very proud. We set about our tasks, which were: 1) To start our work immediately. 2) To see our surrounds, and to get down to the Town of Famagusta. 3) To go into the walled region of Verose, which was the Turkish part. 4) To clean up our camp, and make it habitable. What we got was far from the vision we had in our quality thinking. What we got was – Dysentery. After a few days the entire unit got the "Virile Bug." And we could not be moved. We had to fight it in our Camp, and by ourselves.

We found out that our camp had been used by Mauritian Pioneer soldiers in World War Two. I found out when we were digging a hole to make into a toilet. You see, we were sent to this Camp, but that was not meant to be our permanent Camp. I was digging the hole, when another man shouted to me, "Get out, the ground is moving," and with that I pulled away a large stone. The stench was awful, and if I had stayed longer, I would have plunged into a large pit of excrement – shit!!!!!!! – left there by the Mauritian Pioneer soldiers, and covered when it was full. I did not see the earth moving.

At Katanga Castle, Cyprus, 1955

I had a Triumph 500 Twin motorcycle in Cyprus - the best best bike I ever rode. It was the kind used by the London Metropolitan Police. The ZP registration was the same as the number for Donegal at the time.

Anyway, a few days later, we got Dysentery. The whole Camp was down with it, except about a dozen of us. We had to nurse the rest who had the Dysentery. The Camp was put into Quarantine. Nobody was allowed out or in. A medical officer instructed us what to do, and we did it. We cleaned out the beds and tents of our comrades, who were too weak to leave their beds. It was a mess for about a week, but slowly it improved. The Quarantine was lifted after a month. What we gave them to drink was water with quinine, and hard fried eggs to eat. Some of them were close to death.

World Exclusive... Cyprus E.O.K.A. Terror

I was exactly one year in Cyprus 1954-55, when the troubles started. The Greeks on the island of Cyprus started the *"enosis"* movement, which meant *union*, and it meant that where there had been peace, now there was war.

It was no joke, because like the Six Counties, E.O.K.A. was a Greek terror group, led by Archbishop Makarios, a cleric, who wanted union with Greece... *Enosis*. The

Turks, who ruled approximately half of the Island of Cyprus, were on our (British) side. They did our gate duties.

One very popular guard who did his guard duty left to go Home, but he never got there. He had to pass through a Greek village, but when he got to the village a plank was "swung" out that knocked him off his motorbike. The Greeks then got around him, and beat him to death!!! As revenge, the Turks shot up a bus load of Greeks. Five died. That was a "war within a war."

Dublin Cook Gets Bravery Award

We still went down town to Famagusta. We had our favourite haunts. One of these had an open plan bar that was located next to the pathway, and the road. It was always packed with servicemen.

One Friday evening we were all there drinking ouzo (Greek equivalent to vodka) and *koegh* (beer). It was made in Cyprus. I should know, because I remember visiting the brewery.

Anyway, we were all of us drinking and enjoying ourselves. Next thing someone shouts *Bomb!* The bar was so full that only the man who saw it coming through the window, and the man it struck, knew the hand grenade was on the floor, intended to explode any second. *Bomb, bomb, bomb!* We were all of a panic. Next thing I heard was a loud explosion. We had our drinks all over ourselves.

We then realised what had happened. A hand grenade had been lobbed into our midst by one of five or six youths who then ran off. It hit our cook, who was from Dublin. He calmly picked it up, and with difficulty he threw it towards the open window. Fortunately it fell behind a settee. It exploded. The settee was lifted. The men who were on the settee were thrown into the air. Apart from shock, no one was injured. We tumbled out. We ran in all directions. We took the law into our own hands.

The Cyprus police got through to the military police. We were asked to leave Famagusta. The cook from Dublin got a medal. (I think it was the BEM – British Empire Medal.)

It was lucky the bomb (hand grenade) did not land on the pavement because it would have killed or injured passers-by.

Maralinga – The A-Bomb

This is a Fishing or Angling book, but I must "dwell awhile"on the Atomic and "H-Bomb" Tests that were carried out during the late forties, and lasting into the Sixties. (Christmas Island was the H-Bomb venue.)

Australia was the Atomic Bomb testing grounds for the A-Bombs from the early fifties until 1958 (1952 -1958). Christmas Island was for H-Bombs, which are more powerful. The A-Bombs are less powerful than H-Bombs but are at least ten times the power of the bombs that were dropped on Nagasaki and Hiroshima to end the Second World War and hasten the surrender of Japan.

I am now convinced that if you can get another nation to test your Nuclear Bombs for you, then you're onto a winner. That is what the British did. They had the test grounds in Australia. They got the "Aussies" to test their Atom Bombs in Maralinga, and as you read on, you will find that they (The Brits) also had their "Rocket Range" in the desert at Woomera (400 miles east of Maralinga).

At that time, Robert Menzies was the Prime Minister of Australia. Nobody gave any consideration to the Aboriginal Tribes or Tribe (check the Royal Commission Report on the following pages) who lived there for a lifetime before the white man came to Australia to 'discover it' and shoved the Natives aside or just ignored them completely. I was in that book. I was a Corporal, and we only lived for the day, and if their were any casualties then we had the Australians by the "short and hairy."

During Task Force Antler in the 1957 testings, 9 natives lost their lives. A complete family. They "doubled back" and were lost and died. I was a radio operator, and during the build-up to an explosion, we had to get the Aboriginals free from their homes and sacred grounds, and in some cases, they never returned. Of course, the reason the British went to Australia was they were involved in the "Cold War." The Aboriginals were docile – all but a few.

Older, and with more authority

When the Bombs were being tested, Robert Menzies Government had the press, media and radio stations and the now-infamous Rupert Murdock (who is Australian) write favourable comments and full page articles and programmes on TV in favour of the testing and informing the people that there would be no "Ill Effects" from the fallout cloud. The world's press were encouraged to be on the side of bosses. Fleet Street in London was the "hub" of the News Media worldwide, but it is no more. Wapping is now the "hub" of the print media.

The same individuals have been influencing our lives up to the present day. Mrs. Thatcher broke the miners' strike and their spirit. Arthur Scargill, the miners' leader, was humiliated. This was all part of a right-wing coup. The rampage occurred in

Fleet Street and continued until it has finally been exposed with the charges brought against Rebekah Brooks, the editor of Rupert Murdock's newspaper. The hacking scandal is only the tip of the iceberg. At least after fifty years some kind of justice has been done.

Robert Menzies was only a puppet figure. If you find this unbelievable, read the Royal Commission Report (1985). I will quote from the findings later in this book.

Woomera Rocket Range / Christmas Island

Woomera is 350 to 400 miles north of Adelaide, and the Woomera rocket range is 400 miles east of Maralinga. The H-Bombs were tested (mainly) on Christmas Island. Whole "atolls" disappeared. (An "atoll" is a low lying piece of land, which is used for testing.) Christmas Island is in the Pacific Ocean and at the time was sparsely inhabited. In fact it is now uninhabited because it is so polluted by Radioactive Materials, and it is unlikely to be inhabited ever again.

What Happened When the Bomb Exploded

I am a veteran of Maralinga. Five Atom Bombs were exploded during my term on Task Force "Antler." I was working during the lead-up to four of the five bombs. I was on a football pitch for the explosion of the first bomb that was suspended from balloons. We were all on tenterhooks. All who were not working had to nevertheless be accounted for. Any of us who were working were easily accounted for and were ticked off. Most of the off-duty went to the football pitch. We were about three or four miles away from the explosion and had a clear view of the bomb site. It was like a grand piano hanging from balloons.

Countdown

We had been told what to do. The countdown was continuous, and I arrived at the pitch half an hour before. The countdown was being relayed over a loud speaker. It got to 10 seconds. I, with all the rest, turned away from the bomb. I shut my eyes tight and covered them with my hands. Ten, nine, eight...three, two, ONE. There was a "blinding flash." Even with my eyes shut tight and my hands covering them completely, I was still blinded by the brightness of the flash. From my shoulders to the tips of my toes, I was engulfed by a burning sensation. The blast was so powerful and intense that it caused me to let out a loud gasp of surprise. I turned around. I could see men scattering everywhere and breaking ranks. Many ran but I was rooted to the spot, frozen by the fear.

The next thing I heard was the sound rolling towards us. The noise got louder. All the time I could actually "see" the noise. It came rolling through the air across the desert getting louder and louder as it approached. Then it hit me. It almost toppled me off my feet and I staggered backwards. Believe me when I say that you do not want to ever experience or witness the effects of an atomic bomb explosion. But unfortunately, my first encounter with an atomic explosion was not yet over.

Nuclear Cloud

To my right ten or so of my friends fled with fright. And then the desert seemed to erupt.

The red sand was hit by a down-draught which tore the desert in two ways. First, it was ripped upwards, and then I saw the red sand roll outwards, outwards and upwards. A jet (a Canberra Bomber) shot through the clouds, which by now was the shape of a "Mushroom." This massive cloud began to move away from me. It was high in the clear blue sky, floating a course that was designed to take the "fallout" into the sea, after it took a true course over Queensland. This cloud of red clay was "raining" all over the desert below, and it was contaminated, and depended on the wind to keep it floating, discharging a red dust, which was half the desert it sucked up back in Maralinga.

Actual Photo of Maralinga A-Bomb Test

I was chastened. I was shook. I was shocked. Some had taken to their heels, and I could not blame them. I was rooted to the spot...

No Fishing

I could not do any fishing in Maralinga. There was no water for drinking, never mind water to fish. All our goods, water and food had to be collected from a railhead, 20 miles away.

Adelaide

We did wild things in Australia. We hijacked an aircraft. We asked the pilot to take us to Adelaide, and we made him an offer he could not refuse. When we got to Adelaide, we booked into a hotel for the bank holiday weekend.

Adelaide was known as a city of churches. The city was full of immigrants who had paid £10 for their passage to Australia. They lived in Nissen huts.

The Adelaide pubs opened at 6:00 am and closed at 6:00 pm. At 5:00 pm the immigrants rushed from their jobs to the pubs. It was every man for himself. We ordered six glasses of beer and did not move or go to the toilet. At 6:00 the cops arrived and the pubs closed. The rules were strictly enforced.

We found a night club where you could get a drink. They served the whiskey and vodka in cups and saucers.

Sunday you could not get a drink at all.

Australian Days

During our stay in Maralinga, as part of Task Force Antler, I enjoyed myself, and would not have missed the experience. I wore an identity badge with my photo on it, which was handed in when I left by sea from Adelaide, in the "*SS NEW AUSTRALIA.*" I was demobbed after five years of service in the Royal Air Force, March 1958. It was during the "Cold War" period, when England, France and America, stood firm against the threat of war emanating from Russia and China, with Cuba, Egypt, and East Germany.

I had an experience when I was home on leave during my RAF years which is the subject of this next item. Don't let the date of the following story fool you – it feels like it happened just yesterday.

Ex RAF Man and Sinn Fein Clr. Welcomes Rule 21 Exit

The Donegal Democrat
22 November 2001

The decision of the GAA last weekend to remove Rule 21 from its rule book got the seal of approval from one Ballyshannon man who remembers being a victim of the rule back in the 1950s.

Anthony O'Malley Daly, who recently turned 65 and is now enjoying retirement, was once asked to leave a playing field in Ballyshannon because, at the time he was a member of the British Royal Air Force.

The well-known Ballyshannon man, who served for 20 years as a Sinn Fein Councillor on the Town Commissioners, joined the RAF after leaving school in 1953, and spent five years with them as a radio operator, before later joining the Merchant Navy.

As an 18-year-old he was home on holidays in 1954 from his work, and along with all his pals, he went for the customary game of football on Sunday.

"I went to Legaltion along with the others and there was a game involving Abbey Shamrocks. I was togged out and taking part in the pre-match kick around, but before the game started, an official approached me and told me I could not play," said Anthony, who added that he was aware of the Rule at the time but did not think it would be enforced.

"I had played for Ballyshannon at U-16 and Minor level prior to going away. (My brother Peter was a County Minor Goalkeeper.)

"It is a very vivid memory of being asked to leave the field, and I was very annoyed at the time. I was probably more annoyed by the fact that I was allowed to tog out and take part in the kick-about and then asked publicly to leave in front of all the others," said Mr. O'Malley Daly, who expressed great delight in the rule eventually being changed.

"I'm very glad that the rule has been removed. It has held back the GAA over the years. They should have been able to stand up on their own two feet and not have negative rules like that," said Anthony...

The fact that Anthony was a victim of the rule is even more significant given his support for republican politics over the years. As a member of the Ballyshannon Town Commissioners over the years, he has twice held the position of chairman, and is the only Sinn Fein member ever to do so.

Thanks to the Donegal Democrat for that story. It introduces other topics that I'll cover later, but that's what happens when you try to tell the story of your life. Everything is connected to everything else.

Coming Home

After 5 years in the R.A.F. I was back in "Civvie" Street. I returned to "Inisfail," College Street, Ballyshannon, Co Donegal. I plunged into the fishing, and something a lot more challenging – I got married to one Mary Hanna on May 27th, 1958.

Mary was one of 11 (eleven) children. Her Mother was from the Lough House, away through the Barnesmore Gap. The Glackins were a sept of the O'Donnells, and they were originally from Dungloe and the Rosses.

Mary's Father, David, was an orphan, born in Belfast. He had been a professional boxer. However, he arrived in Donegal Town, met Margaret Glackin, fell in Love, settled eventually in Castle Street, and set up business as a Tailor in a hut on Tirconnail Street. He was in the "rag trade," making suits and other quality hand made "bespoke" items of clothing for many years, until one day he took a hat and cap apart. The reconstructed Hat and Cap were so successful that David Hanna & Sons, Tailors, became David Hanna & Sons, Hatters.

Our Wedding

Mary and I got married on 27th May 1958 in St. Patrick's Church, Donegal Town. Our wedding was the event of the year. It was a morning suit affair. I was taking Mary, the first of the Hannas, who was very well-regarded in the Community. She was attentive to her work in Dunleavy's, where she was Alex Dunleavy's secretary. She was in the Legion of Mary.

Michael McGettigan, the butcher, sang *Ave Maria*. His father was a doctor in Dunkineely.

Mary and I, Dressed in Our Finest

Dada Hanna Leading Mary to the Ceremony

Our Banquet and Cake, with Our Families and Friends

Blessing the Gold and Silver

My brother Peter was the Best Man. Anyway, the tradition of "getting the gold and silver blessed" went well, until I entered the Lounge Bar. There were renovations going on in the Hotel, and I took exception to the Glackins being put into a separate room. Anyway all got sorted.

The Wedding was a resounding success. Dada (David Hanna) went up to the Hotel, and if they said anything to anybody else, they most certainly said nothing to Dada.

The bar was full. The wedding party wore morning attire. I was standing a drink to all in the bar, and all was sailing along well until I paid for the drinks with the two shilling piece in the handful of money mixed up in the Auld Money. Later, when Mary asked me for the gold (which was a rare gold dollar coin) and silver, I had to think on my feet. Eddie Thomas saved the day by slipping me two shillings.

My Parents on our Wedding Day

We went on our honeymoon. We went in a Morris Minor I had rented from Frank Hayes, who owned a bar in Ballyshannon. (It is Max Bar today, but in those days it was Gallagher's Erne Bar, full of cattle during the fairs.)

First we went to Galway to the Banba Hotel. When I woke up the next morning I took an Asthma attack, and after this we went to Tipperary and then on to Cork. To complete our Love holiday, we then ventured to Dublin and capped the trip off with a visit to Belfast.

My Wife

Here is how Joe McGarrigle of the Donegal Democrat described Mary in his book *Donegal Profiles*:

It is not always possible for a mother bringing up a family to devote as much time to outside activities as she would wish. When she has a well-ordered life, however, and is dedicated to a particular cause, it is amazing what she can accomplish. Such a person is Mary O'Malley-Daly, wife of Mr. Anthony O'Malley-Daly, credit controller with the "Donegal Democrat."

Mary's forte is helping young people become adept in swimming and water safety... a short explanation that describes what she is doing, but cannot by any means communicate the extent of her own personal commitment. Mary grew up in a family where caring for others was a daily routine. Her father, David Hanna from Donegal Town, was well-known for his work with young people. His boxing club has been of immeasurable value to the town and has helped mould the character of two generations.

David Hanna had been keenly interested in promoting swimming and even when he passed the three score and ten took his daily plunge at the Holmes beach. Although Mary taught her own children to swim at an early age, it was not until many years later that she became actively involved with her work for the community.

The opening of the new pool in Ballyshannon, costing in the region of €73,000, gave an enormous boost to swimming in the area and this gave her an opportunity to play an active role in promoting the sport. She was conscious too of the more serious side and this prompted her decision to qualify in water safety instruction. She also completed the A.S.A. teaching course, and also a course for teaching the disabled.

Incidentally, Mary's husband was a member of the Erne Club. They did their swimming, training, and held their galas at Creevy.

The Erne Club was affiliated with Connaught, and when the Saimer Club was formed it was decided to continue the tradition...

Mary reflected on her years with the Saimer Club and a touch of pride comes into her voice as the successes reel off her tongue. There were many, but perhaps the most recent will suffice: 1980 Community Games — six medals, including one gold and two silver; 1981 - eight awards with two golds and three silver...

Her own family is amongst the youngsters showing promise. Daughter Orla, representing Sligo Regional College in the All-Ireland Swimming Championships, has had remarkable success – three firsts and a second. A second daughter, Sarah, won the All-Ireland U-18 Life Saving Championships last year, pairing with Sheila McCloskey, and her son, Patrick, has had his share of distinction by getting second place in the All-Ireland finals...

In every town there is someone prepared to devote his or her energies to the welfare of the community. Not all of them with the same dedication, or indeed the same measure of success as Mary O'Malley-Daly.

Our First Wedding Anniversary

What Joe McGarrigle didn't mention is that I taught Mary how to swim. It was on our First Wedding Anniversary, on the Isle of Jersey. I encouraged her to jump into the water near where I was swimming. I said, "If you love me, you will jump in." She did – and she scraped both of her legs on a rock and got a knee injury. She came to the surface and kept her eyes on me, and I pulled her through the clear water of the sea pool. My sister Fidelma and Mary Murtagh were nurses in the hospital in Jersey, and they patched up her injuries.

As you can see, she didn't let that first experience stop her from becoming a great swimmer, and a great swimming instructor. We enjoyed our stay in Jersey.

Moving to London

After our honeymoon, we returned to Donegal and stayed there for the months of June, July and August 1958. I fished the whole summer in the River Eske, Lough Eske, and the River Eany that reaches into the sea at Inver Village. In September, we moved to London together as our first venture as a young married couple (me being the toy-boy as I was a couple of years younger than Mary).

Mary got fixed up almost immediately with a job in the Bank of Australia. One day I was sitting in Hyde Park, waiting for Mary to come back from her work in the bank. Along came the Park Attendant, trying to get me to pay a few coppers for sitting on a deck chair, the property of the London County Council. I told him I had no money. He said, "I don't believe you! You have a good suit." Anyway, I had to vacate the seat. While I was walking away, I looked back. The attendant put his finger to his head, tapped his forehead, and then pointed at me. *You're crazy, man, and with a good suit!!!!!*

We got "digs" in an Ex-Serviceman's Club in Marble Arch. We had to vacate the room each morning and rebook it the same evening. I got a job in the Marble Arch Hotel, washing dishes – big round white dishes. Since then I have become a "sort" of "big white round dishes" expert. I must have washed thousands of dishes, and I passed the inspection test every time. The supervisor came round, picked up a plate, ran his fore-finger down the plate – and if the sound of the sound was like chalk scraping on a blackboard, then I was passed to proceed as I was going. Some skill to have on my CV! I did not contemplate failing the test. I got a meal inside, and when I went to the door, security passed me through with a cooked chicken, you name it!

Cinema Manager Days

Through the Ex-Serviceman's Club I learned of a job as an assistant manager at the Rank Cinema Organisation, and to my delight I got the position. It was based at the King's Cross Gaumont Cinema. Michael Murray, the Manager, had been in the Metropole, O'Connell Street, Dublin, and had only left and departed when he was "head-hunted" by the Rank Organisation, upon the decline of the attendances at picture houses in Ireland and England.

I was sent out on relief duty to other cinemas across London. I loved this job, and all the staff were very friendly and kind toward me. I regularly did relief at Angel Cinema in Islington and the Odeon at Muswell Hill. I enjoyed this immensely.

My favourite cinema was the Odeon at Cable Street in Stepney, near the Spitalfield fruit market. It was a small cinema, and I liked going there on relief two days a week. It had been a Jewish clothing district. However, most of the Jews had now moved to Wood Green to reside and had left Stepney. There was evidence that the older retired Jewish population were still there, and would die there, by the numbers who came to the pictures in the afternoons.

One day I was doing the cash desk. A small Jewish lady pushed her O.A.P. Book and nine pence in at the desk. She got her ticket. She scrutinised me. She spoke, and it was in broken English.

"You a Yiddisha boy?"

"Pardon me?"

"You a Yiddisha, a Jewish-a boy?"

"No, ma'am, I'm Irish."

"Such a pity! And such a nice-a boy, too..."

Cowboys and Wide Boys

Whenever we showed a cowboy film, it would completely fill every seat in the cinema. John Wayne was the Star, unrivalled at the time. When they showed *North to Alaska,* every seat in the place was filled.

I enjoyed getting dressed up for my Cinema Manager assignments

There was seldom any trouble at the cinema. The only worry was that at the end of the night the place was full of empty bottles, containing anything from beer to wine to whiskey to Meth spirits!

There was always an incident. For instance, a woman died in the Hackney cinema. She was an old age pensioner, I wanted to remove her from the cinema without fuss or anybody noticing. I tried to get her out by pulling her, but the next thing I noticed was that the seats were coming too! By the time I got her out I realised that her leg was caught beneath the seat she was on.

At King's Cross we had a member of staff who was epileptic, and the 'Wide boys' used to nag and wind him up due to his condition. A patron would come out to make a complaint or ask the usher to contact the manager, who was me at the time. I was in the office situated at the rear of the balcony. If I rushed down, I would be out of breath before I got there. The staff member would begin to explain what was going on, and the whole incident would be stoked by the wide boys. A shouting match would follow, the initial incident would escalate to a full blown melee, and I would be struggling with the whole affair. Half the audience would now be involved, and I would start asking people to leave.

Cop's Advice

A policeman gave me this advice: "If there is a threat or trouble in the cinema or in the stalls, you are to walk down slowly – and by the time you get there it will more than likely have ended." When, and if, I had reason to call the cops, it would be a black mark against me, because the cops had to report the call, and the manager of the cinema (that was me) had also to fill in a form, six copies – repeat, *six copies* – one for everybody, Uncle Tom Cobley and all... So, when a call came in from the Front Stalls, I would question the usherette as to what was happening. Seeing a staff member on the house phone, the perpetrators normally would leave, but occasionally they would sit it out until I arrived. At this stage of the evening, I would be dressed in my full black-tie clothing.

Michael Murray, me, the actress Mylene Demongeot, and L. Spector at the 1961 London Cinema Managers' Press showing of "The Singer Not the Song."

Some of these yobs were just out to cause trouble, but the likes of Ginger (so-called because of his Red hair) were persistent in trying to 'rise' me! I had to tell them, "Management reserves the right to refuse admission, and I must ask you to leave now." The retort from Ginger and the gang would be, "We paid our money, we are going to stay!" I would tell them that if they didn't leave now, I was going to have to involve the police. That usually did the job, but on one occasion, Ginger thought he would call my bluff and ride it out. I stood over him and persisted that he must leave immediately. Ginger then went over to the wall and took down the fire extinguisher. I knew he was going to release the trigger. He aimed at the screen and then attempted to unload the fire extinguisher. He couldn't get it to work, and he started punching the release, which caused it to jam further. All he could do was try to salvage his attempt at disruption by throwing the extinguisher through the screen. He even failed at this, as the extinguisher landed on the stage in front of the screen. Ginger and his gang ran for the exit.

My revenge occurred the following day during the matinee showing that was frequented by old age pensioners. I heard a voice out in the yard and I could see it was Ginger. He was peering through the fire exit door. With my foot I kicked the bar on the fire exit door. The door shot outwards. I never again saw Ginger, alive or dead!!

Kings Cross Cinema

I spent my Saturdays in the Kings Cross Gaumont Cinema. Each Saturday the Rank Organisation Cinemas held a Boys and Girls Club. We did sterling work. I was enjoying working with children. We did the hula-hoops craze. And road safety with the kids. All these activities were done without the supervision that would be in place today.

Kings Cross Gaumont was a great cinema. There was always something going on – like bulbs popping, as the underground ran beneath the cinema. 1958 saw the rise again of attendances in Cinemas – with the release of *The Big Country,* starring Burl Ives, Gregory Peck, William Holden, and Jean Simmons.

Later I was sent out around the Cinemas as a relief Manager. One night a Bentley pulled up. A man entered the Odeon Dalston to see *The Horse Soldiers,* a John Wayne movie. At the end of the show, he arrived at the office, wanting to give me a tip. I said I did not take tips. Then he handed me a big cigar. I did not smoke, nor did my wife, but I took the cigar. When I got home, Mary and I lit up the cigar in bed – just to take a few pulls each. The next thing we got dizzy, and then we got sick. Non-smokers, both of us. I will remember *The Horse Soldiers*. So will Mary.

The Scrawny Boy

One Saturday in 1960 I got a call to go to the Odeon Hammersmith. I turned up. The Manager told me my duties. I was to stay at front of the house, in the foyer. This I did. I noticed the cinema was packed. I stayed at my post. I heard the kids inside roaring when the Manager introduced this weak, thin boy who took the house down.

After he finished he left the stage. The kids at the Odeon Hammersmith started to "run amok." They piled out into the foyer and started to chant his name. They commenced to break windows. It was like a hurricane or a tsunami. In about five minutes flat the foyer of cinema was smashed up.

Then they were gone. The Manager arrived and spoke to me. My final question to him was, "Who was *that?!!*"

"That was Cliff Richard" – the Scrawny Boy.

(I recently saw him on TV, dressed up with makeup and bare arms. He is trying to look young. He is 72 years old.)

St. Patrick's Day 1960 – the Albert Hall Concert

Peter Wilson, the boxing correspondent for the Mirror, described it as "10,000 (ten thousand) people inside and 5,000 thousand outside fighting to get in." What he was describing was the 1960 St. Patrick's Day concert in the Albert Hall. Bridie Gallagher was the star of the show. Danny Cummins was the compère. Deirde O'Callaghan played the harp. Michael Murray got us the tickets. He was there along with his wife Niamh, me and my wife Mary .We had seats on the ground floor, best in the house.

I remember Bridie Gallagher. She took the house down. She started to sing requests. We started to shout our requests. "They're Cutting the Corn in Creeslough Today" and "The Boys from County Armagh" *Where are the boys that can cooourt them, the boys from the County Armagh?* The requests rang out, with each of us revealing our identity. A person from Letterkenny had a tear in his eye, so had I.

That night in the Albert Hall, Bridie Gallagher was the queen. She sang Irish songs just for us. We lapped it up. She gave us more. All of us sang. A great night to remember.

The Silence was a Roar

It reminded me of the Lough House in days gone by when John Glackin used to shout when the neighbours got home after all day in the bog or saving the hay or digging the spuds. The Lough House was a meeting place. John Glackin used to have a "*meaghle*" at the Lough House, when a person arrived home from America town with goodies for all. The neighbours would come from near and far.

One year John Hanna, Edward Hanna (home from America town) and I said we would fish Lough Mourne. In the evening we would attend the get-together. John got a nice black 3 lbs trout, with his very first cast. We fished it for a full hour without as much as a bite or a rise.

At the dinner all was going good until Uncle Patrick Glackin went out to milk the cows. He came in carrying a Lucozade bottle with a bit of the Donegal Democrat acting as a bung which he says is for Maggie. He attempted to hand it to Maggie, who was out of reach. Enter me, the townie, who reaches up and takes the bottle of milk and says, "That bottle is warm!"

Uncle Patrick says "Jesus Christ, why wouldn't the bottle be warm? Isn't that milk only after coming out of the bloody cow?"

Running the Gauntlet

I studied at London School of Telegraphy, Earls Court, to get my Postmaster General certificate. I ran an open battle with the staff of the London Underground. I could not "fork out" the full fare from Finsbury Park right across London, after having to take the bus from Crouch End, where I lived in Weston Park. It would be a miracle to have avoided the bus fare, which was only 3p. Still, I did avoid the bus fare on occasions, by standing or (clinging) to the "tail." The bus was full in the mornings, and the conductor took his time, so I would just take my time and stay at the back of the bus. When the conductor neared, I just dropped off.

Every morning – running the gauntlet to get Earls Court, where I faced my final hurdle, and that was getting out of the station, turning the corner, walking halfway up a street and into the College, where I was studying at a private establishment a course that would after 18 months get me the Postmasters Certificate.

I knew that I would have no trouble with the Morse Code, or any non-technical procedures, for I had been the best at the Morse Codes, and could take up 30 words per minute, and the sky was the limit as far as interception of Morse was concerned. I could take Russian, Arabic, and any other variation of Morse you could think of.

However as far as the technical side was concerned, I was not brilliant, but I knew I would pass the final exam. It took me two years to get my P.M. Cert. I had to leave the College for three months, then still study until three or four a.m. I returned to the College, took the written exam, and passed...

Being an ex-serviceman, I had another job all along. It was as a Sports Master at Hungerford School, at the back of Islington. Harry Secombe was a regular visitor. I played cricket or football or anything in the school yard, until it was time to go home. The kids carried their house-keys around their necks. They were tough kids. And I often had to defend myself where they would "attack" me (literally), when I gave an off-side or a run out. There were about 50 or 60 kids, and boy, were they tough...

I was studying to pass my exams to get my Postmaster General certificate, so that I could go to sea in the Merchant Navy as a Radio Officer. After two years I got my dream-come-true. My first ship was as 2nd Radio Officer on an oil tanker called "*The Border Chieftain*." I was twenty-two and a half years old.

2nd Radio Officer
The Border Chieftain

The Greyhound

After a six-month assignment on "The Border Chieftain," I found myself back in Ireland under very different circumstances:

From 1963 until I went to sea again in November 1964, I worked on the road where I was wholesaling stationary and Hotel supplies. Cecil Og King was my boss, and we operated from what used to be Kelly's shop (now the bookies). I travelled to all the counties that separated Donegal from the east coast of Ireland, and south towards Galway, but not into the city of the tribes. I drove a VW van, loaded with supplies. I worked hard, and though I was married, I was alone. I froze in the winter.

One day I landed in the town of Clones to stay the night in a prominent hotel. After booking in I walked into the kitchen. There on the floor of the kitchen was a dead greyhound.

Along came the chef. I said to him, "There is a dead greyhound lying on the floor."

He replied, "I know. As I was leaving the kitchen about four hours ago, this greyhound crashed through the IN door, ran twice around the full kitchen, then crashed at full speed out the OUT door. He was poisoned, because he stiffened immediately and, as you can see, his teeth are bare."

I said to the chef, "If he crashed out the OUT door, why is he lying in the kitchen?"

The answer from the chef was, "I dragged him into the kitchen out of the reception, in case someone saw him. Do you want to get the Hotel a bad name?"

Yes, indeed – Get the hotel a bad name...

The Continental Shipper

I served as Radio Officer on a cargo vessel named the *Continental Shipper*. I almost lost my job for telling the truth.

The maiden voyage of the *Continental Shipper* was to carry a load of timber from Victoria, British Columbia, to Japan. As cargoes go, timber is light compared with steel, ore, or machinery. After the holds of the ship were filled, decks were stacked high with rough-cut lumber which was tied down with chains.

There are basically two routes from Canada to Japan – a short northern route or a longer southern route. The Captain wanted to take the shorter route. I showed him the storm warnings that would make the northern route treacherous, but he overruled me. We sailed into a force 10+ storm. The huge piles of lumber on the deck shifted, causing the ship to list.

The Coast Guard arrived, sealed off my radio and took away my logs. They sealed and took the Captain's logs, too. He told them that he hadn't received any storm warnings.

We sailed back to Victoria on Vancouver Island, where crews of stevedores worked to stabilise the lumber on the decks. They had to jettison some of the lumber into the water and spill some of it onto the docks. There was a second accident during the restacking when part of the load toppled into the harbour. Then, when the Captain tried to sail the northern route a second time, tons of lumber again came loose on the deck, damaging railings, funnels, and valves.

We finally sailed to Japan, and when we pulled away from the dockside, the stevedores all cheered. We took the southern route and got there in eleven days.

In Japan the ship was unloaded, and we took on a cargo of steel rods and rolls of sheet steel. That cargo was contained in the holds and did not pose a danger on the deck, but it created a pendulum effect. If it shifted, we would have been in trouble.

The *Continental Shipper* took the steel cargo to South Africa. There the Captain was relieved of his duties and given half an hour to vacate the ship.

My Children, Dara / Orla / Sara / Patrick

I was present when my son Dara was born in the North London Hospital, March 1961. I was at sea off the Philippines when my second child Orla was born. Sarah came into the world when I was in the Russian Black Sea port of Odessa. Patrick, the last of our two boys and two girls, was born when my ship was in the Japanese North Island port of Kushiro.

Dara was chosen Captain of the Under-12 football team which won the District Championship. He went on to become the Captain of the first Aodh Ruadh Minor football team, winning the first of four County Championships in a row. He followed me into the Merchant Navy, where he spent 5 years. Now he is employed by the national Coast Guard at Malin Head. He is married to Mairead Finn, who is from Drumshambo, Leitrim.

Orla is in San Francisco where she owns the Irish Castle Gift Shop on Geary Street. She sells only Irish goods. Orla is married to John McLaughlin, Boston. His Grandmother, 100 years young, is from Kerry.

Sarah is married to John Meehan, a native. John Meehan is a Fine Gael councillor on Ballyshannon Town Council, and employed by the HSE. John has a saint (well, almost) in the family: Blessed Charles Meehan.

Patrick played on the fourth Minor Under-18s football team which won the county championship. He was married to Tanya Zigera, now divorced. He is employed by the City of San Francisco.

Dara, Orla, Sarah and Patrick are recognised swimmers, and recently Sarah, along with James McIntyre and Barry Duffy, swam from St. Johns Point to Creevy Pier (16 Kilometres) to raise funds for Parkinson's Disease. My son Dara did a similar feat with John Maguire last year, and had a struggle from the point opposite Creevy Pier to swim against the severe tide. They had great difficulty completing the swim as the tide turned whilst they were in the water. The swim took them eight hours, with the last mile taking almost two hours to complete.

On the 18th September 2011, my daughter Orla and my son Patrick swam from Alcatraz Prison across San Francisco Bay, against the strength of the infamous currents – a mile and a half of the most dangerous waters ever encountered. Before Alcatraz Prison was finally closed by Bobby Kennedy in 1965 when he was Attorney General, no prisoner had successfully escaped Alcatraz. All funds collected from all swims went to the Parkinson's Association.

Orla and the Healing Priest

There was a priest next door on Tirconnail Street in Donegal Town – Dean Glackin of Killymard, who had great healing powers. When Orla was born, she had a growth on her right temple. The medical opinion was that she had to have it taken off with an operation, and that would leave a scar. We took her to Dean Glackin, who touched the growth with his hands. He said that she would be all right – and she was.

Dara in the River

In the 1960's, Dara and the whole plant – Mary (Mother), Orla, Sarah, and Patrick – were in Castle Street, Donegal Town. While I roamed the World at will, Dara was first up and in the River Eske. Or if the water was too high, Dara was walking up and down the wall, wearing a pair of sunglasses to spot any salmon or sea trout lying in a pool or in a shoal. He knew the tides. He was fearless. Mama was worrying about Dara, and so was everyone.

One evening Dara was "hoking" up and down the River Eske. Next thing he cut his big toe. Within a few days the doctor had to be called. Doctor O'Toole was a west of Ireland man. He was a friend of mine, and my father's. He was a great medicine man, and one evening he duly arrived to lance Dara's infected toe.

When our "cub" spotted the doctor away he went – upstairs and into the toilet. Dara (for whatever reason) hated doctors, dentists, and anybody wearing a white coat. He once had a run-in Dr McEniff, the dentist, who told me, "Take Dara away and never bring him back!"

Dara ran into the toilet and would not exit. Dr. O'Toole left the house and returned to his surgery to see other patients. All efforts were made to get Dara unlock the door, to no avail. In the end, Dada and John had to break down the door, grab Dara, bundle him into a car, and with all instructions they reached O'Toole's house.

Hold Fast

Dada and John held Dara, with Mary and Mama crying over "such a bold boy," and apologies to Dr O'Toole. With a quick, professional swoop Dr O'Toole lanced Dara's big toe, but it was the wrong toe. With the second attempt, sweating because he was small and stout, he managed to lance the right toe – the left was the wrong toe. Eventually, with both toes cleaned and bandaged, the job was done. All was right, again. Once more Dara could head for the river, and that is what he did, early next morning, with two toes bandaged.

"Give Him Plenty of the SSStick"

Maybe "right" is not the correct word, but it will have to do. Dara appreciated the kindness, and concern displayed by Dr O'Toole, and when he got a white trout, Dara sent a fine fish to the doctor. The man with the western accent enjoyed his sea trout, and sent Dara a note of thanks. It countered what he had said the night he lanced the two toes:

"Mrs Daly, I'll tell you what you should do to that boy – Give Him Plenty of the SSStick."

So between Edward Hanna and Dara, there was plenty of fishing and fish. I was at sea, but Mary kept me informed.

I was at home between merchant-navy assignments when a dramatic incident occurred:

Former Commissioner to Get Bravery Award

The Donegal Democrat
17 July 2001

Ballyshannon Town Commissioners this week received news that a former Chairman of the body is to receive an award for bravery 31 years after he risked his life to save others.

Anthony O'Malley Daly, the recipient of the of the award, took the opportunity to underline the importance of water safety.

Now 65 years old and living in College Street, Ballyshannon, he then was a young man of 34 working in the merchant navy on a ship under a Liberian flag when he came home to Ballyshannon for a holiday in August of 1970.

On the 21st of the month as the summer weather was on its way out, he went out checking lobster pots with four of his friends from the locality. The young radio officer and his friends left from Creevy Pier and headed out into Donegal Bay, working their way along the cliffs towards Rossnowlagh.

At a famous lobster spot called Corker, which is filled with dangerous rocks, the men started to pull up one of the pots. The weather had come up slightly and there was quite a swell running; one of the pots got stuck, and as the men endeavoured to bring it in, the boat was hit by a wave.

Deciding wisdom was the better part of valour, the men left the pot and attempted to leave the area. It was then things began to get dramatically worse; one of the oars of the boat broke and the vessel was knocked broadside to the surging surf.

The next wave swamped the small fishing skiff, the one after threw the five men from the boat and into the churning ocean. Of the five only Anthony and one other could swim, with Anthony being the most proficient by far.

He swam two of the men ashore to the nearby rocks, leaving the third individual holding onto the top of the upturned boat. The two men on the first journey were close to drowning before Anthony got to their assistance. One was lying face down in the water and the other was panicking to the extent that he ripped his would-be rescuer's clothes.

Despite these obstacles and the churning ocean, Anthony managed to swim the men ashore while also towing a line from the boat. Once ashore he pulled in the boat which the third man was still clinging to.

At the time, and in fact all through the years, Anthony has not wanted a fuss made about the incident and was reluctant to talk about it other than to confirm the details. However it has arisen many times and was most recently retold at his 40th wedding anniversary celebration in 1997.

It was his wife Mary who eventually brought the matter to the attention of the then Town Clerk, Ms. Philomena O'Sullivan. In 1997 Ms. O'Sullivan had been in touch with Comhairle Mire Gaile, who gives out the bravery awards, for the actions of another native of the town, Mr. Rossa O'Neill, who had rescued a woman from a cliff face in Rossnowlagh.

Ms. O'Sullivan also mentioned the long forgotten deed of bravery of the former Chair of the Commissioners to the Comhairle which resulted in the gardai taking statements from all involved on that fateful day off the rocks at Corker.

Awarded Medal

The final result was the news this week that Mr. O'Malley Daly will be awarded a bronze medal for bravery and a certificate to that effect at a function yet to be arranged.

Speaking to the Democrat, Anthony, who is still working as a FAS supervisor, said he was pleased with news. "I suppose you could say it has been on my mind for 30 years. I'm happy to be getting some recognition," he said.

He said the only reason he had been able to make any difference on the day was his ability to swim. "I don't think it had as much to do with bravery as it had being able to swim. I learnt at the Erne Swimming Club who used to hold their galas at Creevy Pier.

"If I hadn't been taught to swim we all might have drowned that day. I would like to take this opportunity to encourage all people to avail of their local swimming pool and to wear life jackets when they go to sea. My being taught life saving techniques is what saved lives that day," said the modest medal winner who was a Town Commissioner for 20 years and held the Chair of the Commissioners on two separate occasions.

As you've probably pieced together by now, I worked at many jobs over the years. I worked for the Donegal Democrat and for FÁS. I also became involved in politics and served as a Ballyshannon Town Councillor. I was the Chairman of the Council twice, and the only Sinn Fein representative to hold that position for many years.

I was on the Council during The Troubles, and the memories of those years can be painful. I wrote the following article in 2006, a quarter of a century after the Hunger Strikes:

A Personal Reflection: H-Block 25 Years On
1981 Hunger Strike Made Republicans Sit-Up

By Anthony O'Malley Daly
The Donegal Democrat, 10 August 2006

To realise the extent the 1981 Hunger Strike was taking its toll on Republicans, I must go back to when the first Hunger Strike started on Monday, 27th October 1980 by seven prisoners in Long Kesh, and joined by three women on Monday, 1st December.

As a public speaker and Sinn Fein public representative I joined in the campaign to get the demands of the prisoners granted.

On Saturday. 13th December, 1980, a public meeting was held at the Diamond, Ballyshannon. The main speaker was Frank Maguire, MP, and when I noticed the condition of Frank Maguire I got a fright. All his efforts for the prisoners had broken Frank's health. Five days on, the H-Block's seven men and three women in Armagh Prison halted their fast when 'concessions' were granted by the British Government.

However, an explanation in writing the concessions fell far short of expectations. Bobby Sands started the second Hunger Strike on March 1st, 1981.

Frank Maguire died on Thursday, 5th March. My great friend was gone. To me, Frank Maguire was a casualty of his efforts for the prisoners. Still I thought the Thatcher Government would relent, especially when Bobby Sands won Fermanagh and South Tyrone, despite an SDLP call to spoil or leave unmarked their ballot papers, but Bobby Sands died on Tuesday, 5th May, a month after topping the poll, defeating Harry West to become an MP.

I must say that at a meeting in Letterkenny, when Neil T. Blaney T.D. told me Bobby Sands was going to be sacrificed, I knew we were in for a long bitter political battle as prisoners were to join the hunger strike every two weeks.

From the death of such a fine man as Bobby Sands and the position taken by the British Government, added to the knowledge that more were to die before any shift was daunting.

Francis Hughes, Bellaghy, died one week later after 59 days. He had been injured and captured by SAS soldiers after a gun battle in which a number of British soldiers had been killed. Francie Hughes was a well known IRA Volunteer, and a Republican hero, now he had not hesitated to lay down his precious life for his friends and comrades. All members of the movement were shaken to the core. We were waiting for the next to die, and we hadn't long to wait.

Raymond McCreech from Camlough, South Armagh, and Patsy O'Hara passed from this life on Thursday 21st May. I attended every funeral and was standing in a ditch when his brother, a priest, said the last words of Raymond were, "I will be home before you." Patsy O'Hara was buried in Derry on Monday 25th May.

General Election

A general election was called in the 26 counties. Joe McDonnell was nominated to contest the Sligo/Leitrim constituency. Every republican turned out to canvass for the Hunger Striker.

We left no stone unturned from dawn until dusk. John Joe McGirl and Joe O'Neill were issuing the orders and we were doing the ground work with the sole aim of getting Joe McDonnell elected to Dail Eireann on Thursday 11th June 1981. The great Kerry GAA footballer Joe Keohane was stomping the hustings. All hands were to the wheel.

Around this time Charlie Haughey made an election visit to Ballyshannon and felt the wrath of the local Sinn Fein Cumanns. He was jostled and hit with an egg.

39

Myles Byrne, a photographer friend of mine from a national newspaper who was with the FF party, said he never saw the likes of it in his career and told me he would never set foot in Ballyshannon again. *(Myles died in Australia some years later.)*

Back at the election campaign, we were hopeful of success, but Joe McDonnell lost. The Haughey Government lost also, and we marched out of Sligo/Leitrim furious at this loss. After taking a deep breath, we began to pick up political speed for the next challenge that lay ahead.

After mass public meetings, council resolutions were passed by most public authorities supporting our prisoner's demands. Joe McDonnell was a dedicated republican, he had a lovely wife Goretti, and a brave son and daughter, but by Wednesday 8th July Joe McDonnell was dead after suffering sixty one days on hunger strike.

Barely one week later on Monday 13th July, Martin Hurson died unexpectedly from complications after 46 days. On the August bank holiday Kevin Lynch from Dungiven, Co Derry died after 71 days of torture. Next day (Sunday) Kieran Doherty T.D. for Cavan Monaghan died after 73 days. He had been elected on 11th June with over 9,000 first preference votes. He was the eighth republican hunger striker to die.

I was desperate at this stage and questioning the authority of the prisoners who continued to die and the republican movement for seemingly allowing them to die. Each time I spoke from a platform, I prayed for a miracle word or sentence that would move the British government to grant the conditions sought by the prisoners and end what appeared to be an endless nightmare that I and many other republicans were scared for life with anyway.

Sympathy Vote

During a discussion at Bundoran Urban Council on the 24th July a vote of sympathy was proposed to the families of the dead hunger strikers. Clr. Joe O'Neill stormed out of the council chamber after allegations were made by other councillors that H-Block supporters had disrupted traffic and trade in the town by holding protest meetings. This debate concluded with Clr. O'Neill stating that "as long as Joe O'Neill is Joe O'Neill, I'll be on the streets."

In Ballyshannon at a public meeting on the Diamond I was asked to withdraw a band from the parade because a member had said that the same band had previously taken part in a loyalist event. When I could not get this confirmed, I allowed the band to march. After this parade which coincided with the annual Orange march at Rossnowlagh, Co. Donegal, a ranking republican approached me to lead a march at Rossnowlagh to highlight the plight of the dying H-Block hunger strikers. I made an immediate decision being the public representative close to this area that there should be no march or confrontation with the Orange parade. I felt this would be counterproductive as feelings were running so high at this time.

Thomas McElwee, a 23 year old volunteer also from Bellaghy, passed away after 63 days in pain, increasing the number dead to nine. On Thursday 20th August Mickey Devine an INLA volunteer died after 60 days on hunger strike and that was the tenth and final republican to die by the torturous route of starvation.

On the same day as Mickey Devine's death, came good news that Owen Carron, who had been an election agent for Bobby Sands, was elected an MP for Fermanagh/South Tyrone with an increased majority over the UDR major Ken Maginnis.

At long last and after 217 days on Saturday, 3rd October 1981, the hunger strikes to the death finally ended thanks to the intervention of the late great Fr. Denis Faul and the families of the hunger strikers.

Personally those are the facts of the case, but I as a Sinn Fein public representative within the republican movement was almost a broken man, and it was at this time that I began to question my faith (republican faith).

On Friday 21st August 1981 I went to the Creggan area of Derry to view the remains of Mickey Devine. I went into the wrong street and met some youngsters who pointed out Devine's house to me. The house was through a passageway or a short entry, and they said to me, "Mister, you walk through that entry and we will drive your car around for you." I knew what would happen to my car if I had given them the keys! I refused their offer, locked my car and walked through the short entry. When I got to the door of Mickey Devine's house, I was reflecting at the irony of what had happened. I paid homage to Mickey Divine. At last the prisoners had got their demands, but ten men had died, and part of me died ten times as well.

The political landscape would never be the same again.

Moving on to happier memories. Mary and I visited our children in the USA in 1991, and I wrote a full-page article about our trip in the Donegal Democrat.

Angling and More from Boston and San Francisco

By Anthony O'Malley Daly

Mary and I departed for Boston on Saturday, 27th July 1991. I am always struck by the long queues checking-in tickets and luggage – not to mention the tasty meals and drinks served to passengers during the flight. When I am on the ground looking at an aircraft taking off, I am struck by the sheer power, but when I am lodged inside one I resort to prayers and promises, willing the thing into the sky.

All went well and Aer Lingus provided us with a splendid air journey across the Atlantic to the city of Boston, and very busy Logan Airport. My daughter Orla greeted us at arrivals, and took us to our Dorchester holiday apartment. Personal effects put away, fan at full swing to supply cool air, feet up, beer in hand, TV switched on, talk of Ireland and Boston, and somehow the world is (for the moment) all right.

Rest and relaxation can last for just so long, so it was off to meet my old friends such as Tom Sheehan, the bartender for Tom English's pub at Hyde Park, near Cleary Square. Later we were joined by Ballyshannon men Paul Tuohy and Pauric Bromley, and we talked of Donegal's chances in the Ulster Final. We were convinced they would win, but the next day proved us wrong. Sunday morning I was able to ring the local Eire Pub barely 20 minutes after the final whistle in Clones and got the result.

That afternoon we toured the boundaries of Boston - viewed the homes of the more affluent citizens. Then we went to Nantaskit Beach for a swim, which was not so pleasant as the shore line would not recommend itself for a blue flag designation. Now I know that the authorities in Boston are making gallant strides to clear the beaches and clean the image, and they are succeeding, but a mighty lot remains to be done.

Back we went to the local hostelry where we met many from Cork and Kerry. Tom Graham from Offaly, Martin Farrell from Sligo, and Mary Friel and Brian Keeney, who were returning to native parts of Donegal to get married. (*It was not to be. Mary Friel, a former Garda in Letterkenny, passed away in an unfortunate accident.*)

Fishing and Whale Watching

Mary and my daughter Orla had the shops to see and the sights to view, but I was anxious to go fishing. Orla came up trumps. Arrangements were made for us all to go aboard a fishing vessel leaving Hull Harbour at 8am on Thursday 1st August.

The departure point was reckoned to be but 30 minutes away taking the highway, and essentially the right turn-off road, so we were still up at 6am to give plenty of leeway. Things of course did not go exactly to plan for we went past our junction. We were lost and went every which way skirting Hull, to the right. However, in the finish and with good assistance from friendly people we landed at Hull just as the ropes were being untied for departure. We got ourselves and our cold beer on board just in time. As they say in America, "I was all stressed out."

On board including Orla, Mary and myself, were Mark Rodgers, owner and skipper; Kenny Fitzpatrick, mate and fishing gear; Eddie Burke, owner of Doyle's Braddock Bar and restaurant in Jamaica Plains; Bonnie Millar, manageress of Doyle's; Marge Buckley from Cork. The ladies were along for the exclusive tan, and to see the whales. The men were out to catch fish - either Bass, Bluefish or the rare Giant Tuna, and to Whale watch.

The boat "*Final Final*" was a 32ft. Luhrs Tournament 320 sports fish fiberglass cruiser. Fitted with twin 330 h.p. Crusader engines, she could cruise at 25 knots and had a top speed of 40 knots. Why the vessel is called "Final Final" is because the skipper, Mark Rodgers has had many other boats, and did not intend to buy another. But in 1989 Mark went to a boat show to purchase a fishing rod, and came away with his new fishing rod and his new and expensive cruiser. He swore it was his final boat, so he called her – yes, you've guessed – "*Final Final*."

Mark Rodgers, a bachelor, deserves a word or two. He is a swashbuckling American male of the bravo type, the American way of life. He loves his country and stands up for it. Anything he does he is enthusiastic about, so he is keen on his boat, his fishing, his Boston, his sea and his zest for life. Yet he is not blinkered and is kind and considerate. For many years he thought he was of Dutch/German/Scots extraction until his sister traced the family tree to show that he was Irish. His family name is Sullivan from Limerick, and his ancestors can be traced back to 1639.

The mate and general hand of the "*Final Final*," Kenny Fitzpatrick, also has Irish connections. A carpenter by trade, he is known as a fine artist, and being the opposite of Mark he is quiet, and a good listener. Kenny Fitzpatrick is an ex-marine.

40 Miles into the Atlantic

Anyway, outward we sailed from Hingham Bay, past Boston light, and the civil war prison of Ft. Warren, into the main channel and then the broad Atlantic. All the time we sped past numerous boats and dodged crab and lobster buoys. I can understand why crab and lobster is so dear as some of the pots were on grounds fully 20 miles out into the Atlantic. On the way we intercepted a coast guard message telling of the 28ft sailing boat "*Leben*" missing on a voyage to Newport, Rhode Island, and last heard from eight days past. All mariners were asked to keep watch for the missing ship and crew. I hope they were found.

I have mentioned about Boston taking action about its pollution and sewerage problems. Twenty-five miles out we came across a massive platform laying huge pipes to take waste far out to sea. I don't know how long we journeyed, but I noticed that we were out in the Atlantic swell. In fact we were out 40 miles from the shore of Boston. If we had gone any further I'm sure we would have spotted Ireland. Now we were at the fishing grounds, and if you are thinking that so far out the sea would be deserted - then you are wrong. The Stell Wagon Bank was crowded (well, you know what I mean) with fishing boats, Whale watching tourist ships, and Tuna-spotter aircraft overhead. Why they have spotter planes is that Tuna fishing is big business. The Japanese are very partial to tuna, which they eat raw. Any tuna caught can be sold immediately to Japanese buyers, and the prize depends on the condition of the tuna. Mark Rodgers and Kenny Fitzpatrick landed a 550lb Tuna a few years back, and got $15,000 for it.

You might ask "Why sell your catch?" – but what fridge could hold 550lbs of Tuna steaks, and what pocket wouldn't welcome $15,000? Also, the expense incurred to get to the fishing grounds and the gear required, not to mention a very large boat, makes it imperative that one, you catch the odd tuna, and two, that you get a good price for the same.

Bluefish and Whales

The Stell Wagon Bank is not only full of boats and tourists, but it is rich in many species of fish and mammal. The Pilot Whale (small) and the Humpback (big) feed on the plankton and are a source of revenue for the many ships that ply from Boston each day during the season. The Tuna is much sought after as a sport fish for commercial fishing while such as bass and bluefish and others, are fished for sport and considered game fish.

The "*Final Final*" was reduced to 4 knots to hunt for the Tuna and bluefish or bass. Kenny put out 4 rods of the tidewater variety. They were extra heavy 6ft rods with 300 yards of 40 lbs test strain, leaded and a large rubber eel as bait. Later, we changed to a 10 inch plug and a similar sized magnum bait. Mark put out a 6ft. rod with a reel of 130 lbs. breaking strain line, attached with a steel trace, and a bright green squid on a gaff like hook directly behind the boat hoping to lure a big eye Tuna or the much bigger Blue Fin Tuna. No Tuna appeared. It seems the temperature of the sea tended to put them below the 50ft level. On the other hand, Kenny and I hooked some Bluefish and managed to land three. The Bluefish do a strong take and are hard fighters, especially when they see the boat. They have sharp teeth. They fight to the finish and care must be exercised when boarding them. The bluefish is gaffed through the gills. In this method they can be safely returned to the sea if not to be eaten, or killed immediately if required for the table. Their flesh is akin to that of a Mackerel and, also like the Mackerel, they are oily. Many seafood restaurants have them on menus as a class dish.

The event of that sunny day was the sight of the many breaching whales. This giant mammal, this gentle sensitive monster of the deep, secure and confident in its habitat, plunged, rose to the heavens, breached, flipped its mighty tail,, flapped applause like its barnacle scratched fins and in human approach gave the sightseers the show of a lifetime. For me, and all aboard, to plant my eyes on such a scene turned a rare and pleasant trip into a wonderful journey.

By the way, the bluefish weighed each between 10 and 12 lbs. Kenny made them into fillets, when, reluctantly, Mark ordered all rods in and we headed for shore. In the words of Kenny, "The worst part of fishing is having to come in." Even at that, the adventure was not over. The ebullient Mark raced everything to the anchorage, where we had a refreshing swim from the deck of the "*Final Final*" before finally going alongside the jetty. Thank you Mark, thank you Kenny, and thank you Whales.

The Author, with a 10 lb Bluefish

San Francisco

On the 3rd August we left hot Boston and went across the land mass of America to touch down in San Francisco where we were met by our son, Patrick, and his girlfriend Tanya Zigera. Trans World Airlines looked after our flight in an efficient and friendly manner - indeed the return journey was just the same good service.

Here we met old friends in the Rush family - Jackie, Marie, Noel and Rose, Ricky and Camilla, Paddy, Anne and Eamonn. I hope I have left none of them out. Anyway, an Irish bar, McCarty's, was conveniently handy to the apartment, owned by a Monaghan man, Joe Comiskey, and frequented by Ireland's finest from the four green fields. Here I met with Stephen Gallinagh from Buncrana, Pat Feely from Rossinver (Leitrim) and others from the Belleek/Garrison area. At one stage I thought that San Francisco was only inhabited by Cork and Kerry people, but after Down beat Kerry in the All-Ireland Semi-Final, the accents were from Down, Tyrone, Derry – you name it.

A number of things should be said of San Francisco. Parts of the city have banks of fog that roll in from the Pacific. You actually see the fog rolling in to envelop this great city. Indeed you can be in fog in one part of the city and then travel a mile down the road and emerge into clear and hot sunshine. Another feature of SF is how cosmopolitan a city it is with west merging with east, and black mingling with white.

The city streets are the steepest hills I've ever seen, and you have no conception until you drive on them, or take a ride on the famous cable cars. Another daunting aspect of life in this western city is that it is situated on a fault in the Earth's surface and certain of earthquakes. Some are even waiting for a repeat of the really big one, but it may never happen. It does not dampen the ardour and happy outlook of most of its population, who must by now be used to the tension simmering beneath their surface. The roads or streets are in alphabetical order, avenues are in numerical order, and both are wide and spacious and given the hill, it is a traffic offence not to turn you car wheels towards the curb when parked.

San Francisco Bay is spanned by two famous bridges, the Bay Bridge and the Golden Gate Bridge. Out in the bay stands the infamous Prison of Alcatraz – now empty. This establishment once housed the likes of "Machine Gun" Kelly, Al Capone and other notorious law breakers who had to be isolated from society, including the famous "Birdman" of Alcatraz. Robert Kennedy closed this prison in the mid-sixties. A number of Inmates in fact escaped from the confines of its walls, but it was never confirmed if any of the escapees made it to the mainland through the cold waters and currents in the bay. My daughter Orla and son Patrick recently swam from the prison to the mainland, to raise funds for Parkinson's.

The Irish on the West Coast keep in touch with the local news from back home. The Democrat, among other Irish provincial newspapers, is sold at the Irish Imports shop of Louis Roach on Geary Boulevard. Apart from their native Gaelic Games, many of the Irish have taken to Golf. Now there are no John Dalys among their ranks just yet, but they are keen and it allows them relaxation and an avenue to give vent to their frustrations. Sean Molloy who tends bar at Terrie's Lounge could make the grade if he allowed himself a few early nights. Other well known Irish haunts include The Abbey and Ireland 32 – although there could be others I just didn't notice.

Pacific King Salmon

If I fished in the Atlantic, then I had to go on a similar trip in the not so calm Pacific. At 6am on the Friday 16th August, my son Patrick, Sean Liston (Ballybunnion) Con Coughlin (Bantry), myself and 14 others boarded the sport fishing boat called "*The Viking*," skippered by Jan Gobershock, an American of Swedish forbears. To reach Fisherman's Wharf we had to survive an early morning Streets of San Francisco drive with the carefree Sean Liston at the wheel. Suffice to say we got to the embarkation point in one piece.

Off we all set out into the early dawn calm. Past Alcatraz we steamed, and under the Golden Gate Bridge, Danny Timms, our deckhand, allocated our positions on the boat. Rods were provided, or you could bring your own equipment. A license had to be purchased if you had none, and seeing as us four had nothing, the trip and license and use of equipment cost $57. This boat, like "*Final Final*," had the most up to date gear, and the necessary powerful engines. It was 43 feet long by 14 feet beam, with a draft of 4 feet – I thought I better tell you – and it was powered by twin 220hp engines. Going about fifteen miles out to the Duxbury Reef where we were to drift and fish did not take long with such machinery.

The sea was choppy, some were cooking up hot dogs, so stomachs were churning. Mine was not so good either, what with spending half the night in Terrie's listening to Sean Molloy singing and downing numerous "ones for the road." For an old seaman like myself my pride was at stake, so I kept on smiling. The others were in no shape to notice anyway. Hanging over the rails we put our rods baited with fresh spratt on a No. 2 hook, a lump of lead and a strong gut clipped on to a swivel.

A rod holder was provided at each position on the rails with a safety clip, just in case you would drop the rod overboard. The engines were cut out and we fished in a drift with no need to jig the rod, such was the rolling of the boat and the sharpness of the waves. Jan Gobershock, anxious to get one of us a fish, shifted positions many times along the reef. When rods were boarded for the positional shift, all hands took to the cabin, and a bit of sleep.

We were suddenly well into the mid-morning with not a bite, until suddenly Danny the deckhand exclaimed to the surprise of all, "Fish on!" Of course, who had the fish on? Only Patrick O'Malley Daly, and the rod was bent double. All rods were reeled in and the battle commenced. Jan and Danny allowed it was a fairly hefty fish, and a Salmon at that. Naturally I started to give orders such as "Check you tension!" and "Keep your rod bent in him!" and other such expert advice. But Patrick was like father like son, and somehow knew how to handle the situation.

Patrick's First Salmon - His First Fish!

Now you would think in the expanse of the vast Pacific Ocean Patrick would have clear seas, but he didn't. The Salmon got round the rope of a crab cage. We were all relegated to the stern of the ship, but with Jan handling the manoeuvres of the big craft, and one John Van Tassle from Daly City releasing the line with a long gaff, Patrick was free to play the Salmon out for Danny Timms to net it and bring it aboard. The fish turned out to be a King Salmon weighing 28 lbs and as fresh as a daisy, with Sea lice attached. The cameras came out and we gave Patrick our congratulations. Patrick had never been out fishing before, never caught a fish, and on his first trip he landed a major fish.

The salmon's tail was clipped, so we could not sell it.

The King or Chinook Salmon are the largest of the 5 species of Pacific Salmon. King Salmon of 40 or 50 lbs are not a rarity. 28 lbs was big enough for proud Patrick. I was greatly pleased myself. That was the only Salmon caught among 18 anglers aboard *"The Viking"* that day, and when at 1:30 pm the skipper announced to board all rods for the trip back to dry land, there were no objectors. On the way in Danny gutted and gilled the Salmon. On shore the four weary anglers retired to the Fiddlers Green to celebrate. Back at base I cut the Salmon into steaks. Mary cooked some on the spot, and Tanya and Camilla enjoyed the fresh catch from the Pacific. This King Salmon was a hen fish measuring 38 inches long, by 24 inches in girth. Indeed a fine specimen. Well done, Patrick.

Other Visits

Charlie Rooney, Ballyshannon, lives with his wife and family in Daly City, and we met Charlie at the Irish Centre. Later the same evening Charlie took us see the Brooksville Hotel, seat of Lanty and Blanid Molloy in Colma, on the outskirts of the big city. Here I saw a framed copy of the Donegal Democrat 14th May 1965, showing a photo of the then 82 year old Frank Molloy on a visit to his native Leamagoura, Ardara. Lanty Molloy was not on the premises when we called, but we were well looked after by his wife Blanid and her sister Deirdre.

The Democrat is in good company along the walls of this saloon, for festooning the walls are pictures of many of the personalities from the past, including pugilists of the stamp of J.J. Corbett, Jack Johnson, Battling Nelson, Packy McFarland and many other who thrilled mass audiences in the open ring before TV. Also on the front page is a wedding photo of Patrick and Maureen McEniff and the opening of the Tourist Information Office for the All-Ireland Fleadh Rince, showing among others John Tuohy and James White.

Now if you are wondering about Daly City, it was founded by a man called John Daly who operated a "Milk Ranch" around 1890. You can take it from there. Your guess is as good as mine.

My wife Mary entered a shop called "The Irish Castle" and met owner Aquinas McClafferty-Hooley, formerly from Donegal Town. (My daughter Orla has since become the proprietor of "The Irish Castle.")

We fished in the Pacific on Friday, and by Saturday 17 of August we were back in Boston with exciting and fond memories of the many friends we met and made while in San Francisco.

On Sunday 18th of August we were at the Delboy Stadium where Donegal beat St. Christopher's to reach the finals of the Intermediate Championship of New England. The Fennell Family came along to add to the cheers for Donegal. "Gramps" Logue, father of Mrs. Fennell, left Clonmany 64 years ago, and only returned on a holiday a few years back. He still retains vivid memories of how his Native Clonmany was all those decades in the past.

Hurricane Bob

Everything has a happy ending, but sometimes there are a few bumps along the way. On Monday 19th August as we were preparing our bags for departure on Aer Lingus that evening from Logan Airport, we got news that Hurricane Bob was heading for Boston. It struck at midday. First came the heavy rain, and then the hurricane force winds of 100 mph plus. It was batten-down-the-hatches time. A state of emergency was declared for the Boston area. Offices and factories were closed down and staff sent home. In the worst-affected places people abandoned their homes and took to prepared shelters. The television, sometimes blurred, kept issuing information and updating and, mind you, from what I can gather the authorities were leaving nothing to chance. The tunnels were flooded and the bridges were closed because they were swaying. Aer Lingus were still leaving on time – the plane was departing and it was up to us to get there. Anyway, the tail end of Hurricane Bob quickly dissipated, and while we did not exactly depart on time, we got off and landed safely in Shannon. *The Green Green Grass of Home.*

Reflection

And I say this truly. No matter where we travelled and encountered Irish men and women, we found them to be hard working and a credit to society. No family need grieve that their loved ones are in Boston or San Francisco or anywhere else in America for that matter. They are the best calibre of citizen and enhance their workplace. The only pity, upon reflection, is their skills and humanity are lost to this nation – Ireland. God bless and keep every one of them.

I worked for FÁS for a number of years. When I retired in 2001, this newspaper story described some of the programmes I had been involved with:

FAS Retirements

by Conor Sinclair
Donegal Times, 14 November 2001

Colleagues and friends assembled last week in the Abbey Hotel to honour Anthony O'Malley Daly and Timothy Hinchcliffe who have retired from their positions as FAS Supervisors in the Rural Deanery Scheme.

Tributes were paid by Rev Ken McLoughlin, Inver Church of Ireland who said "Over the years Anthony and Tim have made my life very easy with their total commitment as Supervisors and I wish to thank them. I also wish to thank their wives as work often spills over into family life. It is nice to see faces here from past schemes. Only for all these workers on the schemes so many places would have grown wild and derelict. I would also like to thank Canon Harry Trimble who got the FAS schemes going over 10 years ago and compliment him on his vision."

My FAS days - creating a riverbank recreation zone

Canon Trimble, thanking Anthony and Timothy said, "The Rural Deanery Scheme started about 10 years ago and the Community Employment Schemes grew from that. Tim was Overseer on the first scheme and Anthony took over when Tim's health prevented him from continuing. We are grateful to both of them. Without their input the schemes would not have been successful. Rev Brian Russell has now taken a leading role in the schemes. My thanks to you all."

The present Chairman, Rev Brian Russell said "I am very glad that Tim is being honoured here today. Although he has retired on health grounds, he was able to give great help to Anthony. I am also glad that Anthony is being honoured. He has a great pride in his work of maintaining the Protestant churches throughout the area. He always ensured that everything was done well despite his own battle with illness. I wish them both well in retirement."

Anthony, addressing the gathering said, "I feel very emotional today because I am retiring. Canon Trimble gave me this job and it was three very happy years for me. Before I leave I wish to thank the Sponsors of South Donegal Rural Deanery and FAS for three years of happiness. I also thank the organisers of this function and the Abbey Hotel. Thank you all for your gifts and good wishes. A special thanks to Timothy Hinchcliffe and I welcome the new Supervisor, Jerry Ford to the scheme and wish him every success. I will always remember you all for your great kindness, help and consideration."

THE REPORT OF THE ROYAL COMMISSION INTO BRITISH NUCLEAR TESTS IN AUSTRALIA

My story now doubles back to my military experiences and the aftermath of the atomic tests. I was a founding member of the B.N.T.V.A. (British Nuclear Test Veterans Association) – Member No D073. Over the years it became obvious that many of us who were at Maralinga and other test sites were beset with health problems. And a quarter of a century after the tests, the Royal Commission made the understatement of the century:

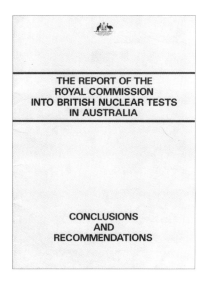

THE REPORT OF THE
ROYAL COMMISSION
INTO BRITISH NUCLEAR TESTS
IN AUSTRALIA

CONCLUSIONS
AND
RECOMMENDATIONS

Conclusion 153. The Royal Commission cannot exclude the possibility that those persons employed as Peace Officer Guards and security personnel at Emu and Maralinga may have been subjected to increased risk from exposure to radiation.

Here are some other conclusions and recommendations of the Royal Commission:

1.   The very first conclusion reads as follows: "The Royal Commission received no evidence to contradict the overwhelming impression that the original decision to lend Australia to the United Kingdom for the purpose of the latter's nuclear tests program was taken by Australian Prime Minister Menzies without reference to his cabinet...

2.   The decision was taken without any scientific knowledge of the hazards that would be involved.

3.   There is no documentation to suggest that Menzies was informed of the long term program that the British had in mind once they abandoned the United States as a possible site for their first test, but it is likely that he was given at least a broad outline...(12.1.15)

7.   There was virtually complete government control of the Australian media reporting of the Hurricane Test and the leading-up to it, thus ensuring that the Australian news media reported only what the UK government wished...

134. (Regarding the Antler Tests that I witnessed at Maralinga:) The Australian government made no decision on the permitted level of contamination from fallout of the Antler explosions.(9.1.36) .

140. Inadequate attention was paid to aboriginal safety during the Antler series.

People continued to inhabit the prohibited zone as close to the test sites as 130 km...

141. Air and ground patrols for Antler were neither well planned nor well executed.

142. Aboriginal people continued to inhabit the prohibited zone for six years after the tests. When they were told to leave the prohibited zone, some of them perished...

There were over 200 conclusions. There were six general conclusions, 148-153:

148. The balloon incidents demonstrate the inadequacy of the safety precautions governing the use of balloons at Maralinga. The fact that the incidents occurred and that the bureaucrats, scientists, and politicians were prepared to give categorical assurances that they could not occur, casts doubt on other assurances given to the public at the time.

We sought compensation for the costs that the nuclear tests had inflicted on us and on our families.

Update 2011 – Nuclear Bombs – Australia

Four years ago after 20 years campaigning, we got our day in court, and we won. The court was the High Court in London. The MoD (Ministry of Defense) appealed to the High Court in London, and we lost. The MoD appeal took a year to get into the High Court. It was Christmas. So we won, and then we lost. We started again. Now we are in the Supreme Court London.

Nuclear Veterans Lose Damages Bid

from the UK Press Association

British ex-servicemen who say they became ill as a result of being exposed to radiation during 1950s nuclear weapon tests in the Pacific have lost the latest round of a legal battle for damages.

But lawyers and relatives said the fight would go on and urged ministers to set up a compensation scheme.

More than 1,000 veterans want compensation and have been battling for permission to launch damages claims for more than two years. The Ministry of Defence (MoD) is contesting veterans' complaints and denies negligence.

My British Nuclear Weapons Tests Medal

Veterans say they were exposed to fallout radiation from tests and say that exposure caused illness, disability or death. The MoD denies both "exposure" and "causation".

The Supreme Court, the UK's highest court, has ruled in the MoD's favour after the latest round of litigation and said the majority of claims could not proceed. A panel of seven Supreme Court justices had analysed evidence at a hearing in London in November and ruled against veterans by a narrow majority (4-3).

Judges expressed sympathy but concluded that veterans lacked evidence to prove links between illness and proximity to tests and said many claims had been made too late. Lawyers are studying the ruling and trying to calculate how many claims will be able to proceed.

Veterans' relatives said they were disappointed by the ruling and called on ministers to step in. "The Government wouldn't lose one vote by compensating the British nuclear test veterans - in fact they'd win a lot," said Rose Clark, 71, of Romford, east London, whose husband Michael - a former soldier - died in 1992 aged 51 after contracting cancer.

Veterans' lawyer Neil Sampson said Britain should follow the lead of other countries and set up a "fair and just" compensation scheme. "The approach that this Government takes is to waste resources on fighting veterans rather than co-operating with them," he said. "There are some things in life that are wrong. The approach of the British Government to this issue is one of those things."

The MoD issued a statement in which a spokesman said: "The Ministry of Defence recognises the debt of gratitude we have to the servicemen who took part in the nuclear tests. They were important tests that helped to keep this nation secure at a difficult time in terms of nuclear technology.

"The Supreme Court ruled today in favour of the MoD that the claims brought by Nuclear Test Veterans were time barred and declined to allow the claims to proceed under the statutory discretion. Perhaps of greater significance is that all the justices recognised that the veterans would face great difficulty proving a causal link between illnesses suffered and attendance at the tests. The Supreme Court described the claims as having no reasonable prospect of success and that they were doomed to fail."

1st April News 2012 – We Lost

This is no April Fool. I received a phone call from Orla, from San Francisco, telling me the news that she had found on-line. We Lost Again, and for the final time. We cannot go any Higher. We were at the Supreme Court in London. The Supreme Court is the highest legal avenue in England. We have exhausted all our legal avenues now. The decision leaves us with no other appeal left, but the "fight" goes on.

Since we lost our appeal in the High Court, London, we have reorganised. The old B.N.T.V.A.(British Nuclear Test Veterans Association) that has been in existence for this past 20 to 25 years, and which I was one of the Founding Members, my number being D073, is no longer in operation. I phoned Bob Smith, Glasgow, Scotland, and he informed me he was not joining the other new organisation. However, I went ahead, signed up, and sent them £100, which was £60 donation and £40 membership.

I don't know, exactly, what our course will be in the future, but I am staying put. My Parkinson's disease that I am grappling with is getting a firmer grip of me each day, and it leaves me with no option.

Nuclear Veterans Association

From: Douglas Hern

Dear Anthony,

Sorry to have so long in getting back to you, first of all dealing with the research on the teeth, the BBC informed me that the results of the tests on the teeth inconclusive and some teeth arrived too late to be included in the shipment to the researchers in Germany. The BBC have so far, although I have requested on numerous occasions for a full report on the research, have failed to supply the request. Teeth are not returnable as they would have been destroyed during the research, but we cannot tell which were used for the research and which were too late, hence I have know way of knowing which teeth were yours any more.

Regarding your query on litigation I have spoken with informed and they have informed me that your name is on the waiting list, this is a list of late decision to the litigation. If we win the appeal, which the Government has laid against our winning decision it will be at the discretion of the Judge as to whether people on the waiting list are included in the litigation or if we lose the appeal no one will be in litigation because we will not be able to go forward with the main case.

I trust you understand all I have said, however if you have any further queries please do not hesitate to contact me by email again.

Best Regards,
Douglas Hern

As I said before, everything in life seems to be connected to everything else. Eamonn McFadden wrote a biographical article about me in 2006, and I have included it here to summarise the first section of Trilogy.

In recent years I have dedicated my life to raising awareness and funds for Parkinson's disease. I am saving those stories for the Grand Finale at the end of this book.

Anthony O'Malley Daly - From the Peace of Ballyshannon to a Nuclear Testing Site

By Eamonn McFadden, The Donegal Democrat, 25 May 2006

When he left Ballyshannon in the 1950's, Anthony O'Malley Daly got much more than he bargained for in the adventure stakes.

From a life on the high seas to the deserts of foreign fields he has travelled the world and seen, in one case, more than anyone would ever want to witness. Born in Ballyshannon in 1935, Anthony was the son of Sarah O'Malley from Sligo and well known surgeon and physician, Patrick Daly from Mayo and spent his formative years growing up in the waterway town. After his school years his first job was as an apprentice baker at Burke's in Ballyshannon. "I was paid ten shillings a week and a bag of doughnuts on a Friday," said Anthony recalling those early years.

But a life of adventure awaited him and he soon made plans to see the world setting off to enlist in the Royal Air Force, only to be turned back because he was too young. Not to be deterred he persisted and was later accepted in 1953 and went to Aldergrove for his training, from which he became a Specialist Wireless Operator with the 264 Signals Unit, a mobile unit that, among other things, monitored Russian radio signals. In his first posting with the RAF he was stationed on Cyprus after the Eoka incident. He spent three years on the Mediterranean Island and thought he was homeward bound in1956, but the crisis over the Suez Canal meant he was drafted there for a number of months until he eventually went to Digby in Lincolnshire in England to await his next overseas posting.

The following year Anthony was on his way with his Air Force colleagues Down Under to the dusty deserts of South Australia. He was part of an RAF Unit stationed at Maralinga, an outpost that has since become infamous for British military operations in nuclear testing.

It was a posting which Anthony believes made a dramatic change to his life and those of his friends and colleagues stationed with him. He spent a year in the desert at a time when five nuclear A-bomb explosions were detonated within a few miles of his RAF quarters. "It was only three to four miles from where the bombs went off. I remember being on a football field when one of the explosions went off. All we were told was to cover our eyes from the blast and turn away and then we saw the cloud go up over Queensland and head out over towards the Pacific Ocean and many of the local Aboriginals perished. It was a pure disgrace," he maintains.

He cites this experience as one significantly linked to his current medical condition, Parkinson's Disease, which he developed in later life. He is now a campaigner with the British Nuclear Test Veteran Association seeking justice for the experience that affected so many who lived in Maralinga during that dark time.

"Some people got cancer and their families got cancer and they are still suffering. I am lucky, I got Parkinson's, but my family do not have any such aliments and are all healthy. Now we are pushing for them (the British Government) to recognise what they did to us, leaving us with no protection at all, just our uniforms," he said.

The Maralinga episode has since been the subject of an Australian Government report commissioned into the British Nuclear Tests in Australia and has identified flaws in the nuclear testing including the warnings given and the inadequacies of the safety precaution and advice.

Anthony returned from Australia by sea on the "SS New Australia" and was discharged from the RAF on his return in 1958. He reached the rank of Corporal and shortly after he returned home to Ballyshannon. Once home he met and married Mary (nee Hanna). With his new bride he went back to England in search of employment and took on the job of a Cinema Manager working in King Cross and Islington in London, back when "an OAP could get in for 9p." A change in career came again when he enrolled at the British School of Telemetry to further his education in communication skills he had acquired in the RAF. Eighteen months after graduation he joined the Merchant Navy, where he spent ten years travelling the world, from Asia to Europe, the Middle East and South America. His last large scale maritime voyage was a trip from Bantry Bay in Cork to Kuwait in the Middle East, on board the largest ship in the world at the time, the "Universe Ireland" with a cargo of crude oil.

Once back on home soil Anthony joined the staff of this very newspaper, the Donegal Democrat, where he was a highly popular member of staff working in the front office. He also became the correspondent for one of his enduring passions which he still enjoys today, angling. "I was given a job with the Democrat by the late Cecil King and for that I am eternally grateful. I spent 20 years in the office and 10 years on the road for them, thirty years there and I mourned the day it left Ballyshannon." During this time Anthony and his wife Mary went on to raise a family of four.

He retired from the Donegal Democrat in 1994, but not one to rest on his laurels he is now an active community campaigner for various charities and is the Chairman of the North West Parkinson's Association. Recently he has been actively involved in the procurement of a Parkinson's Nurse and Neurologist for the North West. Despite living with Parkinson's, you can't keep a good man down and by his own admission: "I may have Parkinson's, but Parkinson's does not have me®."

He still drives, and he took part in this year's NW10k race in Letterkenny, of which he also played an organising role. He remains a committed angler and retained his position as angling correspondent for the Democrat for a number of years after he retired.

No doubt he has tales of "the ones that got away" but he also has the proof of his fishing ability with some specimen salmon and trout taken from the water ways of south Donegal.

Despite an active fishing season this year he is still waiting to land his first salmon of 2006!

I am also including a piece by Ann McGowan which I truly appreciate:

Anthony O'Malley Daly

By Ann McGowan

Anthony O'Malley Daly has often said that "He has Parkinson's but Parkinson's does not have him." Oh! how true that statement is.

I have known Anthony for many years. Firstly it was by meeting on the street and greeting each other with throw-away comment like "How's it going?" to a short chat. In the last five or six years I have really got to know the man he is, and the strength of his will and determination.

He visits the office regularly and we have rare conversation when I misunderstand him. His tolerance is high usually, but there's many a smart ass comment from him where we both end up laughing. One of the things I admire about him is he will not to give in. It is also the one thing about him that drives me mad.

When Anthony sets his mind on something, it doesn't matter how many good reasons you come up with that he shouldn't do it, he will just go ahead. If you won't help him, he will find another way of doing it or another person to help him. I've learned to go with him and don't fight it. It's easier. This book is a prime example of his determination. He has worked so hard on it and should be very proud of it. Hands up – how many people tried to persuade him to forget about it? Mine is up!

Should I say anything about him and his scooter? The Evil Knievel, the Dare-Devil of Ballyshannon. I tell him he is trying to recapture his lost youth by speeding everywhere. We thought we were safe when the car went off the road, but then the scooter appeared. Look out, Ballyshannon and surrounding areas! Someone Up There must be looking after him. Rain, hail, or shine it stops outside the office and in he comes, coat open, no hat, a drink of water, the tablet out, and he's looking for something. Posters, tickets, email, someone to edit his book, or any variety of other things.

When his walking and talking deteriorated, he was always coming up with different exercises to help himself. I'm sure Sarah, his daughter, had a big hand in this. I've been known to try some of these with him, including tapping his speech. The most dangerous example of these was the three-legged walk, which I did with him across the street in front of cars because once we started we were afraid to stop in case we wouldn't get started again. Another case of Anthony living dangerously and my Guardian Angel being around.

People often dismiss those with disabilities and illnesses as though they cannot do anything. They would be making a big mistake in dismissing Anthony. He has achieved more since he became ill than the majority of able-bodied people do in their lifetime. He has a very sharp mind (though not much common sense!) and a will of steel.

I have been on the receiving end of that mind, quite often to my disadvantage. I remember his reply when he asked me to write a story about fishing. I asked him how was I going to write a story about something I knew nothing about. His reply:

"You knew feck-all about the IRA but you wrote a book about it!" Very fecking funny, Anthony! You really had a good laugh about that!

This man has fund raised thousands for Parkinson's. He has raised money for Bishop Tutu in South Africa, for the NW Hospice, and for many other causes. He organised and took part in numerous events. He won Ballyshannon Person of the Year a few years ago. I could go on with the things he has done and achieved and fear those he may do. But he's an example to us all.

He calls me his 'Soul Mate.' If I am, then I am very proud. But I am equally happy just being his friend.

God Bless You, Anthony. If nothing else, you have taught me something very important: "There is no such thing as *can't*."

Photos from My Life and Times

Home from the Sea, with my son Dara

*With my grandson Eoin O'Malley Daly
and the 1998 Angler's Annual*

*Staff of the Donegal Democrat who took over the new premises
on the Donegal Road in June 1980*

Neighbours – front row John Gibbons, Mary Gibbons O'Reilly, unknown person, Agnes Kelly (nee Lally), and Michael Gibbons. Back row: Lily Johnston, Dora McCafferty, and Kathleen Gibbons Cairns on an outing at Creevy Pier.

I loved hoisting the Sam Maguire Cup when the team visited the Democrat offices in 1992

John Hanna (right) and a Belfast man with a magnificent monkfish

*Dada Hanna and the Boxing Club, including Patrick (rear, 3ʳᵈ from left),
David (rear, 2ⁿᵈ from right), and John (front row, 3ʳᵈ from right)*

*Dada and his sons (clockwise from upper left) -
Patrick, John, Edward, and David*

The Hanna Family, 1984

David Hanna and His Family (photo by Conor Sinclair)

My Family - 50ᵗʰ Wedding Anniversary, 2008

photo by Emer O'Shea

Best Wishes

to Anthony O'Malley Daly

Wishing Anthony every success with his book,
Cllr. John Meehan
Ballyshannon Town Council

Best Wishes to Anthony O'Malley Daly
on the launch of Trilogy,
James and Antonia Kerrigan
JK Printing and Photography
071 98 52960

Best Wishes to Anthony
Michael Daly, Editor in Chief
The Donegal Democrat
074-97-40160

Best Wishes to Anthony O'Malley Daly
Gerard Ferguson, Jeweller and Watchmaker
Castle Street, Ballyshannon
071 9858196

Best Wishes to Anthony
Geraldine Og's Boutique
Main Street, Ballyshannon
071 98 52150 geraldineogs@gmail.com
A Beautiful Place to Shop

Best Wishes to Anthony O'Malley Daly
A. Doherty Bookmakers
Market Street, Ballyshannon
071 9851749

Best Wishes to Anthony
Cafe Beag, The Mall, Ballyshannon
Tea / Coffee and Home Baking
Featuring Dee's Cakes
Tel: 071 98 58832 Mob: 086 879 1741

Best Wishes to Anthony O'Malley Daly
Charlie O'Doherty
Doherty's Fishing Tackle
Donegal Town
074 97 21119

Best Wishes to Anthony from
Nirvana Restaurant
The Mall
Ballyshannon
071 982 2369

Best Wishes to Anthony O'Malley Daly
B&B Ireland
Belleek Road, Ballyshannon
Tel: 00353 71 98 22222
www.bandbireland.com

Best Wishes to Anthony from
DecorWorld Ballyshannon
Belleek Road
Ballyshannon, Co Donegal
071 9858193

Best Wishes to Anthony O'Malley Daly from
Old Church Veterinary Hospital
The Mall, Ballyshannon, Co. Donegal
Phone 071 98 51559
vet@iol.ie

Well Done, Anthony

Clippers Barber Shop

Tir Conaill Street, Ballyshannon
Proprietor Ita Doherty

Hours of Business
Tues, Wed, Thurs 11am-7pm
Fri 10am-7pm Sat 10am-5:30pm
Including Lunch

Gent's Cut €10   Wash/Cut €12
Head Shave €6   Children (under 12) €8

Out of Hours Appointments can be arranged by
Phone or Text – 087 2100205

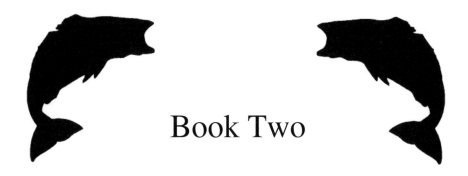

Book Two

Sixty Years of Angling

Excerpts from my weekly newspaper columns
in The Donegal Democrat and in The Sun

and photos from a lifetime of fishing with friends

IDEA

In 1991 I got the idea of writing an Angling column for the Donegal Democrat, with the intention of highlighting the great resource that is available to fishermen in Donegal and its surrounds, and by so highlighting bring attention on the need to protect and conserve this great resource of nature. Since the first article, I have written one each month from January until the end of September, which embraces the New Year's Day opening of the Salmon season on the Drowes to the last day of the game fishing season, mostly the end of September.

With the help of others I have managed to cover game, coarse and sea angling, taking it only from one month to the next, and writing mostly with passion for angling and limited only by my own lack of discipline and mental brakes.

I hope that I have promoted fishing as a recreation, especially among the young, and as an outlet for all ages. I love to hear of people catching a fish and eating it, or returning the fish even if not required. Each angler has his favourite river, lake or sea haunt, and I hope that not a few will read this BOOK, none-the-less reflect with joy on the past season. I look forward with eager anticipation to the coming year, or years.

FIRST SALMON OF THE YEAR 2011 – AND FIRST SALMON OF THE YEAR 2012 – CAUGHT BY THE SAME MAN ON THE SAME RIVER – THE DROWES

IT IS A MIRACLE, YES SIR! IT IS A MIRACLE! READ ON AND SEE THE MIRACLE UNFOLD IN FRONT OF YOUR VERY EYES

An ecstatic angler from County Tyrone has set a record by landing the first salmon of the year 2011. When he caught the first wild salmon within ten minutes of season opening. Ian Martin (46), of Tullyroan, Dungannon, has been trying for the best part of twenty years to catch the first wild salmon of the year on the River Drowes. This year, he set out from home at 4am last Saturday and threw his first cast on the river at 8:30 am. His third cast was to prove lucky, as he hooked an 11lb 8oz. salmon on a stretch of river between Kinlough and Bundoran.

It took him only 10 minutes to take his first cast, hook the fish, play him out, put the net under the salmon and land him. The salmon was caught on the Blackwater Pool, in the Lareen Estate stretch of the famous Drowes River.

Ian Martin - 2011

The bailiffs of the Northern Regional Fisheries Board, the Gardai, the owner Shane Gallagher and his staff, and of course Bill Likely, or Doctor Bill, were also there. About 200 anglers came from diverse places – natives, Germans, French, and some from Japan, were among the hopefuls.

The news spread rapidly. Shane Gallagher, manager of the Drowes Fishery, said the achievement is even more impressive, considering the fish was landed on the fly. "In our 33 years here at the fishery, I would say that this is probably only the third or fourth time that has happened. Salmon are usually caught on the spin. There were between 100 and 110 anglers on the river last Saturday, so you can imagine the excitement when the first salmon was caught so quickly and so expertly."

A second salmon, weighing about 7 lbs was also caught on Saturday, by a German angler called Michael Cruise, who released it back into the river. A third salmon was nearly caught, I won't say by whom, but he got away. I couldn't tell you (although I know) for he was a big salmon, and the guy who nearly landed this big salmon kept exercising his power of speech by speaking to each and every person or angler he encountered in the journey back to the cars, or during the speeches, presentation of the Drowes Cup.

Brendan Faulkner, owner of the Fox's Lair, a Donegal Town man married to a Ballyshannon lady, bought the salmon. The same evening the first salmon of the year got dressed up. There was a tribute buffet held in the Fox's Lair in Bundoran, where Ian Martin was the guest of honour.

I attended the function, got a great meal, a couple Jameson whiskeys. I had a good night's entertainment, got a very tasty meal from Brendan Faulkner, was handed a glass of Jameson whiskey, free and for nothing, and got a welcome re-fill which brought back memories. I got a "junt" of the salmon, which I took Home. All the family got a piece. It tasted like EDIBLE GOLD.

"The Fisheries people are telling me that it's a new Irish Record, which is quite exciting," said Ian. "It was great to land the fish so early, but the downside is I didn't get fishing again for the rest of the day, which was a bit of a pity." Ian, this editor says to you – It's no pity at all. I have not had the first wild salmon, and the quickest I got my first salmon was the 17th February.

That was last year's salmon, 2011. Now for this year's fish.

Miracle On Drowes – One Year On – Same Man – Same Pool – Same Result! Sensation!

You might be thinking that I am repeating myself, or that Parkinson's has finally taken me over. The latter is slowly wrecking my body, but when I tell you this story, God knows what will happen to your – marbles.

Ian Martin went home. He was recognised as a "Great" Angler because, having landed the first wild salmon of the year 2011, his name will always be spoken with pride. His name is inscribed on Drowes Perpetual Cup. He will be photographed. In short, catching the first salmon on the Drowes makes him a made man.

First Salmon On Drowes Goes To Ian Martin – Again!

Ian Martin, now a year older, landed the first wild salmon for 2012, on the tube fly in the Blackwater Pool. The salmon is laden with sea lice, 3 miles up-river, and just short of Lough Melvin. Ian Martin's name will go onto the Drowes Cup twice. People will have to look twice and more times to be sure they have not developed double vision. This year Ian landed the 12 lbs salmon close to mid-day.

Publicity

Yes, Publicity – and that is where I came in. I was on the river fishing when the salmon was landed. The fisheries officers, John Hanna ('cause he was with me), and I all headed for the Shop in Lareen. The salmon was inspected by the bailiffs to see if the fish was fresh run, to see if the wild salmon had sea lice on his body... and was it a Hen or Cock wild salmon? When all these points were satisfied, Thomas Gallagher had the salmon weighed, I noted all his details down, and verified...

Once I had all the details, I rang Paddy Clancy, my brother-in-law. Paddy is a journalist and broadcaster. Naturally enough Paddy celebrates "Auld Lang Syne," and each year he has not a few bevvies / drinks. To his bed he goes "Three Sheets in the Wind and One Flapping," and vows he will be ready to answer the 'phone when I ring with the details. In normal circumstances, Paddy is all business and everything goes swimmingly. However, to sing in the New Year is a trip of tears, after 12 months of endeavour, success and failure. But whoever you are, it is obligatory that you have a "Wee Dram" in your fist as you weep tears of joy, or tears of disaster for the year past, or look ahead, with resolution, to the incoming year.

Ian Martin - 2012

The upshot of this practise is that Paddy Clancy gets into his scratcher (bed), and prays sincerely that I won't ring him on New Year's Day, 1st January, because an Angler / Fisherman has caught a fresh wild salmon. And though Clancy (putting in his surname is a form of recognition or reverence, or both) does not mind the first salmon being caught after mid-day, he is as "grumpy" as a bag of weasels. I have to let the phone ring out. then cut off, then ring him again, three times before I get Paddy to pick up the phone. Sometimes, his good wife will answer, but after the long ring procedure (remember what I just told you), I will hear the "Sound Of Silence" – the void – and you know someone is on the line. The voice of Paddy Clancy will crackle into life, and the faltering words will issue forth – "Is that you, Anthony?" The greeting from me to Paddy is, "Happy New Year, Paddy," and if I was with him the night before, I will enquire into what time he got Home at, and how was he feeling. His wife Bernadette will have driven him Home, but at what time? That is the question.

Paddy has had time to shake himself down, and his years as a professional Journalist clicks in. He knows also that Thomas Gallagher and Shane, his son, who took over when his Father died outside the tackle shop at Lareen, the bailiffs from the Northern Regional Fisheries Board, and "several" others, the "Big Snobs" as my son Dara called them, are close by. He will question me as to the conditions, who got the first wild salmon ("Wild" is the word used on the first day), where they are from, and he might have a word with Thomas or with Harry Lloyd, manager of the N.R.F.B, now retired.

The two big questions are "What size?" (I mean the weight of the fish), and "Was it the first wild salmon caught or landed in the Nation of Ireland?"

Brendan Faulkner got the shock of his life. He knew that if there was a salmon landed he would buy it, but like all the Angling fraternity, he thought that Ian Martin putting up the double was Sensational, and a Miracle.

Salmon, Sea Trout, Snakes

Angling reports for the month of May vary. Some lakes have been fishing well, while the rivers, for the lack of water, have not been so good. the winds for the most part were cold and from a northerly direction.

However, nothing has deterred the Pettigo Tourism Group, who have produced a brochure entitled "Enjoy Pettigo in its Full Colours." I have often been told that Pettigo is forgotten and out on a limb. Well, this brochure shows that Pettigo has struck back, and the product is a beckoning invitation to tourists and visitors.

From an angling aspect I find there are over forty unpolluted and well stocked lakes around Pettigo. The famous Pilgrimage Lake of Lough Derg contains the best Trout in these isles. In and around Pettigo on such lakes as Dunragh, Ultan, Sallagh and other nice sounding stretches of fresh water, you have a choice of game and coarse angling. There are daily and yearly permits for Salmon, Trout and coarse angling. You can bring your own boat and launch it for a small fee or you can hire boats for a slightly larger fee.

Though information, Pettigo is making a virtue of being out on a limb, off the beaten track, and even remote.

The Eske that runs through Donegal Town yielded some small catches of the odd Salmon. John Hanna (on the day after his good wife Mary gave birth to a fine baby girl) caught two Salmon on the system. Since the water abstraction plant and dam was built, the River Eske drains quicker, so rain is needed to swell its flow. The Sea Trout should be arriving in June, and I sincerely hope they get recognition and protection, and a chance to run.

The Eske in Donegal Town, showing the Hanna house and club rooms

On its day the Eske is a joy. To watch a fisherman play and land a Salmon or Sea Trout from a virtual stream running through Donegal Town is something to behold.

Thomas Gallagher, owner of the Drowes River, strives always for improvements. Lately he has constructed three new pools on the upper reaches of the river, and has cleared the Estuary of stones to allow the Salmon to run. The Grilse are running. Tony Guilfoyle from Arklow got one of 4lbs. English visitor Joe Marsh landed two Grilse, fishing very small flies he tied himself. German angler Klaus Bohm got a 10lb Salmon, and of course there is more. It's amazing today how many fishermen have the confidence to tie their own flies and get results.

I know a goodly score of Salmon and Grilse have been produced off the "factory" Drowes River for May, but still reports indicate that the catch is down on last year.

A dedicated German visitor got 16 good Sea Trout off the Erne Estuary at Ballyshannon - using the famous Rogan Gadget Fly. But then on the other hand local and knowledgeable angler Pat Dorrian fished the estuary for a full day recently and drew a blank. Danny Kerrigan is an estuary expert who informs me that the returns are bleak. Better reports of good sized brown Trout are coming from those fishing Assaroe lake (behind the dam), so the advice would be shift location and persist.

You know of course, that the only ideal conditions for catching fish exist only on the day you actually catch fish, and that fishing never fails to surprise - as in the following story from America.

Edward Hanna - the best game angler of the lot - a member of the well- known Donegal family residing in Springfield, Virginia. Edward and his son Karol, who is following in his father's footsteps, went fishing recently on the Shenandoah Valley River. They were after sunfish, blue gill, Perch, Big mouth Bass – up to 40 lbs – and aptly named brown Trout, or whatever. You might say they got the whatever species or selection. Karol was fishing a worm when his cork dipped and he struck. Thinking it was one of the above-mentioned species he played out the catch. When he got it to the net he found that he had hooked and played a 2ft. long poisonous copperhead snake. A rare bite, but not a catch to get bitten by.

Incidentally, a word about fishery protection. Edward and Karol had barely wet a line when the game warden arrived and checked their permits. The game warden was armed and with handcuffs. It seems for the penalty for serious breaches of fishing regulations is not so much that the warden confiscates you precious gear, but he also takes you away in handcuffs.

June angling prospects look promising given (dare I say it) a spill of rain. Grilse and Sea Trout will hopefully run, and you surely won't get the surprise of a snake as there are none in Ireland. And don't forget to return the smaller Sea Trout to help revive the decimated stocks.

Anglers' Ambition Realised

Donegal and District Anglers Association realised a long term ambition when they took over a large part of Lough Eske, the river and the estuary last week. The Association has obtained a 25-year lease from Lord Arran, and it now controls the commercial fishing and the angling rights to the Ridge, the Eske River and the estuary.From now on, anyone wishing to fish the Eske will have to obtain a permit from the Association. For local anglers, the season fee is £20, while visitors can obtain £6 daily permits, a weekly permit costing £25 or a yearly permit for £45. Similar fees exist for the Eany, over which the Association also hold control.

The Eske was at one time among the most important fisheries in the North-West, but poaching and pollution have ravaged the stocks of Sea Trout and Salmon. Now that the Association holds the reins, it plans to resurrect the fishery by restocking the waters with Sea Trout and Salmon. A restocking programme will be undertaken by the members, probably next year, and the Association is hoping that local businesses will support the development with sponsorship.

To try and combat poaching, Association members will mount fishery patrols and the aid of the Northern Regional Fisheries will also be enlisted.

Eske Leased

A notice was published in the Donegal Democrat in 1991 that brought the news that the Eske had been obtained on a 25 year lease by the Donegal District Anglers Association. The lease includes the commercial fishery on the estuary, the River Eske, and a portion of Lough Eske that includes the Ridge, where the Barnesmore River enters the lake. The Association secretary, Jim McGeever, Mountcharles (074 97 35045) Charlie O'Doherty, Fishing Tackle Shop, Donegal Town (074 97 21119) or Colm Kelly, Frosses (074 97 36014) will provide further information and issue permits. This acquisition can greatly assist the Eske system, and the D.D.A.A. are wished success and co-operation in their efforts.

The Drowes fished well for the month of June, and while some large fish were caught, catches of grilse showed them to be small and net marked. The Duff River, judging from the cars parked on the main Bundoran to Sligo road, is getting into full swing. This is a spate river (needs rain) with a magnificent Sea pool.

Ballyshannon fisherman Thomas Gallagher hooked two Salmon on the Duff, but lost both. Further than that I don't know, but I fully expect catches. July should produce the main run of Sea Trout. Don't "pooch" them, don't snatch them, and if you land one by fair means - admire it briefly, return it so that they can survive to create a cycle again.

Angling 1991

The month of July arrived with what was working up to be a heatwave, but as the days progressed it lapsed back into the usual mixed pattern of unreliable weather. I don't have to say much more. Still there are fish to report. Michael McGrath informs me that there is a goodly supply of angling tourists from various continental parts visiting Belleek, Co Fermanagh, and the fish are to be got. The Salmon fishing for July was not that brilliant on the Erne, though Salmon were seen, Michael's prediction is that the king of game fish will be in a more taking mood in August. Many will look forward to that. However, the brown Trout in Keenaghan Lough are of a fine and mainly large stock, and ones of a pound weight are order of the day, with the odd Trout up to 3 lbs. reported. Keenaghan fishes better in the evenings and is for the Fly fishing angler only.

End of an Era - one of the last salmon "shots" in the Erne estuary

Coarse Fishing – The Manchester Gang

FLETCHER, FLETCHER, HALSALL ETC, ETC, ETC. Sounds like a firm of Solicitors. Far from solicitors they are. These men are Coarse Anglers who came to this Country, this County, this Town of Ballyshannon nearly 30 years ago.

John Fletcher

Tommy Cribben

Harry Halsall

In recent years, they have come to Ballyshannon for six or seven fishing trips annually. They hire a bus or mini bus, pack all their kit in, and whatever is left over, is sufficient space for their own young bodies. They purchased a bungalow about mile from Ballyshannon, and the same distance from Lough Melvin.

Michael Fletcher

Callum Fletcher

John and Michael Fletcher are brothers, and they give the orders. John is a Man United "Aficionado" (meaning a fan). Michael is a Manchester City supporter. (I hope I have that right). Harry Halsall, Tommy Cribben, and Paul Andrew are the main force of the cross channel fishermen and friends that fish and promote Ballyshannon and the North West as a Coarse Fishing area. You will see from the pictures that their daily catches of Bream, Roach, and Hybrids, which they keep in a "Keep Net" and weigh at the end of each day's friendly competition – proof that our Assaroe Lake and other Coarse fishing venues are up to standard to hold contests, which I reckon will draw revenue to this area. Among other "Hot Spots" is Lough McNean, which is a bountiful lake in Leitrim, outside Glenfarne.

The Fletchers, Harry Halsall, and others thank Patsy Quinn and Paschal Gildea who gave them permission to cross their properties to fish.

*Tommy Cribben, sea angling -
with an 80 lb Wahoo*

Pike

Fishing for Pike is a skill all on its own. Pike Competitions are very popular events. The catch is weighed, registered for proof, and then it is returned to the water, alive. The amount of gear carried by Coarse and Sea Anglers would make a Game Angler blush with envy.

Now if it is pike you're after, you can travel the short distance to upper Lough Macnean, where one of the best pike fisheries exist. Here there is strict control, only one pike per angler is permitted to be kept, and there is a minimum size. All these regulations are explained prior to the trip being undertaken. In addition, only one hook is allowed so as to lessen the damage done to the pike before they are returned to the water. And if it is sea fishing you crave then trips can be arranged to Killybegs or Mullaghmore.

Back to the Erne itself. Four bream were taken at Belleek, weighing 10 pounds, and using the worm. There is always the story of the fish escaping, and let's face it, what would fishing be if none escaped? The fish who battle with anglers and win out in the finish are usually the biggest, so when I tell you that three Co Antrim visitors out on the Erne trolling between Belleek and Cliff hooked a number of fish, lost them and were disappointed, but then hooked a really big fish that towed the boat before breaking free, to the relief of the occupants of the boat, then you will realise that even with all the species hooked and landed - there is still that lurking, mysterious monster fish prowling the murky depths. What fish it was, and how big, we don't know, but it's out the swimming in the Erne in Belleek. I like that.

What I have to relate next may have very little to do with fishing, but the Belleek and District Trust have purchased a luxurious cruiser for a ransom of money. To hire it for a cruise costs a lot of money, but spread over eight or ten on board then each lot is comparably reasonable.

In 1993 the Ballinamore / Ballyconnell canal opened for cruise traffic, so it's conceivable you can troll all the way from Belleek to Limerick, and you can. It is praiseworthy how all the interests in the pottery town are striving. Angling is part of it. "Promoting gets Promotion."

Always Wear A Life Jacket

The River Drowes continues to fish well, and in attracting many cross channel and continental anglers. The month of April has recorded 120 Salmon landed by anglers. A German visitor caught an 8 lb Salmon fishing the Stout's Tail Fly and following this success with a 14 1/2 pounder that took a No. 12 Hairy Mary Fly. Bob Hutchinson, Ennis, Landed a 10 lb Salmon on a homemade cast tied by himself. Billy Lally from Enniskillen caught 3 Salmon on Saturday last.

Not everybody has similar success, and many arrive and depart without a tight line. However, local anglers John Fahey and Pat Duffy who have the knowledge of the Drowes are getting their share. Lough Melvin has registered moderate catches of spring Salmon. Preston anglers Joe Hindle and John Stuttard netted in the region of 30 brown Trout for two-day fly fishing on Lough Melvin. Ballyshannon, Erne Estuary fisherman, P.J. Coughlin, who likes to get an early start to the season (March), got 6 fine Trout out in the area called The Bog.

Of interest to anglers is the news that the Northern Regional Fisheries Board took 200 Sea Trout from the Erne estuary for stripping in efforts being made to rescue depleted Sea Trout Stocks in the West of Ireland. The rapid decline of the Sea Trout is placing much needed tourist revenue in jeopardy. So concerned is the Donegal and District Anglers Association that they have requested that their members who fish the Eany and the Eske systems to return any Sea Trout they land.

And speaking of the Eske system, Billy Johnston, Donegal Town, got his first Salmon of the season when he caught a fine 12 lb Cock Salmon on Lough Eske on Saturday last. The Fish took an 18 gram Toby on the troll, Billy presented the fish to Jody Gysling of Harvey's Point Hotel and restaurant on the lake shore.

End of April Rain will keep the rivers running and prospects look good for May.

Sad But Brave Irishmen and Irish Women

Recently, I saw a programme about the recession and the effect it is having on the family in Ireland. I was impressed and saddened to know men and women are in cars and buses searching for work from the time they leave their front doors until they man age to return Home at the end of the week. They go as far as Turkey. The "dip in our fortunes" is getting worse, and there is nothing we can can do about it.

We must strive to support them who are or will be on the "roads of life." Hopefully, when you read these few words, things will have improved.

Donegal Reach Final in Boston

At the Delboy Stadium, Boston, last Sunday week the semi-finals of the New England Intermediate Football Championships were decided. In an afternoon when five matches were played in torrid heat. Notre Dame easily defeated Springfield in the first semi-final, and took their place in the upcoming final. The game was always competitive, but Notre Dame always had the edge over Springfield to run out comfortable winners.

Donegal faced stiff opposition in the form of a very good Team called St. Christopher's. Donegal have the reputation of being slow starters, and a second half outfit, and so it proved, for St. Christopher's took an early initiative, and went four points clear without reply. Ten minutes into the game and it seemed as if the "Slow Start" tag attached to Donegal was going to get them swamped.

They had been getting their share of the play, but were not scoring. Then they came to life with a fine outfield shot from Pat Geraghty sailing over the bar to open their account. The Donegal revival was in motion, and the same player reduced the deficit to 0-5 to 0-2 with another left-footed effort.

Pat Geraghty scored again in the 15th minute. Then the tall Jim McGuinness, now Donegal Senior Football Team Manager and Ulster Champions 2011, was having a great game, got onto the score board with a point from play. The teams drew level when John Gildea came out of the backline, and raised the cheers of the large contingent of Donegal supporters risking sun-stroke on the stands.

After 22 minutes of end-to-end play, Donegal eventually went ahead through the boot of Manus McFadden from a free. From this point until the final whistle the Donegal team never lost the lead. With five minutes to half time the spirited St. Christopher's levelled the scores, only for Pat Geraghty to put Donegal ahead with another minor.

Two points per Jim McGuinness from play just before halftime sent the teams to the dressing rooms with the score at Donegal 0-9, St. Christopher's 0-6. All to play for.

On the restart Donegal again lived up to their well known reputation of being a second half team when they put across three points from play through Manus McFadden and Stephen McKelvey. In this period St. Christopher's could only manage a single point. The score went to 0-12 to 0-7 on favour of Donegal who seemed to be coasting into the final. Two points from St. Christopher's reduced Donegal's lead. Pat Geraghty got a point from play, and the lead went up to four points with 15 minutes to play.

However, things are not always what they seem, and Donegal supporters and mentors from Donegal to Boston can verify that. For ten minutes Donegal lapsed, and did not score, St. Christopher's surged, and scored 3 points. With 5 minutes to the final whistle one point separated the striving stalwarts. Donegal were in trouble. Jim McGuinness, suffering from exhaustion and a injury suffered the previous week had to be replaced. *(He is now the Donegal team manager.)*

Siege

The Donegal goal was under siege during this ten minute spell, and but for two important things Donegal would have lost. The first was the inability of St. Christopher's to convert a major chance of a goal. The second, and most important for Donegal, was that goalkeeper Joe Prendergast stoutly defended the net. He allowed nothing past. He blocked all assaults for a goal from St. Christopher's. One point-blank rasper seemed bound for the net when Joe somehow got a firm hand to it and deflected it over the bar. This effort revived the Donegal team, who scored four more points in the final five minutes from Par Geraghty, Tom Geraghey, and John Gildea. There was a point from the opposition. Gladly the supporters heard the final whistle, and Donegal ran off winners, 0-16 to 0-12.

The Donegal Team (13 a Side)

Joe Prendergast (Athlone), Denis McMenamin (Buncrana), Gerry Doherty (Glenties), Paul Kelleher (Clare), Donie McCole, Capt. (Ardara), John Hurrell (Buncrana), John Gildea (Glenties), Manus McFadden (Glenswilly), Pat Geraghty (Galway), Tom Geraghty (Galway), Steven McKelvey (Fintown), Paul Brennan (Athlone), Jim McGuinness (Glenties). Subs: Brian Fennell (Boston), Liam Moylan (Cork), Conie Cremin (Kerry), Paul McColgan (Muff), Paul McCallion (Buncrana), Paul McNulty (Ballybofey), Noel Harkin (Ballyliffen).

Donegal met Notre Dame in the Intermediate Final. Notre Dame have a prominent Donegal connection also. Having seen both Semi-Finals, it should be a hotly contested final. It will take all the urging of team manager Paddy McDevitt and team captain Donie McCole to see a fine Donegal Team through to the All-American Finals to be played in Boston (this year) in September. At an after-match reception held in the Cuchulainn's, Dorchester, I met not only team members but Maureen Doherty (Boston) the club secretary, and supporters Bernadine McCole (Inver), Christina Murphy (Buncrana) who is laundry and cook, and Janine Hammer, the photographer. An entertaining time was had by all, with some talk of home from these fine immigrants who represent Ireland so admirably in America.

And hot off the wires this Wednesday morning the Democrat learned that Notre Dame were accounted for in a keenly contested final. Roll on, the All-American Finals. Note all the Donegal names on both teams.

Three Salmon Caught on Drowes River

Once again the first Salmon of the new year in Ireland was taken on the Drowes River, where over 400 anglers gathered for the first day of the new season. M. McGinley, Sion Mills, Strabane, Co Tyrone, caught his 9lb Salmon at 8:55am in the sea pool at Tullaghan. He was fishing with a Yellow Belly Bait.

Patrick McGinley, with his wife Anna-May had departed for the Drowes in the early hours of the morning, and very nearly turned back when they encountered heavy rain and strong winds through Barnes Gap. However, Mrs McGinley urged Patrick to continue, and he was rewarded the honour of landing the first wild Salmon for 1992 in Ireland.

One hour later Colin Monaghan, aged 17, who caught the first three Salmon last year, landed the second Salmon of the season, with another 9 lbs. fish taken from the pool on the upper reaches of the Drowes, in Lareen. Young Colin was using a red medium Flying C bait.

Then at 11:30 am. the third wild Salmon of the opening day was caught by Alan Kendal, Moneyrea, Co Down. Alan's fish weighed in at almost 7 lbs. and the bait used was a Purple Flying C, in the sea pool.

Presentation

The presentation of Prizes took place at a function in the Drowes Bar, Tullaghan that evening. Patrick McGinley received £200 and the Drowes Perpetual Cup from Cllr. Sean McEniff, Chairman of the North West Regional Tourism Organisation. Rev. Canon Curran presented the second prize of £200 to Colin Monaghan. Harry Lloyd, Manager of the North West Regional Fisheries Board, presented the third placed Alan Kendal with one week's fishing holidays for four at the Lareen Estate.

The first fish of the year was purchased for £500 by a syndicate of Tracey and David Rodgers and Frankie O'Gorman, representing O'Gorman Arms, Imperial Hotel and NW Catering - all from Bundoran. Patrick McGinley donated a substantial sum to the appeal for the Romanian Orphanage Fund. Kevin Quinn from the Embassy Restaurant, Sligo, purchased the second Salmon for £250.

Those wishing to partake of a minute of the first Salmon landed in Ireland in 1992 were invited to a free banquet at the Imperial Hotel, Bundoran.

The soup kitchen, which provides the welcome hot bowl of soup, was positioned outdoors this year. "Chef" Sean Smith from Sligo dished out urns of hot potatoes and soup of shin beef, and the spice to this surprise was that it was served by Hosam Fakhouri, a Palestinian from Jordan.

Thomas Gallagher, owner of the Drowes Fishery, thanked the anglers who braved the inclement elements to fish the opening day on the Drowes, saying, "Today was a good day for angling."

Clare Island Ancestors: The Sea Water is in Your Eyes

My wife and I three years ago paid our first visit to Clare Island. There is a Castle next to the water where all disembark and embark, on or off "The Pirate Queen" Ferry. I was "bragging" about my Great-Grand Father, Austin O'Malley, born on Clare Island - about the fishing disaster, where so many of the drowned were O'Malleys. I told my tourist friend about the big family he had. His name was Michael O'Malley (too). A cop from Baton Rouge.

I will skip some of the details. Such as he knew more about Newport House. And about Queen Granuaile (Grace), the Pirate Queen who sailed the western waters, and was a great navigator. After all, she sailed up the Thames to meet another Queen, Elizabeth the First – and the fact that she was written out of history.

Sea Trout Crisis 1992

The crisis decimating the Sea Trout stocks continues, with (I fear) with no resolution in sight. Such a crisis cannot go much further without the extinction of the Sea Trout stocks, and that could occur as early as 1992. That was the main subject enclosed in a large envelope received by me from Charles Bonner, Dungloe.

Basically, Sea Trout stocks and catches began to sharply decline from1986 to 1988. By 1989 it had reached the realm of crisis. This decline was most notable in the west of Ireland counties of Mayo and Galway, where complete tourist regions depend on the return of Sea Trout to Connemara River and western estuaries.

In 1983 the Sea Trout Action Group or STAG was set up to research and hopefully reverse the decline. What is happening is vast stocks of Sea Trout have disappeared, and any returning to the rivers are small, sickly Trout infested with Sea lice. Here it must be said that the usual sign of a fresh run Salmon or Sea Trout from the sea is attached Sea lice, but what is not usual is for the Sea Trout to be infested with Sea lice. Note also that after a number of days in the fresh water the lice drop off. STAG are investigating the severe infestation and decline in stocks, and they are down to the conclusion that there is a correlation between Salmon farms at sea - the multiplication of Sea lice - and the decimation of the Sea Trout. Naturally this has provoked a clash of interest between the Salmon farmers at sea and Sea Trout interests.

Meanwhile, the prized Sea Trout faces into the shadow of extinction. Nothing is proved or disproved to date, but until a solution is found, and the Sea Trout return, don't keep the Sea Trout - put them back. Donegal and the north West coastal area is not immune either, and while a protection bye-law has been introduced in the West, common sense should prevail here. Meanwhile the investigation is ongoing.

New Club Goes International

The Ballyshannon Sea Angling Club was formed in 1990. There was a need to organise to satisfy the wishes of so many sea anglers in the area, and to exploit the rich facilities of the sea fish grounds out in Donegal Bay.

The club is based at Creevy where the Pier provides safe berthing, and a newly constructed slipway allow for craft to be launched or taken from the sea in the event of adverse weather. In the storms of February 1988, Creevy Pier was torn apart, but was rebuilt by Donegal County Council and funds from the Dept. Of The Marine. A Creevy Pier restoration committee was set up to prompt restoration of the pier with monies from functions this committee built a modern slipway. All of which has lead to this port being a valuable asset to the area, and the efforts of the club.

Now the club has upwards on 50 members senior membership is £10 and junior membership is £6. This fee includes membership of the Irish Federation of Sea Anglers, and allows the members to gain entry to nationwide competitions run by the I.F.S.A. The club also has the use of four half deckers out of Creevy and to date they have organised three sea angling competitions. Now they are going for the really big competition. Their first International Sea Angling competition takes place on Saturday, 31st August and Sunday 1st September. Boats will depart Creevy Pier at 10am over the period of the competition, with competitors booking in at 9am Saturday. The competition will be run under I.F.S.A. rules with each boatman responsible for the safety of the boat.

The angling captain will be responsible in deciding where each vessel is to fish. Drawing of fish in positions will be made on board by the captain. Mackerel will not count, and the minimum length of a fish to count in the competition will be 12 inches - they even provide a count stick. Not more than three hooks be used during the competition, and not more than one rod. For those in the know, a table hook will count as 3 hooks.

The top prize will be carried off by the angler with the best aggregate over the two days, and so on down to the 5th best aggregate. The top junior anglers over the two days will get prizes down to 3rd place. Further prizes will be won by the best lady angler, best overseas angler, best local angler and best variety over the two days fishing and the heaviest fish caught. The competitors are requested to weigh in all eligible fish as there is a prize for the best boatman in the event.

The sponsors have been very generous for at the prize giving in Creevy Pier Hotel on the Sunday evening over £1000 in prizes will be presented. Entry is £12 per rod per day for adults, £6 for juvenile, with the closing date of 24th of August. Completed entry forms can be returned to Christy Higgins, Chapel St, Francis Patton, Knather Road (071 98) 51139 or Danny Kane, Donegal Road (071 98) 51131, all in Ballyshannon.

For a club in existence for little over one year this is a magnificent undertaking. The Ballyshannon Club is wished every success. Anglers taking to the sea are advised to wear life jackets or buoyancy aids. Have a good two days.

P.S. There will be a sick boat in operation to take off any unfortunates suffering from *mal de mer*.

Successful First Sea Angling Competition

The Ballyshannon Sea Angling club, which was formed in 1990 ran their first International Sea Angling competition on Saturday and Sunday last, from their base at Creevy Pier. The event proved to be a resounding success, and will provide the platform for future events. It has placed the area firmly on the calendar for the increasing number of anglers keen on sea fishing.

A total of 78 anglers fished each of the 2 days of the competition, and they occupied not only the local boats but boats from Bundoran, Mountcharles and Mullaghmore. Catches were good over the period, and one angler had 6 different species of fish while another landed a 15kg sunfish - an unusual specimen in Irish waters.

On Sunday evening, the results were announced, and the prizes were presented at a function in the Creevy Pier Hotel.

Results

1st Overall, Eugene Doherty, Donegal Town who received the Ballyshannon SAC shield and £200; 2nd, Jim Barron, Ballyshannon - Trophy and £100; 3rd, Hugh John Patton, Ballyshannon - Clock; 4th, Anthony Doherty, Donegal Town – Life Jacket, Danny Kane, Ballyshannon - Sander.

Individual winner on Saturday was Michael Greene, Donegal Town – Reel.; Individual Sunday, Eugene Doherty, Donegal Town – Reel. The prize for the Heaviest Fish of the competition went to Michael Greene, Donegal Town, who received the AIB cup and £50.

Hugh John Patton, Sean Ferguson, and Dermot Ferguson

Best foreign angler was D. Kurt, Germany, winning a cup and a presentation of cash donated by Peter & Deirdre Schmidt of the Creevy Pier Hotel. Best local angler was Jim Barron – The Gallogley Cup and £50. Anthony Doherty from Donegal Town was best boatman and received £50.

Ladies

1st, Julie Doherty, Donegal town; 2nd Eilish McNeely, Ballyshannon, and 3rd, Siobhan Patton, Ballyshannon. Each was presented with a valuable piece of Donegal Parian China.

Juniors

1st Michael Patton, McGinley Trophy and a boat rod; 2nd Eilish Mc Neely – Trophy and a tackle box, 3rd John Menarry – trophy and fishing net; 4th, Andrew Loughlin – trophy; 5th, Pauric Patton – trophy.

At the presentation function, Francis Patton, Chairman of the Ballyshannon SAC, said they were satisfied with the turnout and success of their first major International Competition. He thanked the participants, boatmen and the many sponsors; the proprietors of the Creevy Pier Hotel for providing soup and rolls for the anglers; the Northern Regional Fisheries Board for launching their boat on stand-by; members of the club for working so hard hard and anyone who assisted in the venture. Over the two sun drenched days, 689 fish weighed in.

Hopeful Start to Angling Season

Like many other aspects of our endeavours, the start of 1992 is filled with hope, anticipation and renewed resolution to the task. Angling in its varied worlds is no exception.

Of the Salmon rivers that opened on January 1st, the Drowes from Lough Melvin has been faring the best. At the time of writing almost 40 Salmon have been landed, and it's well recorded that three fine specimens were landed on the opening New Year's Day. However, don't think that the task of catching a January Salmon is any easier, because that total represents the achievements of a lucky small number of anglers. Hundreds of stalwarts have been out in the cold and rain and frost for exactly zero. Among all the many years I have been fishing I have yet to land a January Salmon, and if I was honoured with catching the first Salmon of the season in Ireland then I would rate that as a form of World Championship. Like all Salmon fisherman I live in the comfort of that ultimate dream.

The size of Salmon landed on the Drowes in January is somewhat smaller than in former years, but all have been wild fish. One scaled 12 lbs, and another recorded up to 15 lbs.

Lough Gill in Sligo has registered a number of early Salmon, but I do not have exact reports to hand.

What I know I have seen from photographs in the local newspaper. Now while Lough Gill opens on the 1st January, the river that spills from the lake does not, and the reason (sensible) that the Garavogue remains shut in January is to allow the spent Salmon or kelts to clear the system.

Hope

While the Angling start to 1992 is showing moderate success to date in some areas, other parts are living in hope. The hope, for instance, that in this crucial year for Sea Trout, the returns to the river will be a vast improvement over over the past three years, when Sea Trout stocks declined so dramatically and disastrously in the West and Northwest.

Hope too that the full international Trout Fly competition scheduled for Lough Melvin on Saturday 6th June will produce record landings and be a big attraction to the precincts. Accommodation has been booked, boats are already in demand, and possibly the home country will win.

Exceptional February Conditions

You may not believe this, but the angling weather and conditions for February were exceptional. The returns reported vary from being very good on the Drowes to only fair on Lough Melvin.

Salmon angling on the River Drowes maintains a hot pace in February to follow the the good start to the season reported in January. Three score and ten Salmon have been landed with the average weight ranging around the ten pound mark. On Sunday, 9th February I was there when Jim Sloan, Lurgan, landed a 9 lb Salmon on the Fly rod. Jim was fishing a size six Silver Rat Fly and the lucky event took place in the Saw Mill Pool.

Travelling anglers are faring the best with Bob Jordan, Omagh, taking a Salmon from the Trout Pool; Neil McQuillan, Larne, getting one from the new pool, and Enniskillen fishermen Billy Lally, Brian McElroy and Dermot McMenamin was the Angler who caught the first Salmon of the decade in Ireland on January 1st 1990. A new fishable stretch has been opened on the lower part of the Drowes, with a catwalk of some 200 meters erected at the Stone Ditch to the sea-side of the new bridge on the Sligo Road.

Lough Melvin

Lough Melvin opened on the 1st February. Seamus O'Dare, from Derrygonnelly,caught the first Salmon on the opening day – a fresh nine pounder. However, returns on the Melvin, for the amount of traffic, have to date been meagre, and can be counted in single figures, which is surprising. I fully expect a vast improvement as the back end of February has seen a goodly downpour of rain for Salmon to run through the system, and over to Garrison.

A number of big (5 lb) brown Trout were landed on the Melvin, but apart from a moment's admiration of them, they were returned to the water. Wait a few months.

Game anglers should be looking forward to March when the bulk of the remaining rivers, lakes and estuaries open. I will particularly be keen to see how the Estuary in Ballyshannon performs in relation to returns of Sea Trout. It will be too early to gauge the recovery of the decimated Sea Trout stocks, but catches at Ballyshannon will be eagerly counted for signs of improvement. Rogan's Gadget Fly and the Stuki spoon are the favourite lures for Ballyshannon.

Nothing in the sea angling line to report, except to say they are polishing up their gear. The seas are rough and dangerous, and the weather is yet too inclement.

Anticipation

Now whether you are a game, coarse or sea angler, you will be searching out your gear, and turning towards your favourite river, lake, pool or bay. So as we drift out in 1992 to our desired sport or recreation in angling, allow me to wish you all success and contentment.

The Quiet Sport Steeped in History

Angling is described as the "Quiet Sport," but its participation level outplays most of the other popular forms of recreation. The very young look forward to the day they go fishing for the first time, the elderly constantly reflect on the occasions they were successful and pine for a return to those happy times.

I am not as active in the pursuit of Trout or Salmon as I have been in the not-too-distant past, and I have yet to land a fish in 1992. However, others have been more active and succeeded in March – which was noted for high levels of water and wind, but mild to the extent that there were virtually snow and ice free conditions.

Erne Estuary

The estuary is providing good Sea Trout fishing at the moment. The experts inform me that it fishes best during March and April. from the Mall Quay to Port na Mara, and westwards to the bog and bottom of the road, catches of Sea Trout have been reported. P.J. Coughlin, always an early starter, has had Trout on most days he has fished. Mark Thompson got seven good sized Trout, and Mark only retains the best, returning the smaller Trout. Patrick O'Malley and Jonathan King are counted among the legions of youthful anglers who are putting up their seasonal count.

Many travelling anglers, with craft, have been fishing this estuary, and I would like to caution them to get to know this waterway and stick to its channels, as with water and tide this estuary can be less than a placid fishing haven. Local knowledge should be sought if in doubt.

New Efforts to Restore Status of Eske Fishery

A well attended public meeting was held in the Abbey Hotel, Donegal, to set up a new angling club, to be known as the Eske Angling Association. Mr. John Hanna, who chaired the meeting, said that it was agreed at a public meeting earlier that the club should be formed and it only remained for them to select a name and form a committee.

He said he was encouraged by the widespread interest the idea received in the community and the enthusiasm shown for an all out effort to be made to improve the Eske Fisheries.

He pointed out that this was something of an historic occasion for the people of Donegal as it was the first time an absentee landlord had given the Lough Eske fishing rights to a body from the community, or to anyone for that matter. He told the meeting of the protracted negotiations they had with Viscount Sudley (Lord Arran) and the successful outcome of these. They culminated in a long term lease being granted, which now passes to this new association. These rights include approximately 100 acres of prime fishing area on Lough Eske, commonly known as The Ridge, together with The Eske River and commercial fishing rights.

He also pointed out that they had also entered into an agreement with the North Regional Fisheries Board for the remaining 900 acres of Lough Eske. "This agreement is for one year initially, but pending a successful outcome of our first year's efforts, this will be renewed annually, in return we will attend to the improvement of the fisheries which will include restocking, protection cleaning river beds and making suitable access points," he said.

Mr. Hanna said that the new amenity would give a tremendous boost to the local economy. "It will provide a certain amount of employment and help tourism. It is planned to train gillies by giving suitable applicants a short course on fishing methods and show the best Salmon and Trout "lays" on the Lough. A gillie should be able to make a reasonable week's pay. "Anyone interested in this work should now apply to Mr. Billy Johnston," said Mr. Hanna.

Mr. Hanna welcomes Peter Nolan into the association. He said he was delighted to see he had been elected to the committee. His father in law, the late Willie McGowan, had been one of the most dedicated anglers in the north west. He had been on the river from his early school days and his tragic death came suddenly while he was engaged in his beloved sport on the banks of the River Eaney. "Peter will carry on the family tradition."

Mr. Billy Johnston said that the Eske Fisheries was at one time reputed to be one of the three best in Europe - but unfortunately this was no longer the case. "The fishing is decimated and it will take a tremendous effort on the part of everyone concerned with the economy in the area to bring it back to the prime position it held in days gone by" he said.

In reply to a local commercial fisherman who said they were concerned about the future of commercial fishing in the estuary, Mr Johnston said that they could not give a definite undertaking about the commercial fishing in the estuary at a given future date because other bodies had an interest there.

Mr. Hanna said that fish in the estuary were in serious decline and the main effort of all of them was not to stop fishing but to restore and enhance the supply. They would not do anything to affect the livelihood of the commercial fisherman. He proposed that the committee meet the commercial fishermen soon to discuss the matter.

Salmon Fishermen Want Monofilament Legalised

Inshore fishermen in the NorthWest have
renewed their campaign urging Marine
Minister, Mr Michael Woods, and the Northern
Regional Fisheries Board to permit the
introduction of monofilament nets for the
Salmon fishing season now approaching.

At a meeting of the Donegal Salmon and
Inshore Fishermen's Association in the Mount
Errigal Hotel, Letterkenny, it was asserted by the Salmon boatmen that it was
fundamentally wrong to attempt to control a fishery by limiting its technology, and
insisted that the most effective gear available are nets of monofilament type.

The fishermen were adamant that the use of monofilament nets makes for greater
safety at sea, plus the advantage of higher quality catches, and reduced loss of gear.
The meeting demanded that the use of these nets be fully legalised.

The fishermen also highlighted their full acceptance of the need for Salmon
conservation, and said they have, in the main, complied with regulations governing
the importance of Salmon stocks conservation.

The meeting also discussed the embarrassment and annoyance felt by Salmon crews
during the fishing season at the strong naval presence positioned in north western
waters, and that the round the-clock fishery corvette patrols throughout the entire
Salmon fishing season. The fishermen claimed that the super vigilance maintained
by the authorities off the Donegal coast was continuing whilst foreign fishing
vessels were plundering fish stocks elsewhere along the coastline.

Reference was made to the strong force of naval personnel and Gardai that was used
on one occasion during the Salmon fishing season to bring a half decker fishing boat
into a west Donegal Port.

Eany Fishery Will Not Open

The commercial fishery on the Eany at Inver will not open this year and the fishery
may remain closed for a four-year cycle, the Northern Regional Fisheries Board has
confirmed.

The Donegal and District Anglers Association has sold its rights on the Eany to the
Fisheries Board and the Board has also acquired the commercial fishery. The DDAA
retains the right to be the only club with permission to use the fishery. Board
Manager Mr. Harry Lloyd said that the fishery was nearly at the point of extinction
and the board has taken a decision in principle to close the commercial fishery this
year definitely.

The board intends to seek scientific advice from the Department of the Marine and from the central Fisheries Board and it hopes to carry out an assessment in the summer so that the level of juvenile Salmon and Sea Trout stocks can be ascertained.

Considerable restocking is likely to be necessary and it looks as if the development of the fishery could prove to be quite expensive. It is the boards priority to develop rod angling on the Eany as this would increase the tourism potential of the area and provide the employment not only through jobs as gillies and river workers but also through creating a need for new bed and breakfast or hotel accommodation as well as other services associated with increased visitor numbers.

New Eske Body

A new body, The Eske Angling Association, is expected to be formed at a meeting in the Abbey Hotel, Donegal, on Monday night, 6th at 8pm.

Last Friday night, a public meeting called by members of the angling community in the Donegal area attracted a large number of people. At the meeting, it was learned that the Northern Regional Fisheries Board had agreed to lease their portion of Lough Eske - about 900 acres - to the new Eske Angling Association and that the fishery will from then on be jointly managed by the fisheries board and the Association and its trustees.

Under new management, it is hoped that a programme of protection, restocking and management can be undertaken with a view to restoring the fishery to its former status as one of the leading Salmon and Sea Trout sources in western Europe.

Negotiations have also been going on with Lord Arran and terms have been agreed with him for a 25-year lease on the 100 acres of Lough Eske and the river and commercial fishery under his ownership.

Please take notice that angling for Salmon and Sea Trout with rod and line will not commence until 1st May, 1992.

The Duff

This spate river needs rain for fish to run, and goodness knows enough rain fell around these parts, but it is still a bit early. Four Salmon have been caught to date. Two taken by Billy Lally from Enniskillen, fishing a shrimp.

The Eske History 1992

I said - A great system, sadly going steadily downhill, for want of attention and respect.

Eddie McGowan (RIP), who lived beside the River Eske at Drunlonagher caught the first Salmon of the season when he landed a fine 13-pounder from the Mill Hole, fishing the worm. The date was Friday 3rd April. On Friday 17th April Billy Johnston took his thirteen year old daughter Billie Anne Johnston onto Lough Eske where Billie Anne hooked and landed her first Salmon at the Ridge, trolling a green and gold 12g Toby. The fish weighed almost 15 lbs. This beautiful Salmon was immediately presented to the American Ambassador to Ireland, Richard Anthony Moore, and his wife Ester, who were spending the Easter break in Harvey's Point.

The very next day I caught my ten pounder fishing an 18grm blue and silver Toby at Corraber, on the North side of the lake. I saw the pink flash and I knew I was in a fresh wild Salmon. The Johnston Family extended their winning streak when sons Robbie and Ivan got a Salmon each on Easter Monday. On Easter Monday I fished the river Eske down from Miss Jenny's Bridge, losing two casts for the venture, so over-grown is the river.

I mentioned the highs and lows of angling. Well one German visitor, Gerhard Seller from Bavaria got his high when he landed a 10lb Salmon on a visit to Lough Eske with his wife Udar. Gerhard comes to Ireland regularly for the fishing. In 1983, on his first visit, he caught a Salmon, and he has had to wait nine years of trying to catch a second Salmon. The American Ambassador came to Donegal to purchase a Hanna Hat. Gerhard Seller came to Donegal Town also to get a Hanna Hat. Possibly there is a link between wearing a Hanna Hat and getting a Salmon on the Eske. Anyway, John Hanna claims he has the successful recipe. If you wear a Hanna Hat, you end up with a Salmon.Glencoagh Lake

This small lake just outside Mountcharles. St Naul's Angling Club held a Trout fishing competition on Easter Sunday. The results have already been published, and it seems Ballyshannon fishermen virtually swept the board. Mick Lally, alias Miley from Glenroe, presented the prizes at a culmination function. (Glenroe has now been taken off RTE.) Sixty-eight Anglers fished in the competition, and fifty-five good brown were caught. The prize for the Heaviest Fish was claimed by a one-and-three-quarter specimen.

Highs and Lows in April

April was the kind of month that if you got a fish, it put you on a high, but if you didn't, then you got a low. The American Ambassador got a Salmon without wetting a line, but a Ballyshannon youth who got a trip to a famous western fishery returned empty handed. With angling, sometimes you can't catch fish, and other times you can't stop catching them. Anyway April weather was variable, and that is not "kicking for touch."

Thomas Gallagher of the Drowes fishery informs me that the snow and sleet on the mountains kept the temperature of the water cold. Easter brought very cold weather indeed, and April is the gap between the end of the spring runs and the start of the grilse. I finally landed my first Salmon.

Drowes

Such is the reputation of the Drowes that Thomas Gallagher is a bit disappointed that only fifty plus Salmon have been taken during April. Literally hundreds of anglers travel regularly to fish this river. Successful anglers, to mention just a few, were local man John Fahy, with three fish; Chris Sinclair, Bangor, a Salmon of 13 lbs on the 17th of the month; Sam Gourly, Omagh, 10 1/2 lbs on the 23rd; J. Sands, Magherafelt, caught a 12 pounder on the 19th April; Maurice Cullen, Portadown, and Gary Crooks, Belfast with one apiece in the early days of April. I have said it before and I will say it again - such rivers as the Drowes and the Duff, and such lakes as the Eske, Melvin and Glencoagh are tourist factories, generating clean jobs, protecting the environment, and churning revenue.

The Moy

At the start I mentioned the highs and the lows of angling. Well young James McIntyre, of Assaroe View, Ballyshannon recently experienced the low fishing. James went for a days fishing on the Moy in County Mayo. He didn't get to fish the Ridge Pool, which is one of the most famous and sought after stretches in Ireland, but he did fish the Moy Estuary for Sea Trout. James drew a blank, but enjoyed his trip, and he isn't really down or hitting a low, because he can fish his local (and just as famous) Erne Estuary, where he has been successful in the past.

Far-way rivers may look more inviting, but home waters are the hero.

Salmon the Rhine

That shook you. And if Salmon used to run into the Rhine, then they made their way as far as Switzerland.

Jody Gysling the owner of Harvey's Point Hotel comes from Switzerland, and he tells me that the Swiss are very careful and appreciative of whatever they have left. Fishing is expensive there, and most of all potential anglers have to learn about fish and fishing before they are granted a license and allowed to fish there. They are tested in their knowledge of what they can retain and what they must return. They place great value on their waterways and their fish. I hope we are not going down a destructive torrent by taking the cycle of fishing events for granted.

Heinz Joachim Innelbagh with Irish-bred salmon caught in a tributary of the Rhine

Specimen Catches in May

The really good weather of the last week did not hide the fact that the month of May arrived with cold weather and high levels of angling waters. Hopefully the sunny state will remain for as long as possible, and we anglers will lift our eyes from the lakes and rivers, to view with contentment the swift flight of the swallow arrived from southern continents.

Sea angling is getting into its stride, with calmer seas, and the Ballyshannon Sea Angling Club are holding a members' competition on Sunday, 31st May, departing from Creevy Pier at 10 am. If you want to take part, join the club.

The mayfly and olive hatches appeared the second week of the month, after the cold spell. Two specimen Salmon and a specimen Trout were caught during May.

Melvin

A visiting English fisherman, whose name escapes me, got a 2½ lb Brown Trout in Hill's Bay. The cold temperature of the water is not tempting this multi-trouted lake into full production just yet, but one of these days, and be there when it happens. Seventeen Salmon are reported taken off the Rossinver and Garrison end of the lake. One was taken on the Fly, and the other fell to the trolling method. Wooden Devons, Brown and Gold, Blue and silver or Yellowbelly on the end of about 40 yards of line are most in use.

Melvin Competition

The 12th Annual Lough Melvin Wet Fly International takes place the 19th, 20th and 21st June. This international event is organised by the Kinlough & District Anglers, with prizes worth in excess of £3000. First prize is a 19ft. fibre glass lake boat, plus the J. Cassidy Perpetual Cup, and the list of winners goes to 12th place with a prize to the value of £40. There are additional prizes for heats winners, the heaviest fish and boatman's prize for the heats and the finals.

Boats will leave Breffni Pier each day of the competition, returning at 6pm for the weigh-in. The entry fee of £35 covers boat, engine, boatman, and the evening meal. All competitors are requested to wear life jackets in the interest of safety. With a list of over 50 sponsors, and the efficiency of the Kinlough & District anglers over the years, this international event is a Premier occasion in the angling calendar.

Drowes

In the year 1990, several hundred Salmon were landed from this river during the last month of May. While 1992 has not repeated the hefty success of 2 years ago, nevertheless two specimen Salmon were taken during the month. An Armagh fisherman got a 24 pounder, and a welsh angler Arthur Fogerty got a 21 lb 4 oz fish. The grilse arrived by mid May, and they are scaling between
3 and 6 pounds. So far they are in good condition, fresh with Sea lice.

Local anglers to register Salmon are Eddie McFadden, Ballyshannon, with two Salmon in double figures, fishing worm; Jim Mahon, Ballyshannon, with a 12 lb Fresh Salmon at the new bridge on the Bundoran to Sligo road - the bait used is described as a dilapidated Silver Devon. Sometimes Jim has all the luck. Peter McSharry, Larreen, using a No. 8 Garry Dog Fly, got a Salmon in the Island Pool. Peter kindly thought of me, as that is my favourite pool.

Silver Devon

Grahame Tuck, Surrey, England got seven Salmon for his weeks holidays, but then Grahame does it all fervently, and let's face it, he has not the same river of plenty in Surrey. He fished early morning and late evening with the Fly.

Pettigo

Pettigo is 120 miles from Dublin, and 95 miles from Belfast. And the Pettigo Tourism Group in conjunction with the Pettigo and District Angling Club have produced a small compact brochure detailing top quality mixed coarse and game fishing angling holidays. There are so many outlets for fishing in and around Pettigo that you can choose to fish for Salmon, Trout, Pike, Perch, Roach and Bream, and I'm sure even a few more species.

The brochure is completed with maps showing just where Pettigo is, and the location of the rivers and lakes. The participating accommodation is listed along with specific rates to lure the interested angler. The effort is a credit to the endeavours of all concerned.

Final Comment

A final comment of the month of May I will leave to a German angler, just arrived, when I met him on the river Drowes, I enquired if he had caught anything. "Nothing yet," he said with accent, "But not bad for the first day." You thought they had no sense of humour!

July in the North West and in Boston and San Francisco

I have been away visiting my family in Boston and San Francisco, and in the journey doing some fishing. However, fishing here at home has been somewhat sparse in certain areas due to the prolonged dry spell. Up to mid-July we have had virtually nine weeks of good weather. Salmon and Sea Trout cannot run into the systems and are hanging about in the estuaries, where they become easy prey for illegal activity. Rivers such as the Drowes and the Eske have the added difficulty in that domestic water is being extracted in ever increasing amounts to supply Donegal Town, Ballyshannon and Bundoran. This is of necessity and no complaint can be voiced now that the supplies are in place. But how long can this situation continue without detailed thought regarding the co-existence of both demands, allowing that water is a greater demand, and the "well" slowly going dry with Ozone penetration, and the Greenhouse effect possibly taking its toll? Anyway, for now we are all right because the rain has started. The rivers will flood and the fish will run, so that the end of July offers better prospects for anglers.

Boston

Kenny Fitzpatrick and Eamonn Dunsworth (Limerick) took me fishing in Boston. We went to Houghton Pond and Beach at the Blue Hills Reservation in the precincts of Boston. This lake or pond holds Trout, Rainbow Trout and largemouth Bass, and two giant turtles. Part of the lake is roped off for swimming. Eamonn was fishing light rod and gear, with one small Fly, for Trout, and Kenny went after largemouth

Bass. There is a bag limit of 6 Trout per day, reduced during the spawning in September/October. No limit on Bass.

Kenny and Eamonn are dedicated anglers, and like the mould of American fishermen they return most of what they catch – keeping only what will provide a meal.

As we fished, sunfish were spawning along the shoreline, rather like the Char in their turn in October and November in Lough Eske. The shore was dotted with early morning fishermen, and I saw landed largemouth bass of about two to three pounds. The bass are rapid and strong strikers, and play like a fresh white Trout – never giving up and jumping all around the place. As the Trout were not rising to the Fly, we concentrated on Bass. The baits used were the rubber worm, which is reeled along the bottom, to attract the bass. Kenny tried most lures in his bag, and then fished live shiners. Eamonn was way on ahead of us, but when we did again meet, both had caught two largemouth bass, which was enough for a feed.

I did not see any Trout being taken, but they are of the usual pond size, with the odd one to 6 or 7 pounds. Believe me. Not only do they fish in this pond, but they swim in it, and just to cap the morning off a group of white robed Evangelists arrived and proceeded to baptise by immersion some half dozen persons in the sweet waters off this multi purpose facility.

I came away from Houghton Pond with a new appreciation for the keen value Americans place upon their receding recreational opportunities, against the background of threat. I will finally remember this angling chance by the big mosquito bites I endured. Houghton Pond in Boston must surely be a Mosquito Headquarters. My thanks to Kenny and Eamonn.

San Francisco

I had experienced the sea fishing for Salmon in San Francisco the the last visit, so on this occasion I headed for the river - The Russian River. My son Patrick and Tanya Zighera made the arrangements. So on Thursday, 2nd July, Patrick and I made an early start in the general direction of Santa Rosa, some 60 miles from San Francisco. I came ill crossing the Golden Gate bridge in the midst of dense highway traffic. Odd thing was – the brake wasn't working too well on my side of the car.

Actually, when I got used to the traffic, the journey was pleasant through the rolling, earthquake prone hills surrounding that city. San Quentin Prison was passed, and I liked the romantic names of Sonoma Country Line, Redwood Highway, Eureka, Bodega Bay, Napa and Petaluma Valley. We were crossing the famed wine and champagne country, and, no, I did not encounter any of the Falcon Crest soap opera stars. Anyway, this about fishing, and to make a long story short we arrived at Monte Rio where Patrick and myself had the full USA breakfast of ham, eggs and mash, not forgetting the black coffee.

Not knowing anything about the Russian River, we visited King's Sport and Tackle Shop in Guerneville and got a brochure about the river. We were too early for Chinook or Silver Salmon which start migration in the fall (Autumn). We got the drift of the river in Monte Rio and with the advice of Rial C. Allen mounted our gear, keeping one eye in the direction of the game warden would appear from. The rods and equipment were kindly lent to us by Noel Rush, out from Castlefin.

Fishing a Mepps with a tail on it, I was quickly into a nice bass, which I beached. Now don't ask me if it was small mouth, big mouth, large or striped bass, but it played gamely before capture. I returned the fish in case it did not fulfil the regulations, and then we would be in bother. Patrick, fishing a plug bait with a lump of lead for distance and depth hooked and landed a slightly bigger bass, and it got freedom also. Soon we tired of the location, and ventured up river, but try as we might, we only got bass, with plenty of swimmers crossing our water and numerous other tourists, so at three in the afternoon, satisfied, we reeled up and departed.

I thought I felt a slight earth tremor, but Patrick said the sun was getting to me. You know the song about mad dogs and Irishmen go out in the midday sun. Once again I was impressed with the American angler, and his efforts to protect and sometimes strive to restore what we demand and take for granted.

Back across the Napa Valley we drove until the shaky city of San Francisco (and its famous fog), hove into view. Then it was back to slamming on the brake on my side of the car to little effect. Thanks to Patrick and Tanya for organising the trip to Russian River, and to Noel Rush for giving up his gear.

Boston (Again)

This has nothing to do with fishing, except that water is involved, but on our return to Boston my daughter Orla had organised for us to be part of the 4th July celebrations of American Independence day on the Charles River in Boston inner harbour. The fireworks display took place on the 5th July, having been postponed the day previous due to heavy rain, but if you think you have seen fireworks, then believe me, you have experienced nothing until you have seen the renowned Boston Fireworks to celebrate 4th July. Our thanks to Kevin Scanlon and the crew of the "Iduna" and to Billy Hegarty and crew of the "Sea Hag" For allowing Mary and myself witness what is truly a wonder of this world. Thank you, Orla.

Erne Estuary

The commercial fishing has started on this estuary. Skippers and crews have paid a hefty license fee, and equipped boats. I am the chairman of the Erne Estuary Salmon

Fisherman's Association, and the returns to the boats so far have been drastic. If there are no returns to the commercial fishermen, then the prospects to the angler are bleak too. This once famous Salmon river is now degraded and decimated. In the past it has been closed to commercial netting so as to rejuvenate the River Erne and increase the stocks. All schemes have at most produced only minor success, if any success at all.

While in San Francisco I read about the impending catastrophe facing the great Sacramento River Salmon where dams have been built to divert water. Because of poorly designed spawning grounds, the fish shun reproduction, or die in a feeding frenzy at the base of spillways. The result is dwindling stocks. Equate that disaster to the river Erne – where no more "A silver shoal of Salmon rolls in among the crew." An answer must be found.

Litter

I hear an anti-litter campaign on the media of late, and of course, it's never too late. So, finally for July, I ask the angler to play his/her part. And by example teach the minor fisherman, who eagerly trudges to the water in excitement of landing a fish, to protect, respect, conserve preserve our domain from the ravages of litter, that leads to death dealing pollution in the future. Avoid litter, prevent pollution.

Eske

The level has been very low to mid July. John Hanna took a number of dead Sea Trout from the river recently. What happened to kill them is not known. The northern regional Fisheries board and the Eske anglers are jointly organising a river clean-up. First phase will commence from Timony's Turn to the Mill Hole. If you want to assist, make contact.

On Sunday morning last I fished unsuccessfully the pools below Miss Jenny's Bridge. On my return to the roadside I met Herbie Moran, from Lough Eske and Coventry. We spoke. Herbie said, "40 or so years ago we could go to the pool and pick the Salmon we wanted." The good old days, long past, and I suppose little regard was on the Salmon then – such was the quality and choice. The Eske Anglers have acquired three boats from the NRFB for letting to anglers to fish the lake.

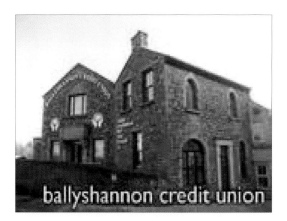

August Angling

In August time the rains came. It rained sometime over the bank holiday weekend, and it rained again into the second and third weeks. I didn't pray for rain, or do a rain dance, the rains just came and the fish ran into the rivers and lakes – just what the angler wanted.

The seas around out coasts were calm one day, and in turmoil the next, making a challenge to the sea angler to get it right before venturing out. The mackerel are still about the coasts, and are the best bet for salt water casters, but be very careful fishing from rocks along the shoreline.Records

A specimen brown Trout was caught on Durragh Lake, near Kilmacrennan, by Billy Doherty. The fish weighed in at 13 lbs. 3 ozs. Billy was pictured with his record catch in an earlier edition of this newspaper, so it remains for me to say congratulations to the keen Kilmacrennan fisherman.

Gweebarra Bridge

On Tuesday 18th August I was crossing the Gweebarra Bridge and spotted two men fishing off the bridge. Barry Threlfal and Maurice Boyle, both from Dublin, were fishing the incoming tide of the estuary for flounders or flat fish. They had half a bucket of flounders already landed, and they were using lugworms as bait. I thought they were fishing for white Trout, but you have to go to the shoreline for that.

Eany

The Eany cascades out of the Bluestack Mountains, and when you can see the Grey Mare's Tail of white water after the rain then you will know the Eany is fishable. This river is about 16 miles long until it enters the sea at Inver. The local Donegal & District Anglers Association have put this river into the care of the northern Regional Fisheries Board, and commercial fishing has ceased in the estuary with the result that more fish are getting into the system.

Good catches have been reported for August. Count Douglas O'Donnell visiting his kinsman Vincent O'Donnell, Landed 3 Salmon over a two hour period. from the Devlin Pool. Jim McGeever, Mountcharles, Secretary of the D & DAA has had four fish between the Devlin and the flag Pool. The grilse have averaged 5 pounds. Patsy McHugh, Inver, got seven grilse, spinning the Toby or the Flying C (Condom); Willie Ward, Inver, three grilse on the spinner; Michael McLoughlin, Mountcharles, got four Salmon at the Bony Glen Pool. When the grilse were running, two visiting anglers took 25 Salmon from the Bony Glen on worms, and I think that's a bit much – maybe its envy on my part.

Ronnie Drew

Enter Ronnie Drew, the vocalist and guitar player with The Dubliners, who is celebrating "Thirty Years A-Greying." Ronnie had just one previous outing as an angler, without success. Anyway, John Hanna,

Edward Hanna, Ronnie and myself enjoyed two wonderful days fishing, and having the craic on Lough Eske over the August weekend. No Salmon, but Ronnie landed a number of Sea Trout and the local brown Trout on the Fly, and was thrilled. He is now hooked on fishing, and will return.

Teaching Ronnie Drew about Fly Casting

Edward Hanna, Ronnie Drew R.I.P., John Hanna, and me. I wish this photo wasn't stained.

I was teaching Ronnie the art of Fly casting (imagine), and his favourite flies are the Hairy Mary, Fiery Brown and the silver Rat, or words to that effect. Welcome to the fraternity, Ronnie Drew - "A free man on Sunday."

(Sadly, Ronnie Drew died in 2008.)

World Record Sea Trout Caught and Returned

A 30 lbs. Sea Trout was caught by Randolph Harrison from Mill Neck, New York, fishing the Rio Grande River in the Tierra Del Fuego region of southern Argentina. This massive fish was weighed, measured, photographed, and then released. It is being claimed as a world record for a Sea Trout caught on the Fly.

Drowes

Thomas Gallagher and the Drowes anglers can be pleased the system is fishing so well in August. In deed, as the month progressed, and the condition of the river improved, so too the catches increased.

Reiner Troester, Duisberg, Germany, got a Salmon on the worm at the Four Masters Bridge; Cees G. Snel, France, fishing at the sea pool, landed a 5 lb grilse using a No. 14 Garry. I never would use such small flies. Others to record catches of grilse are Pat Ruane, Dublin, with one from the Island Pool; Bob Jordan, Omagh, Got two on the worm at the New Bridge; Neil McMullin and father from Larne got three Salmon, and Mervyn Armstrong, got two. Chris Pringle, Monaghan, at the wash stones fishing the Silver Rat and The Hairy Mary got three grilse. The wash stones seem to be a good place to wait on the run arriving. Mark Carty (13) and Brian Carty, Holywood, Co Down, got a Gilaroo Trout apiece fishing from the jetty at Lareen.

Not bad for a river opened since 1st January.

Finn

This vast river system is fishing well for Salmon and Sea Trout, and that is good news. Manus O'Donnell, a member of the Ballybofey and Stranorlar Anglers, tells me that they have 60 members in their angling club. They allow about 20 outside members to fish their club stretch. The annual fee is very reasonable. They control a stretch from Corraine Burn at Dooish to Murphy's at Dreenan, and the members volunteered protection on a rota basis. The Foyle Fisheries provides them with a dinghy, an outboard engine for patrol duties. Club members also trim and maintain the riverbanks. All methods of angling is allowed, except prawn or shrimp, but members mostly fish the Fly. There is no bag limit.

When I say the Finn is vast I mean from its source at Lough Finn it runs for 40 miles, and the Reelan River is a tributary. For the record, Manus O'Donnell caught a 29 lb cock Salmon on the Clady River in Gweedore in 1990, on the worm.

September Fishing Spree

As the results of the rain that fell during August, the fish ran into various freshwater systems, making the reports for September excellent for the most part. The September weather was good, the water conditions were great.

Donegal senior football team won the All-Ireland for the first time in ideal conditions, and anglers of all persuasions joined in the fantastic welcome of the cup holders received as they entered the county of Donegal across the Drowes Bridge that spans the famous river.

I'm told the GAA writer "The Follower" is an avid angler, when he gets the time. Indeed, how many of the victorious team are anglers also? It would be of interest to search out.

Drowes

The conditions during September for this river were ideal, Despite frost at night towards the back end of the month. Some 150 Salmon were caught by a host of eager anglers. Most of these fish proved to be in good condition. However, some fish have been returned to the water. Anglers here have been using the Fly or spinning for their results.

Daryl Kennedy, Moira, Co Down, got six Salmon ranging from 14 lbs to 5 lbs in weight. Daryl, you will recall, landed the first Salmon of the season in 1982, when he was ten years old. His keenness has not waned. David Hutchinson, Ennis, fishing in the Island Pool landed a 12 pounder, but lost five fish on the same day. Swiss angler Danny Assolari took one Salmon from the Eel Weir, and another from the Black Water. Dave O' Brien, Ennis, caught a great Salmon of 16 lbs. and a smaller fish from the Scott Pool, and at Lennox bridge. Alfie Marshall played a fresh fish on the Fly in the deep water; Joe Murphy, from West Clare, got two, while Ian Louth, a Meath man, caught a seven pounder.

The popular Fly of the moment involved in catching a lot of Salmon from the Drowes is the Gold Thunder, designed and tied by Bob Hutchinson from Ennis, Co Clare. This Fly is a variation of the Thunder and Lightning. This river has had a long season, having opened on 1st January. By closing date at the end of September over 1200 Salmon will be recorded as caught by anglers in 1992.

Assaroe Lake

There is more to fishing than game angling. John Fletcher, Michael Fletcher, Paul Andrews and Harry Hallsall, all from Manchester, are proof of this. They are coarse anglers. John Fletcher and friends spent a week fishing the Assaroe Lake shores at Ballyshannon the early days of September, and no day did they not record 30 pounds of coarse fish. These fish are put into a keep net until the end of the day's fishing then the bag is emptied, with all fish returned to the lake.

John informs me this lake holds coarse fish to competition standards. Assaroe Lake, he said, contains Roach of quality and specimen size. Bream to four pounds, which would be considered as good, and also quality Perch in abundance. The four cross channel visitors had the lake to themselves, and enjoyed their fishing vacation. This venue of angling has yet to be exploited here.

Owenea

This river is managed by the Northern Regional Fisheries Board, is a spate river and is 16 miles long until it enters the sea at Ardara, having passed Glenties on its productive journey. I got a report from Bosco McGill, Ardara, a member of the local anglers association. Generally there has been a good run of Salmon into the Owenrea River, and more importantly the Sea Trout numbers have improved over the recent season. Bosco got a Salmon of 5 lbs at the Ridge Pool, and a sixteen pounder was landed from the Holly Bush Pool.

On 1st September, Jack Smyth, a resident of Portnoo, and member of the Ardara Anglers Association, hooked a 22 pounder at Poul a Tuorn. Jack was fishing the Flying C, or condom, as this bait is popularly known. It took well into the hour to land this specimen Salmon, and Jack, having no net, deftly gilled the Salmon to end the struggle.

Some years back 25 lbs. was the specimen weight for a Salmon, but that has been reduced to 20 pounds. I got a 20 lb 4 oz salmon and duly collected my Specimen Badge.

Poetry

The quiet sport of angling prompts many facets of human response. Edward Hanna is exiled in Springfield, Virginia, with his wife Breege, son Karol and daughter Clare. You can imagine his thoughts wandering back across the broad Atlantic to his own Lough Eske, where he spent many youthful days fishing in contentment for the sage Salmon and the fiery Sea Trout. To fill the pain Edward has composed a poem about Lough Eske, entitled "Twilight in Corraber" (Corraber is an area on the northern portion of the lake). See what you think of a sample stanza:

> *"As I threw a stone across Lough Eske,*
> *It skipped above the lake,*
> *And my memory cleared of present things*
> *T'was if I was awake.*
> *And fishermen stood boldly*
> *At Callaghan's point they fished,*
> *The most precious things they ever caught*
> *Were memories of this."*

Keenaghan Lake

The annual boat/shore Trout Fly competition took place on the 13th September. This is now fished for the Gussie McGonigle Memorial Perpetual Trophy, with the proceeds going to the Ulster Cancer Foundation. Thirty entrants fished this competition in good conditions, with plenty of Trout landed. The winner of the Gussie McGonigle trophy and a fishing rod was Johnny Ray, from Belcoo, Co Fermanagh, with a Trout of 26 ounces. Second place went to Pat Love, Derrygonnelly, for a Trout of 16 ounces. Pat got a landing net. Third spot went to Joe Flanagan, Omagh, Trout 14 ounces, and the prize was a box of Rogan's Flies; 4th, Gerry Kearne, Trout of 13 ounces, fishing bag; 5th was Sean McCann, Belleek, who won a leg of lamb, locally sponsored. At the weigh-in at the Border Inn, Gerry McGonigle sincerely thanked the sponsors, those who gave donations and said that £300 had been raised

Late Gussie McGonigle, Belleek with 26lbs. and 18lbs. Salmon caught using Shrimp on the Duff River

Gussie McGonigle R.I.P.

for the U.C.F. The raffle for the Melvin Brooch was won by Sean Dolan, Bonahill.

Eske

The banks of this river are being steadily revealed a great river, once in decline. All concerned are to be praised for their efforts to rescue this three to four mile stretch with immense water character, and potential. My good friend, Francis Kennedy, Donegal Town, got a fine Salmon of 10 pounds in September, which was fully deserved. I got a four pound Rainbow Trout at the Abstraction Dam just down from Sean McCauley's and further got an eight pounds Salmon on Lough Eske, trolling a Toby off Callaghan's Point. On Saturday 26th September, Billy Johnston got a nice fish, again on the Toby, near Roisin. Billy also landed a big fish from Fox's Pool, above Miss Jenny's Bridge, flying a small Fly called the Garry Dog (I think). Of course Billy had to do it the hard way. Midway through playing this Salmon Billy's reel fell into the river, so he had to net the reel before the Salmon.

Finally on the lake - a number of char experts were out investigating and researching the ten thousand year old resident of Lough Eske (Char). They were using light tackle in their efforts to catch one. Four year old Veronica Beir, daughter of one of the party, was holding the rod when she informed her father something had taken the bait - a Mepps. What had taken the Mepps was a 15 lb Salmon. Some anglers say this lake is "Dead water". Well, Veronica Beir and her party have proven this to be wrong. The answer is to join the local anglers who are making the effort. Don't be a knocker...

Melvin

The Kinlough and District Anglers held their end of season Trout Fly competition on Lough Melvin on 26th September (Saturday). Fishing was from 11 to 6 pm. departure from Breffini Pier, outside Kinlough. 54 boats took part, and 74 Trout were caught. Conditions were not ideal with calm waters and frost the previous night. Prizes for the heaviest bag catch were - winners Jackie Mahon, Sligo, and H Patterson, Belfast, who caught 9 Trout weighing 5.66 lbs. They received £200 each.

Second with eight Trout, were Freddie Steel, Banbridge, and Ken Hutchinson, Agivy, Derry, for two holidays of two weekends at the Abbey Hotel, Donegal Town and the Maghery Hotel, Bundoran, to the value of £150 each. 3rd, with 5 Trout, Trevor McKearn, Dromore, and Brian Gordon, Belfast, who won £75 each. The Bannerman Perpetual Cup for heaviest Trout went to Harry McCafferty, Letterkenny, for a Sonaghan Trout of 1.04 lbs. The presentation of prizes took place at a dinner in the Maghery Hotel, Bundoran.

Two Salmon on River Drowes Opening Day 1993

Two Salmon were landed at 9:30am on the January 1st opening day on the River Drowes to herald½ in the new year in the northwest. Tommy Bateman (33), a lift engineer from Carrickfergus, Co Antrim, caught an 8lb. Salmon at the Crooked Hole Pool at Lareen using a 16 gram red Flying C, and Peter Keane, (48), a fishery officer, from Irvinestown, Co Fermanagh, landed his 10 lbs. Salmon from Briney's Pool, above Lennox's Bridge, on the main Bundoran to Kinlough Road. Peter was fishing a purple shrimp on a single size 6 hook. As both fish were caught at the same time, the honour of landing the Salmon of the season was shared.

Crowds

The opening day of the 1993 fishing season started at 8:30 am under the supervision of the Northern Regional Fishery Board staff. Game anglers from virtually every county in Ireland, and many visitors from abroad, in total numbering some 300, braved the blustery conditions in attempting to catch the first Salmon of 1993.

The Drowes river, with some sixty pools, was in good condition. New catwalks had been put in place over the winter period, and the water level was deemed to be ideal for catching Salmon.

However, the honour of the first Salmon of the new year was swiftly claimed by the River Liffey, Dublin, with a 9:05 am report of a fish having being caught.

Honours Shared

Lucky fisherman Tommy Bateman and Peter Keane shared the £200 prize for the Drowes, and both names will be inscribed on the Drowes Perpetual Cup. The two Salmon were purchased by Frankie O'Gorman and the Rodgers family of the Imperial Hotel, Bundoran, for £500, and were on the menu of a free function held in the hotel last Sunday. And is also traditional a donation was made to a good cause. In this case £200 was donated by the owner of the fishery, Thomas Gallagher, to the mentally handicapped at Cregg House, Sligo.

Presentation

The presentation of the prizes took place at an enjoyable ceremony held in the Drowes Lounge, Tullaghan, at the closing of the opening day. MC was Clr. Tony Ferguson, who thanked all who had helped to make the day a success. Clr. Frank O' Kelly also spoke and presented the prizes, and Thomas Gallagher thanked the staff of the Northern Regional Fisheries Board, Gardaì, The Drowes bar, and Bill Likely for their help and assistance.

Comfort

Nothing is more traditional on the opening day of the Drowes than the soup kitchen, manned by Linda McSharry, Lareen; Hosam Fakhouri, Palestine; and Sean Smith, Sligo. The main ingredients for the hot urn were One cwt. Potatoes, 4 stone carrots, 1 stone onions, celery, and undisclosed portions of meat.

A poem was nailed to the entrance called "The Salmon's Refuge," which read:

> *Welcome to Lareen, Happy New Year*
> *All anglers from far and near,*
> *The soup is ready, spicy and hot,*
> *To cheer you up if none is caught.*
> *Then Try Again And It Is Our Bet*
> *A "Big One" Will Jump Into Your Net.*

Back to Basics

January was for rain and more rain. Storms and more storms. The lakes are bulging with water, the rivers working full time to gulp such torrents through their systems. The spent fish will have every opportunity to make an exit to the refreshing sea, and the fresh spring fish will accept the obstacle free invitation of gushing water to run into and through the rivers of their destiny. So while the opened rivers were high for angling for most of January, all systems will be given a reasonable chance of good fishing in February – notably the Melvin. Going back to a bit of spawning, I am told most of the locations were average, but the Eany redds counted about average and good.

The Opening

The news to me so far is that two Salmon were landed off the ever reliable Drowes on the opening day of 1st January. As already reported, and since then upwards on 30 have been taken.

Eddie McFadden, Ballyshannon, got his January spring Salmon fishing the worm, in the place he frequents, the Stakey hole. Pat Duffy, Bundoran got one early on and followed it with another fine fish mid-month.

Two Salmon were caught on the Lennon, on the 1st January, and a number of Salmon have been landed upstream by anglers from the Letterkenny district.

Lough Gill, Sligo made Ricky Rebozzi and his two sons happy then they caught a 12 pounder on new years day. That's it for January 1993. Tight lines.

Mild February

Good returns After the dire conditions experienced in January, the weather improved to mostly mild conditions in February. Water levels started to recede. More anglers ventured to their favourite haunt, and a steady run of Salmon was observed.

Drowes

Over sixty spring Salmon caught here for the month. No real "whoppers," but what is wrong with an average size of 8lbs weight and a few 12 pounders! John O'Connor, Cahir, Co Tipperary, got his 10 lbs. Fish at the Island Pool fishing a flying Purple C. James Quinn from Cullyhanna, Co Armagh, fishing an O'Reilly shrimp Fly, got a 12 lb Salmon at Lennox's bridge – accompanied by Big Tom McBride of country and western singing fame. Local fishermen John Fahy, Kinlough, has three Salmon do date, and James McCartan, Down footballer of note and fame, landed a 10 lb Fish from the Wash Stones, spinning. The river is in good condition water-wise and should continue to produce in March.

Prospects

Heavy rain at the end of February has left the rivers in flood. Apart from the impending cold spell forecast the prospects for continued game fishing look good for March, and it will be interesting to see who registers the first Salmon from the Eske, the Finn and the other great rivers of Donegal.

I.T.F.F.A.

The Irish Trout Fly Fishing Association have been in contact with me with a list of the major competitions organised for the year. Here is the list, venue and date: The National Championship, L. Sheerin, April 24th ; Leinster Championship, L. Owel, May 9th ; Connacht, L. Conn, May 23rd; Munster, L. Lein, May 9th; Ulster, L. Melvin, June 12th. The inter provisional Championship takes place on Lough Owel, Sept. 11th. There are club qualifiers, leading to the club team finals on Lough Conn, and the association are in the process of organising a youth team (under 18) to participate in the Youth Home Internationals.

Melvin

Lough Melvin opened in fine style on the 1st February, again the mild weather allowed some twenty boats out onto the water. Frank Gallagher, Garrison, got the first Salmon trolling a Yellow Belly. Frank's fish weighed 8 lbs. And was a fresh run, and he followed the first day fish with a second Salmon, a 10 pounder, on 2nd February on the brown and Gold Devon. Aiden O'Dare, Derrygonnelly, got the third Salmon on the 3rd day, again trolling a Devon.Others to register Salmon were Pat Mulligan, Enniskillen; Bob Beatty, Derrygonnelly, with two Salmon; Denis (father) and Sean (son) Maguire, Garrison, got a Salmon apiece on Sunday 21st February.

An interesting feature experienced on the Melvin to date is the quantity and quality of Brown Trout taken. These big Trout are varying in size between five and twelve pounds. Robert Gilmore, Kesh, and angling mate, got a Brown Trout of eleven pounds and another weighing twelve pounds. Latest reports coming from Sean Maguire of the Melvin Tackle Shop, Garrison, says that the water has muddied somewhat at the end of February, but there is a hatch of Duck Fly making those magnificent Trout rise. About twenty Salmon were caught during February.

March Lamb and Lion

I still say that February and March are the worst months of the year, and they are very deceptive. More people / anglers go down with colds and flu's – to my reckoning – than at any period over the winter months.

March comes in like a lamb and leaves like a lion, they say, and this March was no different. Even in the period of one day the conditions were so changeable that one hour it was warm and the next it was very cold. The water levels were low, and invariably such would deter one angler and encourage another. Most of the fishing systems opened the first of March, so the rush to the river or lake has increased. The spawned eggs of the Salmon should, about now, be leaving the safety of the redds to embark on life in the open stream, so don't wade into the rivers.

Slieve League Anglers

The Slieve League Anglers' Association, based at Carrick, had a signing ceremony in the Bridge Bar, Carrick, on Friday 26 March. Minister of State, Pat the Cope Gallagher, TD. Attended the official signing on behalf of Udaras Na Gaeltachta for a long term license for Teelin Fisheries over to the Slieve League Anglers Association. A limited company has been formed to run the fishery, with an active 12 member board. Chairman is Francie Cunningham, Secretary Donal Ward, and Treasurer Smith Campbell. Now under control of the S.L.A.A. Are four rivers – Glen, Yellow, Owencheskna and the Grove, the nine lakes feeding the four rivers and four other lakes in the district, all flowing into Teelin Bay.

The system holds Salmon, Sea Trout, Brown Trout and char. Annual membership is £25; weekly £10; and daily £3. Pat the Cope Gallagher was presented the first permit issued. This fishery system is described as the best in Ireland for its size.

Good luck to the efforts of the Slieve League Anglers Association.

Drowes

Dare I say it, but Thomas Gallagher was not happy with the results for March. The low level of the water might have had a bearing, but "only" 60 Salmon were recorded. Harry Corbett hooked, but lost a Salmon on St. Patrick's Day - I would have liked to have seen Harry land his fish, but that is the way of Salmon fishing.

One day you can't catch them, another day you can't miss them. Take the case of Billy Ray, Glengormley – landed two Salmon and lost three. Denis Brennan, Cookstown, got a 12 lbs. Fish with the red shrimp in the black water. Ray McCullogh got a Salmon from the Black Water, and using the shrimp. Paul McGivern, a ten pounder from the lower Island Pool, fishing the Gary Tube Fly.

The Perch Hole yielded a Salmon to Paul McClement, Belfast, on the Hairy Mary Fly. John Fahy got a four lbs. Grilse, full of Sea lice, which is unusual for so early in the season. Not bad for a disappointing month.

Melvin

The lake is fishing well at the moment, and returns for Salmon and Trout for March good.

To start off with, a picture saves a thousand words. Mark Thompson, Ballyshannon, shows the 8lbs. Brown Trout he caught on the 10th March. Mark was trolling a blue and silver Toby, 7 gram. Here is a short list of others to register fish: Frank Gallagher, Garrison, 8lb Salmon on Brown and Gold Devon on the plantation Shore; Barney Lawn, Boa Island, 8 pounder on Devon at the sand at Garrison; Johnny McCloskey, Enniskillen, caught two fish trolling the black and gold Devon; Chris Fahy, Dublin, a 12 lbs Salmon on the Thunder and Lightning Fly at the pump house in Hemmings Bay on 20th of the month of the month; Pat McSharry, Lareen, got a 2 lb Gillaroo Trout on the Golden Olive in Lareen Bay.

.

What is a Sewin?

I'm told it is a Welsh Sea Trout. The story is that John Hanna from Donegal went over to see the victory of our rugby team in Cardiff, and came back with the Neath & Dulais Angling Club newsletter 1993. Reading this newsletter I find that a number of Notable fish were recorded in 1992, among them a magnificent Sewin of 17 1/2 pounds weight. How would you like that on the end of your line?

Trout fishing on the Neath and Dulais rivers is mentioned as good, with fish of 1 lb plus caught, and the best one landed being 4 lbs 10 ozs. This Trout netted the senior angler Gary Davies a trophy at the AGM. This angling club is very organised to produce a newsletter, and maybe it is the case of more the struggle, the more the interest and effort. The largest Fly caught Salmon was a six pounder, and a cup

Sewin

has been donated for presentation to the winner of a night time Fly fishing competition – so what is a Sewin?

Florida

My brother Peter is just back from Florida, and he brought some brochures and fishing journals. Fishing inshore and offshore is a big industry in that part of the USA. Could you handle a 350 pound Thresher, a 60 lbs. Striped Bass? One photograph pictures a 800 lbs. Giant Tuna, another a Mako shark of 275 pounds.

Billfish are taken on the Fly and grouper are a popular species with the American angler. Depth-finders are used to locate Gator Trout, and Sea Trout are fished along offshore beaches. North America's only coral barrier reef lies six miles off the Florida Keys, and like ecosystems worldwide, this reef is under threat. All in the fishing is varies and plentiful, and the climate is warm and dry. However, be satisfied with the temperature conditions prevailing in Ireland, put up with the colds and flu's, because Florida can be torn apart and drenched with torrential rains and powerful and destructive hurricanes.

Finn

Manus O'Donnell tells me that the Ballybofey and Stranorlar club stretch of the Finn has produced a below-average ten Salmon during March. There was enough water, and cold weather. Most anglers are waiting for milder conditions to attempt the Fly in preference spinning. Frank Neeson, Ballybofey, got an eleven pound Salmon on the minnow at the pot. Downstream in the Killygordon stretch is fishing well, as is upstream at the Cloughan area, and on that hopeful note, I will finish.

Eske

This system has had the worst start in returns for the Anglers in thirty years.

Charles Doherty, who is up and out early, and has the river fished before the rest emerge from slumberland, caught a ten pound Salmon; Eddie McGowan and John Hanna escapee Rainbow Trout – Eddie got his on the River and John hooked a big Rainbow while trolling on the lake. These fish are not natural products of the Eske, so what effect their arrival will have on the system is not known. Again, there was plenty of water, and the work on the river reveals pools I never knew existed. Indeed everything was in favour of the angler, thanks to the effort of the Eske Anglers and the Northern Regional Fisheries Board, but disappointment to date.

Drowes

The cosmopolitan Drowes is fishing well. The Salmon taken during April were nearly all big twelve pounders and upwards. About 100 fish were landed, and they fell to every bait from the Fly to the Fly to the Flying C, to the worm and shrimp. I met Norman Huston, Magherafelt, coming off the river on Saturday 24th April carrying his 9 lbs salmon caught just below the Eel Weir Pool, on a size 10 Ally Shrimp Fly. Norman was so proud as he told me that the previous Salmon he caught were of the six pound variety. He showed me an Islander reel his brother David sent from the Vancouver Island of Canada, and ascribed his success to the reel, expensive as it may be.

Melvin

Ballyshannon angler Gerry McNamara is doing well on the Melvin, and tells me that the lake is covered with the Duck Fly hatch. Some upcoming events: The competition for the O'Connor Cup will be fished on Sunday 30th May, leaving noon and returning to Breffni Pier for the 6:30 pm weigh-in. This is a wet Fly contest organised by the Kinlough and district Anglers. Contact Thomas Kelly.

The Ulster Club Wet Fly competition takes place on Saturday 12th June, Breffni Pier, from eleven to six. This competition is for clubs affiliated in Ulster only.

Erne Estuary, P.J. Coughlan Benefit Day

The estuary epitomises the good and the bad for April. I met Gerry McDermott wending his weary way home with a handful of rods, and when I asked him about his luck he indicated the returns were bad for the long trudge down the Erne Estuary.

On the other hand, PJ Coughlin seemed to hit it at the right time. One day he had seventeen Trout, another day six, and then two outings of two fish each time. PJ landed one white Trout over three pounds weight, and he was fishing Rogan's Gadget on the tail and the gosling on the dropper. The white Trout are in good condition at this venue. The south side to the limit is the favourite spot on the estuary. Other to get fish are Mark Gibbons and Keith Mangan, all from Ballyshannon.

Sea Angling

There are fourteen affiliated sea angling clubs in Donegal – that's according to Gerry McGowan. Anyway, Gerry is floating the idea of possibly running a competition, possibly in July, for these clubs to take part, and he wants a reaction, if interested. The embarkation point will be Creevy Pier, and the categories would include one for The Best Club of the Year, yet another for Best Angler of the Year. And there is more.

Sea angling with Patrick O'Malley Daly, me, Ronan Hanna, Dara O'Malley Daly, Seamus O'Neill, Pearse O'Neill, Turlough Craig, and John Hanna

May – A Taste of History

You anglers will know how the month of May fished. So I won't go into any detail – except to say that towards the end of the month, it was dry, water levels were low, the grilse began to run, and the poachers struck at many venues. The Sea Trout are in trouble. However, let's start with a bit of history that will be of interest, and comparison. It concerns the Drowes River.

Drowes History

I have been handed a page from "The Salmon Rivers of Ireland," written by Augustus Grimble and dated 1913. Make comparison, if you wish, between 1913 and eighty years on in 1993. According to the author the river opened 1st February, while the nets at the mouth of the river started a month later. It states that the whole fishing was virtually over by 1st June, except for the occasional grilse. "Fresh-run fish are often seen entering the fish in January, and Rogan reports from Ballyshannon, which is but a few miles away, the capture in the Drowes and Lough Melvin is about 120 fish, averaging 10 lbs. between the opening day and the middle of May."

Anglers in Ballyshannon, circa 1913

Many of you will not recall the Marine Hotel, Bundoran, but back in 1913 this establishment was said to be "quite comfortable and about a mile from the river (Drowes), for which no waders are wanted." Permits and tickets to fish the Drowes could be purchased from R. Deacon, Fishery officer, Bundrowes Bridge, and the angler was burdened with the following strict conditions: Artificial Fly only to be used. No fishing with worm, shrimp or bait of any sort. No spinning with any lure, real or artificial.

During the time no one is in residence at Lareen, six rods per day will be let, but when anyone is in residence at Lareen only four rods per day will be let. When the water is open to six rods, the angling will be from the lower end of the black Water Pool to the sea. When only four rods are let, it will be from Monolek Bridge to the sea. Each day ticket, 12s. 6D ; weekly ones, £3, available for six days. No angling after sunset. The angler arriving first at the river will choose his station to commence fishing, and the next comer in order may take up any position left, which is four hundred paces from any other angler, up or downstream. Anglers may keep one fish a day, providing they catch a fish a day, but all over and above one fish must be sent to the fishery office.

Hundreds can fish the popular river now, and all forms of legal angling are allowed. I could see the present day angler confining to one fish bag limit. Right.

The Grimes Family
and
Finn McCool's Pub

extend our Best Wishes
and Congratulations

to Anthony O'Malley Daly

Finn McCool's Pub
Main Street, Ballyshannon

After several years in the Donegal Democrat, my columns were also published in The Sun Newspaper:

Sun Newspaper – Fishing Guide to the Best Waters in Ireland

Welcome to Sun Sport's own special spot for Irish anglers.

Each week I'll be bringing you news of the latest in the fastest growing leisure sport in the land – and on water, of course.

We'll share knowledge of the best pools, the new events, the ones that got away and the most rewarding waters.

Who fishes where and why? Ask the Lord Lieutenant and find the answers here.

Ireland

The mighty downpours of recent weeks were disastrous for many rivers as they burst their banks. Not all rivers were affected, however – the Eske in Donegal and the Drowes in Leitrim avoided flooding. My advise to anglers on rivers in a brown flood in the rest of the country is to fish the worm in those conditions, and then the Fly as the water recedes. The worm is bringing good returns of grilse on the Ballysodare River, South of Sligo. Three Salmon were taken at the Butt Falls alone in one morning. They weighed from 10 to 12 pounds.

Northern Ireland

The entire Erne system in the north is up – and running. Thanks to recent rain the river is in perfect condition and flowing just right for Roach and Bream.

Enniskillen angler Tony Cursley decided to have a mess-around at the manor house section, and instead of using the usual big hooks for Irish style fishing, he went ultra fine. Using a size 22's hook to a 1 lb. Line, he netted 106 lbs. of Bream, hybrids and Roach on a single bronze maggot. And thanks to the increased flow, all the town sections are now producing excellent catches.

If you're looking for a 200 lbs net of Bream, then the newly pegged section at Magho, seven miles past Belleek, is the place to head for. There is a landing stage which puts you straight into deep water.

The River Bann appears to be a waste of time around Portadown, and although New Ferry is Fishing well for Bream and hybrids, water skiers make life difficult.

While the rain has certainly freshened up Northern waters, Southern ones are unfortunately still a wash-out.

New Evidence on Trout Lice

The discovery by fisheries scientists of twelve infested Sea Trout in the Dargle River at Bray recently, hundreds of miles from the nearest marine Salmon farm, has cast serious doubts on the theory that Salmon farms are to blame for the collapse of Sea Trout stocks in the west of Ireland, according to the Irish Salmon Growers Association.

"The fish, which were discovered by scientists from the fisheries Research centre at Abbottstown, were infested with the same species of lice that have been found on fish in the west of Ireland," the ISGA say in a statement.

A spokeswoman for the ISGA said that "While the results are not conclusive, they certainly bear out the claim that some other factor than Salmon farming is contributing to the collapse. Perhaps the sustained witch hunt against our industry will now end, and all sides of the debate can go forward together to solve this problem once and for all."

June for Arranmore Rainbow Trout

I had heard of the wild Rainbow Trout on Arranmore Island, and now I have some information to pass onto you anglers – thanks to a communication from James O'Donnell, secretary of the Cumann Iascaireacht Slat Oilean Mhor, the Arranmore Angling Club. The club was formed in 1989 and though they have only 12 members they have endeavoured to make yearly improvements to their system. A successful application for lottery funds meant that they were encouraged to bring back life to the eight lakes they have available on the Island, and with the aid of a small grant the members commenced a restocking programme. They got Rainbow and Brown Trout from the hatchery in Glenties, and all indications are that the Trout are adapting well to their new environment as quite a number of large Trout, both Rainbow and brown, have been caught.

The largest lake on the Island is Lough Shore, which is believed to be one of only two lakes in Europe where Rainbow Trout are self-perpetuating, and this to me means wild Rainbow, which is unique. And how these Rainbow Trout came to be in Lough Shore is quite naturally a tale in itself. Naturally enough, there are two versions, and that makes it all the more interesting.

Rainbow Trout

Between the years of 1905-1907, a Mr. C. Maude of Glen House obtained the fry from Hanlon's hatchery in Dungloe as C. Maude's brother, a Captain Maude, was a marquis of Coyngham, and the manager of the Dungloe hatchery. The second is that the fry came from New Zealand by an officer in the royal navy.

The local club have received assistance from the Northern Regional Fisheries Board, Donegal County Council, Rionn Na Gaeltachta and the island Comharcumann who completed a walking system around the Island taking in the lakes under the jurisdiction of the club. Rionn Na Gaeltachta this year have helped the club purchase five lake boats, which are available to anglers at very little cost.

The progressive dozen or so members have more plans for their club and the enhancement of the Island economy in that they intend to build a boathouse, construct a picnic shelter, and plant a belt of trees around the lakes. This angling paradise would be well worth a visit to see if you have the flair to catch the famous breed of Rainbow Trout.

Incidentally, the club members would like more information regarding the Rainbow Trout of Lough Shore, so if you can assist please forward text to the writer. I leave you on this subject with the names of the other lakes on the island – L. Na Meena, Acheskey, Na Muc, Cnoc na gCarn, Lar, Mion an Mhuillin and Seschin.

Melvin

During June the Ulster Trout Angling Competition was held. Ninety boats took part in this popular contest and a total of 289 Trout were caught. At stake were 16 places on the Ulster team for the Interprovincial Championship to be held this September, 50 places to qualify for the 1994 National Championship.

First place in this ulster championship went to D. Paul, Agivey Club, with ten Trout weighing 7.18 lbs; second was A. O'Dare, Derrygonnelly, eight Trout at 5.54 lbs; and third place went to D. Gault, Ballymoney, with seven Trout at 5.23 lbs.

Eske

Weather and water are near perfect for fishing at the moment, and having said that, conditions may well have changed when you have read this. You will remember the Sea Trout entering the Eske were infested with Sea lice and in bad condition, but recent reports from the members of the Eske Angling Club indicated that the Trout coming out of the sea are now in much better order. However, members continue to return all white Trout. Young Pauric McGlynn landed a 16 lb Salmon on Lough Eske on Sunday last fishing an 18 gram Toby. Fair to say that the Salmon runs are not up to par, when compared to the amount of hours the Angler puts into this system.

Drowes

Good returns from this prolific river. Jack McMillan, Ballymena, got seven Salmon for a week's worm fishing. Cathal Gallagher, Askill, fishing a green Toby, got an 11 lbs. Salmon at Melly's High Bank. This was Cathals first Salmon after a long apprenticeship, so congratulations are in order. Chris Pringle, Monaghan, was lucky with three fish on the blue shrimp Fly in the Trout Hole, and Dermot McMenamin, Enniskillen, took five Salmon, again on the worm. How is it that all these fishermen can get the Salmon in twos and threes and I am still on zero? Maybe getting out on the flowing water has something to do with it. I counted approx. 300 Salmon/grilse taken and recorded from the Drowes for June. Good luck to them all.

Finn

The lower stretches of this river are not as good as the upper parts right now, as the Salmon and grilse are running right through. Most of the fish are small grilse, with the odd large Salmon being taken. The pot area at Dooish, above Ballybofey, is producing good returns, also at the Cloughan Stretch at Glenfinn, Some of the results are – my contact Anthony Murray got three grilse from Murphy's Pool using a number ten golden shrimp, and an even smaller 14 Yellow Dog Fly.

Danno Laverty, fishing a Trout Mepps, came in with a 13 lbs. Salmon, and two small grilse, with Sea lice attached. Imagine these fish are running right through, and are somewhere about twenty miles from the sea, and have Sea lice. Anthony Murray tells me that for the month of June use small baits, and I guess his returns are sure proof of that. The flood on this river should ensure goodly returns right into July.

Wet Fly International on Lough Melvin

The Wet Fly International on Lough Melvin attracted 200 anglers who caught 483 Trout. The Melvin has Brown Trout, Ferox Trout, Sonaghan Trout and Gilaroo Trout. The Brown Trout can be found almost anywhere in the lake while the Sonaghan or Black Trout stay mainly out in the middle. The Gilaroo are available close to the shore.

First prize went to Joe Deery, Belleek, Co Fermanagh, who won an 18 ft. lake boat sponsored by John Maher, Tipperary. Galway's Toby Bradshaw, grabbed second prize - £350 and a fishing holiday at Lareen Park in Leitrim on the banks of the Drowes. Third prize went to Brian Minagh, Athlone – fishing tackle worth £250.

Eany

Moderate fishing reported from this spate river. I have told you before, but I'll tell you again – this river is fishable when you see the Grey Mare's Tail gushing out of the mountains, but don't ask where the grey Mare's Tail is, or you might not get the right answer. Jim McGeever, Mountcharles, was spinning at the Iron Bridge when he got his grilse of 4lbs; Albert Johnston registered his Salmon, and brother Billy was successful with an eight pounder just below the Devlin. Fish are being taken from the falls also, and as this river is now in good order, it is worth a try.

Albert Johnson

Cooked

The Gilaroo Trout have the gizzard of a chicken. The original story – and there are a few versions – is that a woman in the Dartry area gave St. Patrick a chicken for Good Friday. He went to the waters of the Melvin, dipped the chicken in the lake and it disappeared. Patrick instead was left with a fish in his hands which the woman duly cooked and which he ate. The Trout which St. Patrick took from the lake then on it had a chicken's gizzard in it, thus the name Gilaroo.

The flies to fish on Lough Melvin are the Bibio, Green Peter, Connemara Black, Sooty Olive, Claret and Mallard – and in sizes 8, 10, 12.

The Drowes is the river which flows from the Melvin and which opens for fishing on New Year's Day when, nine times out of ten, it produces the first wild Salmon of the year caught in Ireland. This fish usually fetches £500 from some local business person and part of the funds go to charity. Over 300 Salmon and grilse were caught on this river in June. Cathal Gallagher, a local angler from Askill, got the first Salmon of his career – an 11 lb Fish, with an 18 g in Melly's High Bank stretch. Chris Pringle from Monaghan got three Salmon at the Trout hole with a blue shrimp Fly and Jack McMillan, from Ballymena, landed seven Salmon for his weeks fishing mostly with the worm.

With water levels suitably high, July prospects on the Drowes look promising. Any legal method of angling is permitted on the river, but the 90 odd pools respond to a Silver Rat, Silver Doctor, Thunder and Lightning, worm, shrimp Mepps, Devons or

Toby. Thomas Gallagher is the owner of a fishery and there is accommodation readily available in the locality or in the Lareen Estate.

Lough Ennell, near Mullingar off the Tullamore Road, fished great for the May Fly and returns of Trout were moderate to good in June. The Trout are big on this stretch of water, and fish of 4 lbs plus are not uncommon.

On the Derravarah 10 miles north of Mullingar the angling fraternity are having a problem with speedboats. One suggested solution is for the speedsters to remain out in the middle of the lake over the deep. Is there a problem in other areas similar to this one? Let me know.

Bream are on the rampage in Northern Ireland and Runcorn angler Bob Bryant caught 81 of them in a single session at Lough Muckno. It is great news for the 60 match fishermen trying to win next weeks £1200 prize in the Muckno 100, a brand new 4 day angling competition. Toome Shore, where Bob – who normally spends all his time catching tiddlers on the Bridgewater Canal – had Bream to 6 lbs in a weighed catch of 230 lbs. on legered red Maggot and worm, will be included in the festival. There was an almost identical catch reported by Rodger Bell from Staffordshire, who was enjoying a fishing holiday at Eonish on Lough Oughter, part of the Erne system in Cavan.

Rewards

The mighty river Shannon is in better form and anglers travelling this weekend can expect to do even better than Peter Harwood, of Boston, Lincs. He got 97 lbs of Bream at Shannonbridge while using a swim feeder rig with worm and sweetcorn. Quality Roach and large hybrids are a feature of big catches on Northern Ireland's River Bann at Portglenone.

Early morning fishing has brought rewards on the Broadmeadow stretch of the Erne in Enniskillen. The best peg is at the mouth of the mooring inlet behind the forum, where legered caster is accounting for nets of Bream in the 4 lbs Bracket.

Friday, 6th July 1993

Good reports of salmon and grilse returns on many rivers. The Liffey is having its best year ever. Ned Brennan, a member of the Dublin Salmon Anglers and the Leixlip District Anglers Association, caught a 6 lbs. 8 ozs tagged Norwegian grilse recently. It was one of three fish Ned landed that day. All took the worm, fished on a

No. 2 hook. The Norwegian salmon was confirmed as a wild fish. The tag has been forwarded to Norway to find out its history and to claim the small reward.

Spring fish are being caught on the Liffey right now and all are above the 10 lbs mark. Grilse are also running steadily, entering the river at Ringsend. The best stretches are at Leixlip, CPI Lucan and at Island Bridge. Favourite baits are the worm, Flying C and the Mepps. I got my first salmon of the year when I landed a fine 12 lbs. cock salmon from the Devlin Pool on the Eany just outside Frosses in Co Donegal. I was fishing a Flying Purple C.

Flying Purple C

Pools News. News. News.

There were 20 salmon landed that day from such pools as the falls, Hughies and Devlin. The river is managed by the Northern Regional Fisheries Board, and fished by anglers from the Donegal and District Angler Association.

Day or season permits are required, and you will be asked for your documentation. Because the worm is so deadly on this river, the Angler is restricted to one hour per pool and the shrimp is banned. Naturally many of the fishermen in the know on this river fish the fly, and small ones at that. They don't believe the motto: "The bigger the fly, the bigger the fish." The best salmon and grilse fall to really small flies. Incidentally, when this spate river is fishable, you will see the Grey Mare's Tail tumbling out of the Bluestack Mountains.

The river dropped two feet in about three hours on the morning. Well known Donegal Angler John Hanna fished it with me. A great run of Sea trout enter the Eany, but members are encouraging fishermen to return any white trout to the water. A bag limit of three salmon is in force. It is hoped the inquiry announced by Marine Minister David Andrews to determine the cause of the Sea Lice infestation that has decimated this White Trout will produce a solution.

Fabulous

Up the North, Bream were almost running up the fishing lines on the River Erne at Belles Isle. Peter Cody from Grimsby was on a fishing trip to Enniskillen when he latched into a fabulous 134 lbs haul of hefty Bream. The 28 year old welder couldn't get his legered maggot and caster hookbait into the water fast enough.

In the beautiful surroundings on the Duke of Abercorn's estate, Pete plucked Bream to 5 lbs from the shoal. And he scored another "Ton" of fish – the other occasion was a 116 lbs net of Bream caught the day before on the Erne at West Isle.

Ireland's Roach record was rattled twice during the week when fish of 2 lbs 12 ozs and 2 lbs 13 ozs were caught at Monaghan from a Carrickmacross lake. The magic of Monaghan is also doing the trick when it comes to Bream where Des Wilson from Blaney hammered out 170 lbs from Lough Muckno. The Shannon is producing Bream to 6lbs. from pre baited swims. The North's Erne system appears to be in limbo although the Trory Shore is still good for Bream and hybrids.

Meanwhile, the Eske river and lake got a flood and a nice run of grilse came up the river and into the lake. White veins of water gushed down the surrounding mountainside. The Eske Angling Club members appeared from everywhere. Joe O'Donnell from Mountcharles got two grilse.

Hans Peter Mecshele, Fly Fishing, got a grilse on the Ridge portion of the lake, and John Hanna landed a 6 lb grilse using a No. 8 two hook Black Doctor fly at Corrober. Despite a water obstruction point on the River Eske, it remains in good condition for quite some time after a fall of rain. Extensive clearing and renovation work has been carried out on the river to make the pools and banks more accessible, so this river which flows through Donegal Town is worth a try just now.

Powerful

Now the news from the powerful Blaney is both good and bad, and I will explain.

Michael and Mary Donnelly got three 9 lbs. Salmon on the Hairy Mary Fly at Clohamon. That's the good news. The bad news comes from Derek Nally of Bunclody, Co Wexford. He tells me that the river is having its worst ever season. Derek is chairman of the Slaney Rod Fishers Association, an umbrella organisation for the various interests and angling clubs connected to the river.

There has been a bit of a late run of grilse, but the big 20-25 lb Springers did not materialise this year. Derek cites the following reasons for the decline in the Salmon stocks: Drift netting at sea. (Jack Charlton came out strongly on this point last week.) Drift netting in the Wexford/Enniscorthy Estuary. Poaching & Pollution. Cormorants, a protected species, coming up to 30 miles upstream to devour the smolts.

Three Salmon were caught on the Garavogue, which runs through Sligo City. The younger generations are enjoying a good run of Sea Trout. They are using size tens in Teal and Yellow, Bibio and Connemara Black, 12g Tobys and size 2 spotted Mepps. Some sea trout weigh up to 2 lbs.

That is great news.........

Warmer

Everybody is catching Bream at the moment. Warmer weather has put the fish into an obliging mood and anglers are bagging up. Martin Oaks and Richard Wilcox from England had five great days of sport in the Belturbet area. The pair did best of all at Lough Dooley where they used ground bait swim feeders, red maggots and worm, and in five hours of solid fishing Oaks had 108 lbs and Wilcox had 118 lbs. Two more holiday makers, Jack Hennifer and Mike Hargreaves from Bolton, spent a week in Cootehill. They caught Bream to 6 lbs and Rudd/Bream hybrids weighing 3 lbs in a wonderful session on Annamakerrig Lake. One of the heaviest catches came from Gulladoo Lake, near Carrigallen, where Peter Johnston from Mansfield loaded his keep net with 132 lbs of Bream, Roach and hybrids taken mainly on Red Maggot.

Friendly

Ted Smith of Barton Smiths Fishing Tackle Shop, near the Hyde Bridge, informs me that it only costs £10 to join the Sligo Anglers, who control the top end of Lough Gill. It's a friendly society that was founded in 1927.

The best part of the Garavogue is between Hyde Bridge and the New Bridge. Bernie Fox, of Sligo, caught a fine 25 lbs. Salmon, fishing the worm, in the Falls Pool of the Ballisodare River.

An Irish-based English angler won the Mucknoo 100 coarse fishing competition on Lough Mucknoo in Castleblaney, Co Monaghan. Gordon Simms, originally from Bolton but now resident in Cavan, took a total of 131 lbs of fish to win the event. Arthur Judge, Ballinasloe, was runner-up on July 23rd 1993. Mighty Competition. Mighty draw for tourists.

Cavan Fishing

Cavan is a town surrounded by 25 lakes and two rivers, and it's bang in form with everybody filling their boots – and their nets – with big fat fish.

Pat Cunningham took a whopping 311 lbs of Bream on legered Red Maggot Fly in a single session on Baird's Shore. Fellow angler Andy Finnegan took 268 lbs.

During the same period. Cork is an area normally associated with beaches, mountains and jazz, but the bream are now there now in great numbers and almost blocking the fabulous River Lee.

Perfect coarse and game fishing in Cavan and the Finn, 40 miles from Donegal. Finn rises in the Republic, but permits are issued by Foyle Fisheries.

Mayo's Barry Casburn stopped off for a spot of sport on the Lee Reservoir and bagged 33 Bream weighing 107 lbs. Legered worm was the best method.

Sweetcorn is becoming a dominant bait in Ireland and was used successfully by Stan Harrison and Mick Sheehan at Killygowan Lake near Belturbet. Using swimfeeders and casting 35 yards, they hooked Bream to 6 lbs and hybrids to 2 lbs. In a net-full scaling 230 lbs between them. You'll finds virtually perfect conditions this weekend on the River Erne system from Enniskillen to Cavan.

The mighty Shannon system is carrying a touch extra water, but good fishing at Portumna and Banagher indicates no harm is being done.

Recent rainfall has meant a lot of heavy water on stretches along the Finn River which divides the twin towns of Ballybofey and Stranorlar in Donegal. Some stretches of this 40 mile river system are taken by clubs, and some are private areas. Although this river rises in the Republic, you require a Foyle Fisheries License to fish. The bailiffs come from Derry.

Anthony Murray tells me there are plenty of grilse and Sea Trout in the river. The run of sea trout has been particularly good. Gary Murray got six sea trout up to 1lb. One morning recently and followed it with five more the same evening. Gary was fishing a size 12 Alexander and a number 14 Peter Ross. The salmon and grilse are rising, but taking short, and the angler will have to be quick. However, the Cloghan Stretch, which is eight miles upstream from the Twin Towns has plenty of grilse.

London Aer Lingus Workers Do Well on Holidays

Aer Lingus London workers Liam O'Conner, Trevor Glassup and John O'Shea have completed a fishing holiday in Ireland. They were very successful offshore in Donegal Bay, where they got 50 and more.

Mackerel are plentiful along most shores now, and they are a tasty dish. I'm all for anglers who fish to eat and don't leave wasteful dead fish to rot on Pier sides.

And finally, I've been contacted by David Ivors, 26, the Commons, Thurles, Co Tipperary. David wants to take up trout fishing. Is there an angler in the area who can assist him on his quest? If you can, David Ivors is at the above address. I'm sure by now, David Ivors is an accomplished angler, has caught loads of salmon, sea trout, brown trout, and if he gets this book, I would appreciate him to contact me with what occurred in his life, and please send me a photo of a fish he caught. I will hold a space.

International Ladies' Fly Fishing Championship

Ireland hold the prestigious International Ladies' Fly Fishing Championship on Lough Conn, Co Mayo in September. This year's tournament is the first on these shores, so let's hope Ireland's ladies put up a strong fight to repel the English, Welsh and Scottish invasion. It will be rough and tough stuff, so Michael Smurfit's Kildare Hotel and Country Club has come to the ladies' aid to prepare them for the confrontation. The complex has agreed to put its excellent angling facilities at the disposal of the Irish Ladies Flyfishing Association this weekend. A private lake is on the golf course and the River Liffey runs through the grounds at Straffan. The team will be under the watchful eye of resident angling expert Sean McManmon, who is also the estate manager of this luxurious facility.

The Irish Ladies Team is: Anne Geary, Mary Geary, June Curry, Rosemary King, Kate Lennon, Mary Kelly, Betty Hayes, Miriam Gallagher, Mary McGovern, Myra Cosgrove, Susan Byrne, Mary Brady, Lisa Cloney, Mary Harkin and Maureen Lyons. The lakes the ladies will be practice on have been stocked with Brown and Rainbow Trout and they will wet-fly fish from boat provided.

Carrick River

From the mountains of west Donegal through the Village of Carrick and into Teelin Bay flows the Carrick River.

Recently the waters were acquired by the Slieve League Angling Association. Donal Ward, secretary of that association, tells me the river is fishing superbly at present. With rain the spate has been flowing for five to six weeks, allowing the Sea Trout, Salmon and grilse into the system in great numbers. In common with the Eany and the Eske the local association has done fine work alongside the Northern Regional Fisheries Board in clearing the banks to accommodate the angler. Carrick got an early run of Sea Trout with Sea Lice, but the July and August runs are clean fish and the regular size.

Favourite haunts for these game fish are The Falls or the Salmon Leap Pool and The Junction Pool – where the Carrick and Yellow rivers meet. Permits are £25 a year, £10 per week and £8 per day. The association report many anglers from Northern Ireland and over seas finding this good system. A refreshing feature is that since the local anglers took over the river and cleaned the Banks, poaching has diminished.

Donal Ward got a nice 5 lb Grilse on a number 10 fly Curry Red Shrimp. Another Angler landed a fish over 16 lbs at the Junction Pool on a Black Flying C.

Charlie Bonner sells fishing tackle in his shop on Dungloe's main street. He is a member of the Rosses Anglers. Charlie is also an international trout fisherman who represented Ireland on the five man team that fished the international competition at

Camuloops, Canada, last June. He finished second on the Irish team and has qualified for the World Contest to be held mid-August 1994 at Ringeby, Norway.

Anyway, the Rosses Anglers are one of the most active associations for angling in Ireland. They have in excess of 100 members and watch over 130 lakes encompassed in a region of West Donegal from the Gweebarra Bridge to Crolly Bridge.

Salmon

The Selection for fishermen is between Brown trout, Rainbow Trout and Salmon and at moment the new old story is – there is plenty of water. The Brown Trout Rise in size to 4 lbs. The sea trout are anything to 3 lbs, depending on what lake is fished. In a competition held in conjunction with the Mary from Dungloe Festival, a Trout of 2lbs. Took the competition. Permits are £3 per day, £5 per boat per day, £5 per week and £10 a year. This is great value in anybody's money.

The Rosses Anglers are holding a two day competition over Saturday 7th and Sunday 8th August. It will be fished in lakes Dungloe, Meela and Tully. The winner will come in with the heaviest Trout. The prize is the valued Bourke 17 foot boat. You can enter, at the usual time, at the Wee Bridge on the Glenties side of Dungloe. All are welcome to come along and try their skills in this fly cast out contest.

Brendan Kenelly came all the way from Tullamore, Co Offaly, to show me a photograph of a Ferrox Trout he caught on the worm from the Tullamore River. This trout was taken from a deep, slow, unfinished stretch of river. Revive it so other anglers can come out and fish?

Lord Arran leased his portion of The Eske System around Donegal Town to the local angling association for the Nominal fee of £400 per annum, for 25 years.

Ted Malone, expert sea trout angler and author of books on fishing, has invented a new salmon fly – a version of the Donegal Blue – to commemorate this royal gesture and included it in revised editions of his book "Irish Trout and Salmon Flies." Called the Arran Blue, the fly is made up thus: Tail – none; Body – Bright blue seal's fur; Rib – Oval silver tinsel; Front hackle – Peacock's blue neck hackle, tied umbrella fashion.

The Arran Blue

Ladies Who Fish

The ladies who fish are the members of the Irish Ladies Fly Fishing Association, and while it is the men or gentlemen who normally set out at weekends to occupy themselves with their favourite sport, pasttime or recreation, it is now accepted that women are taking up angling in ever increasing numbers. The Irish Ladies Fly Fishing Association was set up in 1990 by Ann Geary in Co Mayo, and has taken part in the International Championship each year since. In 1991 the championship was held in England, in 1992 in Scotland. To date the best Irish performance was placing third in 1991 against England, Scotland and Wales.

The international team draws its anglers from the 32 counties, and many of the Ladies have upwards on 40 years experience. So while ladies who fish are not new, the formation of the International Team is. The team is : Mary Geary, Mayo (Team captain), Anne Geary, Mayo (team manager), Mary Brady, Dublin; Susan Byrne, Offaly; Liza Cloney, Dublin, Myra Cosgrove, Clare, June Curry, Antrim, Mary Dowling, Cavan, Miriam Gallagher, Sligo, Mary Harkin, Dublin; Betty Hayes, Limerick, Mary Kelly, Mayo, Rosemary King, Derry, Kate Lennon, Wexford and Maureen Lyons, Dublin (Secretary).

Mary and Anne Geary are a mother and daughter combination. Mary Kelly is a nurse in the Sligo Regional Hospital, and Miriam Gallagher works in the North Western Fisheries Board. Rosemary King is a games mistress at Colraine High School. The team is currently preparing for the international event to be held in September on Lough Conn. This will be the first time the contest will be held in Ireland. Good luck to the Ladies, we hope they emerge Victorious.

Lough Errig

George Kelly, P.R.O. Of Fintown Angling Club, was in contact with me to say that the club which was formed last year is doing well. Lough Errig, which is drained by the River Glenleghan and forms part of the Gweebarra system, has had a good run of Sea Trout. George Kelly Jr. got one of 1-3/4 lbs, and in a local competition a three pounder was taken by Michael McGeehan.

In an open competition held during July on Lough Errig the winner was Patrick Walsh, Loughanure, with a 1 lb 9 oz Sea Trout on an Invicta Fly, and winning a fishing rod to the value of £100. Second place went to Dinney Sweeney, Loughanure, who won a buoyancy jacket, with a brown trout (1 1/4 lbs). James Kelly took the junior section, to win a wallet of flies, for a Brown Trout weighing 1 lb. The Fintown Angling Club has some 40 members with 15 lakes to look after, and stocks some of them. However, most contain a natural stock of wild trout.

Pettigo Angling

Kitty McVeigh traveled all the way to Ballyshannon to present me with a brochure - "Angling around Pettigo – Information regarding its Rivers and Lakes." I have to say in Pettigo they are really alert to the potential of its precincts, which include not only prime salmon and trout fishing waters, but coarse fish and country walks as well. Chairman of the Pettigo angling club is Michael McVeigh, Secretary Pat Britton, and the area is well worth a visit.

Sea Angling

Mackerel are teeming about our Donegal shores at present. At Creevy one evening recently 40 fishermen were shoulder to shoulder plucking Mackerel from the sea. Charter craft are available from Mullaghmore, Creevy and other ports.

Wrasse, Pollock, Whiting and Shark (some up to 50 lbs) are fine sport and can be cooked and eaten. Check if the sea is calm, get the weather forecast, and wear a life jacket. The boats are safe and waiting, and there can be nothing better than a day at sea in the sun. Seamus Goan tells me that when the Mackerel are close to shore that the farmer takes it as a sign of rain to ruin his crops. Nothing truer at the moment.

Disturbing News from Cork Harbour

Cork Harbour is one of the finest in the world. So, it was disturbing to hear about the two fires at chemical plants last week and the admission that some solvents had been discharged into the Harbour itself.

With this in mind, and the possible effects on salmon and the sea trout, I contacted John Buckley, Secretary of Cork Salmon Anglers Limited. John informs me there appears to be no ill effects to the marine life of Cork Harbour or the Salmon that run the river Lee, YET! The authorities themselves maintain the discharges into the waters were 98% water and 2% solvent. John himself was just about to go out the door with fishing rod in hand to fish the River Lee. The fishing season so far has been one of the best for many a long year. An excellent run of spring salmon enter the River Lee, with fish between 7-10 lbs weight. John got one at 16 lbs, and now is catching grilse of 4-5 lbs.

Grilse are called Peals in Cork, and the Lee is now fishing well for them. Favourite spot at the moment is the Killen Stream, and the Monroe Killer Fly 6 on Esmond Drury double hook should yield results. The free fishing part of this lovely River Lee runs through Cork City and the Lee fields in the suburbs.

Visitors should fish the water weir. Apart from the Salmon and Peal, the Lee also carries a good stock of brown trout up to 2 lbs. The CSAL is a limited company who own a majority of the waters of the Lee and rent additional stretches. They have about 80 members, 50 of which are share holders who pay £35 annually, with ticket holders on £135 a year. Visitors are charged £10 per day.

Returns for last year showed 600 Salmon recorded as landed. Sea Trout were never in the river Lee in any quantity. However, I finish this subject on a cautionary note. Despite so-called reassurances, environmental groups and myself remain concerned about discharges of chemicals into Cork Harbour and elsewhere too.

Now for the Easky River, which is crossed by the Workhouse Bridge on the main Sligo to Ballina Road. It enters the sea at the village of Easky, close to Killala bay. George Lindsey is one of the five original members of the syndicate that owned the part of this system from the Bridge in the Easky to Fortland Falls, upstream a distance of one mile.

Sting

There is a sting in this report too, in that the Central Fishery Board and the North Western Fisheries Board are endeavouring to acquire the Easky to develop it.

Basically, they want to control the system and curtail the poaching, along with issuing a maximum of 50 permits. The anglers and farmers with land along the banks of the river are objecting to this move, and claim they were not properly consulted. They also reckon the CFB plan is seriously flawed. A compulsory purchase order taken out by the NWFB was due into effect on 6 August last.

Whatever the outcome of this dispute, which involves not only the anglers but Declan Bree TD, member of the Dail Labour Party of the Government, one of the results is that the River Easky will almost certainly suffer before there is a resolution. At the moment the river Easky is full of salmon. However, Sea Trout are only a shadow of former run, due to their lice infestation.

There is some fine fishing in the area. The Easky claims the Title of best small river in the west. And figures tend to prove the point – 800 salmon and grilse caught to the end of July. George Lindsay got six grilse recently during the days fishing. All were 3-5 lbs. He caught two using a number eight Red Shrimp Fly, the remainder on the Flying C.

George tells me that fishing is totally free on the owner stretch at the moment. All legal methods of fishing are permitted from the fly (which is favoured) to the lemon and gold Devon. The mood of people regarding the Easky is known, but why not get along to the riverbank of the best small river in the west – you won't be disappointed. I only hope they resolve their dispute, and soon.

Good Runs of Sea Trout

There has been a good run of sea trout on one of Donegal's principal salmon rivers, the Owenea, although generally the stocks are well down on previous years. In fact, so much so that anglers are returning to sea trout. This spate river rises in the Glen of Glenties, and enters the sea at Loughros Point after a 16 mile race.

Excellent water conditions prevail at this moment with the river in prime condition for most of August. The Owener is experiencing the biggest run of salmon on record. The average grilse caught weighs in at 6lbs. Local association members Pascal McHugh and Alan Watson caught a beautiful fish of 14 lbs each. Alan took his Salmon on a number 8 double hook red shrimp, while Pascal got seafood fishing a red Flying C 15g.

This river is owned by the Northern Regional Fisheries Board, and fished by the Ardara Anglers Association. Visiting anglers need permits running at £6 per day, £16 per week and £40 for the season. The recommended baits are worm, Flying C (red/black/natural) and the red curry shrimp fly in single, double or treble hook, sizes 10 to 4. No shrimping. Bag limit three Salmon a day. The six best pools on the Owener are Gavigan's, Brian's, McGill's, Billy's, Holly Bush and the Poulateorann Pool. Friendship and accommodation awaits the angler in the tidy town of Glenties and the tweed town of Ardara, who can supply permits, fishing tackle and information at (075) 41262.

Next we go to the New Lake, at Dunfanaghy in north Donegal. This extraordinary lake was formed in the 1920's as a result of a severe Atlantic storm. Nowadays the lake is run by the Dunfanaghy Anglers Association who issue daily permits at £5.

The Shannon Estuary is Fishing quite well at the moment with two specimen weights landed by shore and sea anglers. Rodney Smith from the Shannon town anglers was ashore off Poulnasherry near Kilrush when he caught a 46 lb Stingray. The specimen weight of 30 lbs, with the Irish record standing at 51 lbs. Also in the estuary a group of anglers on board an Atlantic Adventurers boat out of Kilrush landed a 105 lb six-gilled grey shark. The Irish specimen weight for such a shark is 100 lbs.

The Shannon Estuary is also the scene of the next outing of the Limerick Sea Angling Club when they fish Labasheeda, Co Clare on Sunday 29th August. One of the most active sea and shore angling clubs in the region, the members are hoping to land some big tope from the shore. Check in at 11am in Casey's Bar, Labasheeda, and guests are welcome.

Wild Salmon

The rain continued into August. Rivers and lakes remained high, and by the end of the month most waters were still a foot above normal – such was the rainfall.

Water temperature was normal – such was the rainfall. Water temperature was normal for the time of year, and the exciting part is that plenty of salmon and grilse came out of the sea, into river and lake.

Drowes

Approximately 100 salmon or grilse were landed here. Don Stevens, Kinlough, got five grilse fishing in several parts of the river, using a Green and Copper Toby.

Some anglers have all the luck. Brian Carty, Hollywood, landed three grilse at the Four Masters Bridge, using a Hairy Mary and Shrimp cast of flies – size ten.

Darryl Kennedy, Moira, took a sea lice laden fresh eight pound Salmon shrimping in the Blackwater, and Bernard McCullough, Ballymena, got one Salmon at the new Bridge, and another from Melly's High Bank Pool, fishing the 12 gram Green and Copper Toby.

Melvin Competition

The end of season Wet Fly competition will be held on the Melvin on Saturday 15th September, with £800 in prizes. Angling commences from Breffini Pier from 11 am until 6 pm, with the weigh in on the pier. The Kinlough & District Anglers are the organisers. Entry forms through Thomas Kelly, Kinlough, Co Leitrim, phone (071) 98 41497. Don't say you did not have ample notification of this event, which is always a great day out.

Eske

John Hanna is the only man to score on this system, with two Salmon in the one day. John got a 7 lbs. Salmon in Corraber, and then followed it with a glorious 12 pounder on The Ridge, using a silver and copper spoon called The Kerry Boy.

On reaching shore, to great excitement, Jody Gysling, proprietor of Harveys Point Country Hotel, acquired the smaller salmon, had it sent to the kitchen where the chef prepared two immediate and nice steaks, for a most enjoyable meal of fresh wild Salmon, flushed down by a bottle of white wine, accompanied by all the delicate courses, and within a very short while all seemed calm, tranquil and manageable with this earth. I have no other reports of any fish being caught out of this depleted system.

Tiddler?

And finally, a 46 year old American lass named Nadine Cloer was fishing off the Florida Keys recently when a six foot barracuda "just shot out of the water like a torpedo" and bit her on the arm, hand and hip. Poor Nadine needed 170 stitches to the wounds. So may you all think yourselves lucky when you catch a tiddler, and remember not to get too close to it!

Barracuda or Torpedo?

Edward Hanna

Didn't I get a letter, with fishing cuttings enclosed, from Edward Hanna, now residing with his family in Springfield, Virginia, within recent weeks? Here are some of the details.

Fish "snagging" (that's foul hooking or snatching) is to be banned permanently in the State of Michigan, after October 25th 1993, thanks to a bill passed by the state legislature. (Imagine!) Three stretches of Michigan River had remained open to snagging – the Big Manistee, the Pere Marquette, and part of the Sable River. (Now read why).

Snagging has been allowed since the mid-1960's on the theory, since discredited, that Pacific Salmon could not be caught fairly (in the mouth) on the spawning run. Fisheries chief John Robertson said "snagging did not follow the strong tradition of fair sport in Michigan" (a good one).

Another cutting told that scientists who study the ocean migration of Atlantic Salmon say there are only about 250,000 two-sea-winter fish on the wintering grounds off Greenland. They say 18 years ago there were about 850,000 salmon there, with at least two winters at sea. The rivers of North America need at 200,000 multi-sea-winter fish to maintain minimum river populations. The causes of the decline include overfishing by commercial fishermen, and a drop in temperature of the wintering grounds water, thus decreasing ocean productivity. (It doesn't sound good). What quantity is required to maintain Irish rivers?

European Pike Challenge

Anglers from across Europe will descend on Lough Derg for three days next month to take part in the European Pike Challenge.

With prizes worth £5,000, the competition has already attracted entries from Germany, France, Italy and the UK, not to mention a strong Irish contingent as well. In all, up to 250 anglers are expected for the event which will also bring a very welcome end of season tourism boost to the beautiful village of Killalo, Clare. Lough Derg is regarded by experts as one of Ireland's premier pike fishing lakes and is perfect for the event which starts on September 20th.

Pike Competition, Ballyshannon Anglers

A new dimension to this year's challenge will be the permitted use of dead bait which should ensure larger pike are caught. The largest Pike ever recorded anywhere in the world was caught in Lough Derg. It weighed a full 90 lbs. The record was set almost 100 years ago and is yet to be beaten.

North Atlantic Salmon Fund and Greenland's Fishermen Press for Ban

Government Officials are coming under increasing pressure to ban drift-net fishing for Salmon off the Irish Coast. Now the chairman of the Limerick Sea Angling Club, and one of the best known anglers in the midwest, Jim Robertson has added his weight to the appeal. "It's about time the Government stepped in to end this kind of fishing," he fumed. "The recent agreement between the North Atlantic Salmon Fund and Greenland's fishermen means a suspension of drift-net fishing for Atlantic Salmon in that region. "And that means the only place where drift-netting for Atlantic Salmon now takes place is in the waters around Ireland and Britain. It's time it didn't!"

13th Rosses International Angling Festival

This weekend it will be Lucky 13 for the pretty town of Dungloe in Co Donegal as the Rosses International Angling Festival gets under way with up to 80 foreign fishermen taking part.

Now in it's 13th year the event has attracted competitors from Britain, Germany, Scotland and of course, Northern Ireland.The anglers luck is also in as a fine run of sea trout has just been reported for the area. "The fishing year will be excellent this year," said Garda Sgt. Joe Joyce who is chairman of the event. "Recent rain and the run of Sea trout into the competition lakes will make the weekend a memorable one for the visitors."

The anglers will fish three local lakes using wet fly and the winning team will take home the Bank of Ireland Trophy and £500 in cash. There is a fish counter on the Dungloe River which feeds the lakes and already over 1200 sea trout have passed through so the weekend should result in some good bags.

Salmon Not Taking the Bait

The lack of rain in other parts of the country has affected fishing and led to a disappointing salmon season so far. In the Mulcair in Limerick and in the Feale in Listowel, the salmon have not been landed in any great numbers even though the Shannon Regional Fisheries Board say the fish are in the rivers. Now in the final month of the season, anglers are hoping that the dry weather will end and some rain will bring better fishing conditions.

The fish that are landed seem to go for the purple shrimp at the moment, especially in the Mulcair. The mixed season was confirmed by Brendan Coulter of Cavan who is secretary of the National Course Fishing Federation of Ireland. He said the fishing has been patchy and he was disappointed at the lack of good bags on Lough Muckno during the past few weeks. The problem seems to be a drop in water temperature.

Favourite

Due to floods, Connacht anglers plumped for Loch Bran for their winter league match. However, the fishing was not good with only small weights. Section winners were Pascal Weemes from Mullingar and Charlie Greeves from Drumsna. Charlie has four wins and is hot favourite for the booty. When Charlie was hauling in a slab of 4lbs, a fellow angler asked him if he ever did the lotto. "Never," said cheeky Charlie. "Well with your luck, I reckon you should start," came the reply.

Big Fish in Tralee Bay

It is a different story on the sea angling front with some good catches and specimens taken recently. Fishing particularly good at the moment is Tralee Bay in Co Kerry where huge monkfish and skate have been landed. In fact the 23 year old record for stingray has been broken. Set in 1970 by John White shore fishing off Kilfenora Strand in the bay the record stood at 51 lbs. However, there is now a claim for a 64 lb. Stingray before the Irish specimen Fish Committee.

The fish was caught by Michael Wall at Derrymore Point in the bay. Richard Kelter one of the leading members of the Tralee Bay Sea Angling Club says they are delighted with the new world record. A 56 lbs Specimen monkfish was landed on the *Oceaneering* skippered by John Deady out of Fenit in Co Kerry.

Two specimen fish in Clare Two specimens were landed during the outing to Labasheeda in Co Clare held by the Shannon Estuary Anglers. Neil Pop had a 10.6lbs Bulhuss, Frank McGeehan had a 10.4 bullhuss while Colin McDaid caught a 10.6 lbs Thornback Ray. The full results were: 1st Colin McDaid of Tralee, 2nd Rodney Smith of Shannon, and 3rd Neil Pope of Limerick. The junior prizes went to Paul Sheehan and Dominic Martin.

Jaded Japanese Business Leaders

Jaded Japanese business leaders are flocking to the cool mountain streams of Kerry to learn the art of fly fishing.Over three days, they are given expert instruction by one of Ireland's best known anglers and coached in age old skills. In a move that also appeals to the Hi-Tech Japanese, their progress is video taped during their stay in Kerry.

The man behind the venture is Michael O'Brien of the Anglers Paradise School in Killarney. He is confident he can teach a beginner to fly fish in three days. "Kerry is ideal for fly fishing," he said. "There are many rivers and lakes, a wide variety of fishing is available. In Japan at the moment there is a big move towards fly fishing and they come here to acquire the proper techniques. The Japanese are interested in learning the art of fly fishing and when they go back home they use their new skills to catch catfish."

In addition the great numbers of Japanese Visitors to Kerry, Mr. O'Brien also reports that the rivers and lakes are fishing well. "In the brown Flesk River at the moment the biggest numbers of salmon for the past 50 years have been seen. "At Killorgan there are huge numbers of Sea Trout. Anglers spinning and using the worm are landing fine catches." he said. In the winter months visitors to the Anglers Paradise School avail of lake fishing and they arrange barbecues on the small islands. A whole accommodation package is also available.

Picking the World Team

Anglers from all over the country travel to Oughterard in Co Galway next Saturday (18th September), for the Inter Provincial Championships organised by the Trout Anglers Federation of Ireland. Teams of Anglers from the four provinces compete for the Irish title but an added interest is the fact that the top two rods will qualify for the Irish National Team to take part in the World Championships to be held in Oslo, Norway next year.

One of the Organisers, Mr. Vincent O'Reilly of Headford, Co Galway, has been Captain of the Irish team for the past four years. "While our record in world class fishing has not been great, we are confident that the team will produce a good performance," he said. Now the National Chairman of TRFI, Mr. O'Reilly has pulled off a major coup by attracting the World Championship to Ireland for 1995. "We would have 26 countries taking part in three locations in Galway. It will be a great boost to Irish angling and a valuable contribution to tourism," he said.

The decision to select Ireland was taken after leading figures in the world body fished in Galway with Mr. O'Reilly. "They were very impressed with the quality of the water and the range of fishing in the west," he said.

National Pike Championships '93/'94

The ninth qualifying competition of the 1993/94 National Pike Championships was held last Sunday on Swan Lake near Lough gowns. A total of 94 anglers turned up from as far away as Keady, Ballina, Limeick and Athy. Fishing was very slow at the start. The shore under the road usually produces good numbers of pike, but on Sunday only a handful of small pike were taken here, which probably accounts for the fact that no local angler qualified, as they all fished this area.

Swiss Angler with Specimen Pike

For the second qualifier in a row, an Athy angler caught the largest fish. Jerry Cullen had the only double figure fish, a pike of 10 lbs 2ozs. Dublin anglers who have not been in the frame recently came back well with two qualifying and another just missing out in sixth place. The top five anglers on Sunday's event, who qualified to fish in the final in the final of the championships are; 1st Dom Gallagher, Duleek, 4 pike 12 lb 13 oz.; 2nd Jerry Cullen, Athy, 1 pike, 10 lb 2 oz.; 3rd Ray Fitzgerald, Dublin, 3 pike, 8lb 15 oz.; 4th Mark Brown, Dublin, 5 pike, 8 lb 13 oz.; 5th Gary Quinn, Donore/Drogheda, 3 pike, 7lb 13 oz. Dom Gallagher won the Gilladeer Bait Trophy.

Charity

A charity Pike Competition in aid of Carrickmacross Recreational Centre will be held on Lough Muckno at Castleblaney next Sunday. The Prize fund will depend on on the level of entries but there will be a minimum of £400. The entry fee is £8, and interested Anglers should check in at the Black Island Car Park at 11:30 for a 12 noon start.

The Dublin Pike anglers Association are holding a Pike Competition on Ballyhoe and nearby lakes next Sunday. A bus will pick anglers up at various points about Dublin and later drop them off at the same points.

Opening of Salmon Season

New Years' Day will see the opening of the Salmon season. The following are the rivers and lakes that have a January 1st Start: River Liffey, Dublin; River Drowes, Donegal/Leitrim Border; Rivers Lackagh and Lennon in North Donegal; Lough Gill and part of the Garavogue River in Sligo; Carrowmore Lake, Belmullet, Mayo. Permits can be gotten from the Local contacts, and each angler will require a state license. A full national license costs £25, the district license is £12. Under 18's pay £8, and the general daily license for all ages is £3.

Harry Lloyd, manager of the Northern Regional Fisheries Board tells me that judging by the extent of spawning salmon and trout the angler can "Look forward to a good season, everything being equal, and there is every indication of good runs of fish." For the angler on the Liffey and the Drowes the landing of the first Salmon of the year will net a £200 bonus plus the likely £500 sale price. The honour of the first salmon in Ireland has gone to the Drowes 13 times in the last 14 years, the Liffey getting the other honour.

High-flying helicopter pilot with the Shannon based marine rescue service, Martin Raynor, has been named the Boat Master Angler of the year in the Limerick Sea Angling Club. He was presented with his award by club President Senator Brendan Daly at the annual dinner held in the Shannon Rowing Clubhouse in Limerick. The Shore Master Angler trophy was won by Rodney Smith, of Shannon, while Declan Maxwell won both Junior titles. Declan is the son of Bill Maxwell of the Aughinish Club who is a member of the Munster council. The occasion also honoured Mick Fitzpatrick who fished for Ireland at the World Championships held last October in Sardinia.

Anglers had to wait until the 15th day of the season before the first River Drowes salmon was landed by Tommy Bateman, Carrickfergus. He was fishing the middle pool, above the Four Masters bridge, with a bunch of worms on a No2 hook. The salmon was a seven pounder, with sea-lice with tails attached – fresh indeed. That was two weeks after Denis Moloney landed the first salmon of the year from the Liffey. There have been few other successes, although Michael Carty, Sligo, caught a 7 lb. Salmon on Lough Gill trawling near Church Island at the top end of the lake Friday 14th January. The Embassy Restaurant bought the fish for £70. Seven new records were established by the Specimen Fish Committee last year. A carp of 27.78 lbs, Pike (lake) of 39lb 3oz.; Flounder 4.91 lbs; Grey Mullet 9.10 lbs; Electric Ray 72.5 lbs; Stingray 64 lbs; and a torsk of 10.66 lbs. The top specimen taken by a youngster was claimed by 14 year old Maurice Gorman from Mullingar for a lake pike of 30 lbs 7 oz from Lough Ennell.

17lb Salmon – Specimen Pollock

Conditions during the month of March were disturbed – wet, cold and windy. It must have upset many an angler's plans to go to his safe haven and catch a fish. However, fishermen are a hardy breed, and the harsher the conditions the more effort an angler will put into his favourite pastime. The harsh conditions must have affected the estuary in Ballyshannon, because to date I have not gotten any reports of sea trout returns to the Krill, Stuki, Gadget or Gosling. A 17 lbs. Salmon was caught on the Drowes, and a specimen Pollock taken off Killybegs.

Prime Minister (Finnish But No Fins)

Finland Prime Minister Esko Aho took time out to spend a day fishing the Drowes River in the Northwest. Keen angler Aho, 40, battled in vain through wind and rain in a bid to bag a salmon from a river running at a mighty torrent.

Aho, in Ireland as part of an official two day visit, headed straight for the water but soon found out that the fish were not biting. "It's a pity I didn't catch anything, but I still enjoyed it very much," Aho said. Even expert gillies Peter McSharry, Don Stevens and Thomas Kelly failed to entice the fish with a Flying C, Devons and Tobys after guiding the team to such pools as the Black Water, Island Pool and the Tinker's Hole.

Aho is a dab hand at fly fishing, but the stormy conditions ruled this method out. "I will return and hopefully next time I'll be able to fish the fly and have a bit of better luck," Aho added.

It's No April Fool

The Sun Friday, April 1st, 1994

Today is April 1st but it's no cod that I'm optimistic about the overall results of the 1994 season so far. The Owenea River at Ardara is in flood at the moment, but I expect results from locals and tourists over the Easter holiday. The natural or red Flying C should be tried for the angler spinning. The banks of this river are ideal for the fly fisherman. So the Shrimp fly, Hairy Mary or Jock Scott size number 8 would be ideal. And for you wormers, try a bunch on a size 2 or 4 single hook – the size two being the best.

Darren Maguire - First Salmon

Two fine salmon have been caught off the River Eske near Donegal Town. A local angler using the natural Flying C bagged the fish at the dam above the town. One salmon had a mountain of sea lice attached.

Luck

If you want to try your luck there, permits are required from the Eske anglers. And they can be bought from Donegal Town fishing tackle dealer Charlie Doherty on the Main Street. Small size 8 locally made patterns of the fiery brown, golden olive or Donegal blue will produce results. But any sea trout caught must be returned under the rules of the local angling club.

The River Drowes is shaping up well for the holiday weekend. Flood waters have receded to ideal levels. A Northern Ireland angler got a 17 lbs Spring salmon on the worm below Lennox Bridge. Chris Kitchen landed two salmon (10 and 11 lbs.) at the Money Pool, fishing the shrimp, and Brian McKilroy took a 12 pounder from the Mill Pool at Lareen. In all 50 salmon have been taken for the month of March. I hear that there is excellent salmon fishing on the Killarney Lakes. A total of 41 salmon weighing 366 lbs have been lifted, with most taken on the trawl from Lough Keane.

In the West, the Greenfields / Birchall area of Lough Corrib is the place to be, with the trout taking the duck fly, and anglers taking the trout. Coarse fishing on Garradice Lake at Ballinamore and along Connolly's Shore is producing Bream in batches of 50-60 lbs. Changeable weather could assist or hamper anglers here.

Further north, skipper Anthony Doherty set out from Killybegs with a deck load of anglers and they caught a Specimen pollock weighing 12.12 lbs using Mr Twister. The Connacht heat of the Angler of the Year will be held on Lough Scur on Sunday 24th April, and the draw will be in Drumcong at 11 am.

Shares certificates are again causing problems. Why, you may ask? What's £12 for good all-year round fishing, when you know your £12 is being put to good use for restocking, and building roadways into fisheries?

Increased

The second leg of the Dublin Pike Anglers Junior League will be fished this this Sunday 24th April. The juniors are in two sections – under 15 and under 18. Weights from the first leg were very low, so at the end of the third leg there will be prizes for all juniors. Go for it!

Like other regions of Ireland, from today the Northern Regional Fisheries Board will charged increased permit fees to visiting fishermen for angling on state managed salmon, sea trout and brown trout fisheries here in Donegal. The Owenea River, Owentocker River, Ardara Lakes in the Glenties, Ardara areas – Eany waters and rivers in the Frosses, Inver districts – and the Eske River and lake (in conjunction with the Eske angling Association) in the Donegal Town area will charge non-local members permit charges at £10 per day or £35 per week. This will be in addition to the state license, which is also required.

The rational prompting this move is that in the past the cost of fishing these waters was considered very inexpensive. The board carried out a survey of visiting anglers back in 1992 which demonstrated there was a "willingness among visitors to pay substantially higher charges for salmon and sea trout angling." Such charges, claims the board manager Harry Lloyd, "remain relatively inexpensive when compared with international salmon angling prices" and are cheaper than the average price charged for fishing on stocked trout fisheries in Britain and Europe.

Funding

This situation arose because of the persistent shortage of the finance necessary for investment in fishery development, protection and for management, and to avail of substantial amounts of EU/Exchequer funding for fisheries management from Europe. The aim is to improve the mentioned angling systems to achieve "Branded status" in the international market, thereby attracting increased angling visitors, and revenue, so as then to increase employment for additional fishery officers.

More visitors and anglers pump up the local economy, and visits bring revenue to many local outlets. A key element in the complete strategy is to employ more protection staff to protect the fisheries. Apart from the regional board's role in this drive for improvement, the Donegal County Councils, the Enterprise Board, Fàs Force, Bord Failte, North West Tourism, Udaras Na Gaeltachta, the Office of Public Works and the Vocational Education Committee will be expected to help in this drive to improve angling revenue and create jobs.

Creevy Co-Op

I am a member of the Creevy Co-Op by buying a share, and I serve as a committee member. I bought a share – one of the first. The share cost me £350.

It is increasing year upon year. We are an attraction, and have a fishing vessel skippered surveyed every year. We take tours out fishing, whale watching, diving. A few months ago, we opened a big hanger for fishermen and others to store their boats. The hanger is our pride and joy. We have cottages that we rent out to visitors, restored, and all in good condition. Now you can walk from "The Foot Of The Road" round the coast to Rossnowlagh, a distance of 5 miles or more.

The President Comes to Creevy

Creevy And District Community Development Co-Operative Society Ltd. received a visit from our popular President Mary Mc Aleese to launch our new charter angling boat, a 33 ft Aquastar, the "*Duanai Mara*," on Saturday 31st July.

Her Excellency, was a neighbour of the Goans in Belfast. Mary and I received our invitation from the Co-Op, from Molly, and we were very excited and proud.

The Co-Op looks upon the purchase of our charter Angling Boat as a great achievement. We see it as the "Flagship" to the hard work Molly Reynolds and our staff and Committee have put into the Creevy Co-Op. We have three new Holiday Homes constructed. Michael Patton, supervisor of the FÁS project, and the men and women who are working day and daily to make Creevy a great place to go for a holiday. We have constructed a paved pathway from the Foot Of The Road right around the coast to Creevy Pier, about two miles. Then you can carry on walking to Rossnowlagh, about another two miles. The four or five mile walk skirts the coastline. Yesterday, I actually saw a man hail a taxi in New York, the peace and quiet is so peaceful.

Molly and Margaret are so active in getting funds that they are like ferrets in their efforts. They got LEADER money and received backing from The International

Fund for Ireland. A few months back, we had a packed house when we opened a large boat house and offices. This ceremony was performed by Cathal Goan. Now anybody who wishes to become a member or book the boat can contact us on 071 98 52896 or e-mail creevy@:iol.ie. Seamus, Mandy, and Ita Goan are Resting.

Champagne Breakfast and Thomas Harvey

For about a decade Jody Gysling, owner of Harvey's Point Hotel on the shores of Lough Eske, held an Angling Contest between the Swiss guests and the local fishermen, the Eske Anglers. I fished it every year, along with John Hanna. His brother Edward was in America. Billy Johnston was one of the regulars.

One year we took Thomas Harvey along. Thomas Harvey was a very well known gillie on Lough Eske. He could row all day, and he knew every haunt where a salmon could be lying. The day we took him out for the competition, we took a nice white chair for Thomas to sit on. It was to honour him, because we knew the experience Thomas Harvey had, and the time he spent on the lake. Thomas said that if his client for the day got a salmon,

Swiss Guests and Irish Hosts

he would row him from dawn to dusk, but his client got only one salmon for the day. The reason was if the client got two or three salmon, he got a greed. So Thomas (by his own rules) thought that one was the regulation, but more was too much. He then rowed the client where Thomas knew there would be sea trout. Or brown trout. The brown trout could go to certain size, and then there was sea trout. Lough Eske sea or white trout were renowned, and it was not unusual to run into a shoal out in front of Harvey's Point Hotel (favourite point), or at Rosheen, Coraber, the Ridge, where the Barnesmore River enters the lake.

Ted Malone, a river and lough expert, claimed the best stretch (for white trout) on Lough Eske, was a drift from Clady Point (with a west wind) across to the island, and he proved it. But I have digressed. I was telling you about Thomas Harvey.

King For a Day

Thomas Harvey was king for a day, and more, if he got his clients a salmon. The Champagne Breakfast was the full monty, and to set off with such a pile of packing was the delight. We all assembled later for lunch. The check-in took place at 6pm. I am pleased to say I won the trophy. I was in seventh heaven. The day ended with a slap-up meal, drinks, and a sing-song, and jokes.

Watch Maker

An extraordinary announcement about Thomas Harvey... He was a watchmaker, and anybody who set eyes upon his work was astounded.

He was a great friend of John Hanna's, and he knew John was a great angler, but he used to say, "John, you're a bad fisherman. You have them (salmon) all JAGGED!! You will spoil it for the other anglers!"

The late Thomas Harvey had a brother, James, and a sister- in-law, Bella, who looked after various holiday homes and the Ardnamona Hotel. They were all great people.

Lough Sheelin Brown Trout

I said that the brown trout were usually small, and John and Edward Hanna, and many more anglers, would fish for brown trout or brownies if they wanted a feed of light (but very tasty) brown trout...

When they went ashore to take a smoke, or drink a beer, or swallow a mouthful of whiskey, a fire was lit, and the brown trout (or white trout) was gutted and put onto the open flame. When they were ready, they were eaten. And, on occasions, I would eat a trout and enjoy it...

Edward and John and Jim Thomas were experts at cooking fish on an open fire. Indeed, Jim Thomas was an expert at eating fish or anything, never mind cooking...

In the early days, Jim Thomas would often take us back to the National Hotel, do up a steak for us (John, Edward, and me), and, I kid you not, you would eat your own fingers to get at your steak. And you would go to war when you saw Jim Thomas prepare and eat a steak. His steak.

Jim Thomas is dead now, and so is his wife Lorraine. *"Those were the days, my friends, we thought they would never end,"* are the words of a song. But they did...

Salmon & Sea Trout Decline in Donegal

My letter published in The Donegal Democrat, 22nd February 2007

Sir, I am a fully paid up member of the Donegal Eske Anglers Association for the last fifty five years. It is the only system I fish with now but when I was younger, I fished the Eany River - a great spate river which entered the sea at the graveyard pool near Roses Pub in Inver village. I also fished the best parts of the Drowes River and had a boat bought for 32 punts on Lough Melvin that becomes the River Drowes at Lareen Estate and enters the sea at Tullaghan. I fished for king salmon and silver salmon in the mighty Columbia River in 2002 and I won the first Derby Grand Prix of that season by landing a 37 lb Chinook or King Salmon. The way it worked was that when you got a big fish you registered it on the board, and whoever got the biggest salmon during the period was the winner. I just scraped through with only ounces to spare. Nevertheless, my salmon was the winner and I felt so proud.

Cut to the Chase

Now we must cut to the chase and get down to brass tacks. I am going to risk life and limb by expressing my opinion on how we have arrived at the published plan to close the Eske River and Lake, the Lackagh and the Lennon.

Anglers have arrived at a situation that has been festering for years – that there is not enough salmon escaping the many interests that block their passage from their natural predators to the spawning grounds e.g. seals to drift nets, draft nets and several other forms of trapping salmon...

Years ago the monks who lived in the Abbey Assaroe in Ballyshannon used to have salmon gardens. When the tide was out they built pools and when the tide came in the salmon went into the pools or gardens. When the tide went out again the salmon were trapped in these pools/gardens. However, there were thousands of salmon in the rivers of Ireland, that is far from the dire situation we now find ourselves in as we enter 2007. The seal is protected and naturally they continue to increase and multiply to the consternation of fishermen. A seal will seldom eat a complete salmon but will snatch a junt from the shoulder or belly of the fish and leave the mutilated fish useless.

My Experience

I fished from Arranmore Island for a season in the late sixties when I had 1800 yards of drift net 30 mesh deep nylon net with red corks on the floating back rope and lead, manually placed on the sole rope, to keep the net in place. We had only a small share of the catch because some half deckers and trawlers had eight to ten thousand yards. Sometimes during the night we were 'tided' to find the next morning that someone with a bigger net was in front of you. This boat had fish, we had none, that was annoying. However, the fact that all boats used nylon meant you could only fish at night and not during the day, and if it was a calm sea overnight the fleet docked mostly empty handed, but when the sea was choppy and dark the salmon would be stuck in the back rope on the surface.

Enter the monofilament net which was clear gut and with a streamlining of the complete net this allowed fishermen to go chase salmon day and night in both good and bad weather, calm or rough seas. Naturally this increased the catches of salmon.

Now enter the famous bag net in the late 60's and this was the scourge of the salmon. It comprised a section of net which was held by a person on shore or anchored to the shore, as the salmon identified land marks in his or her quest to arrive back to the place of his birth. It would be confronted by this length of net which it could not go through or under. The salmon would then swim out along the blocking net into a bag that had a net open, the main boat anchored the net and there, for greater success, a smaller boat with a fisherman holding the rope which he tripped capturing the salmon, further increasing catches from a diminishing school of salmon.

Ballyshannon Estuary

What really is at stake here is not so much the demise of the salmon as the ending of a tradition where for a month or 16 days draft or drifting, lying under canvas in the case of drifting or sitting beside a fire among the sand dunes in the dead of night down the channel looking back at the town of Ballyshannon. What contentment, what a bonus. I fished the channel at Ballyshannon and it was so pleasant that I could take pleasure in the sight before my eyes. "Go on" shouted the bud when a fresh salmon splashed like the entry of a rocket into the water to break the contented silence, and spur the sleepy fishermen into action as the eager crew rushed to shoot the net around the salmon, no war cry matches the "go on" - It is more than a call to arms.

It's both a war cry and an anthem to the fishermen. All that would end if the channel was closed. You would think that as an angler I would welcome the end of draft netting and I would, but to me tradition is hard to let go and these fishermen deserve full and proper compensation for a lifetime of effort and toil.

The lovely nights among the sand dunes will be lost forever. The fisherman who said he was going to fish the channel at Ballyshannon for a share of nothing, has more to lose; more than meets the eye and by the way, after the cementation company were employed to harness the rushing waters in the mid 50's, the Erne's wild fish began to decline and large salmon were seen in pools of water dying and nobody was allowed to take them. When the works were completed catches in the estuary and the ESB share dropped drastically.

The river could not revive itself and in 1972 the ESB ceased taking its share of salmon and in that year there were only 321 salmon caught by the fishermen -this reduced further to 7 in 1973.

The channel was closed for a total of nine seasons at various times. The river did not increase stocks by being closed. It meant that the powers that had locked out the fishermen threw away the key and abandoned the Erne Estuary to its own devices. These closures far from improving the stocks in the river system (from source to sea) resulted in near extinction of the famous Erne salmon. Our lack of concern eventually resulted in its extinction. This has happened and we are all to blame nor will all our bleatings bring it back. Salmon caught now on the Erne Estuary are hatchery fish.

Some anglers and net fishermen saw all of this coming and while I was one of those to express concern, I did little or nothing about it. Here I must mention and praise some of the anglers and fishermen who! saw what was coming and attempted to do something about it. The Erne Estuary Fisherman's Association was reformed in 1986 with myself in the chair for the next twelve years. We endeavoured to implement changes to the fish pass and the smolt pass with minimal success. On a lighter note during this period at a meeting of the fishermen I told the members that there would be no fish in the estuary and that we were wasting our times going down. One member replied "I don't care, I'm going down to get my f*****g share out of it." The net result was that the river Erne died a tragic death.

Eske and Eany

One of the names that spring to mind in relation to these rivers is my old pal John Hanna of Hanna Hats fame. John is one of the best anglers to catch a fly and who almost single handedly took on the poachers that were rampant on both rivers. We would be out fishing when John would spot something wrong. He and his brother Edward would go ashore and confront the bad guys. My motto was to leave it to the authorities but I went along for the sheer hell of it (quaking in my wellies). John even attended court to ensure convictions of these individuals and as a consequence was under constant threat. I called him the salmon sheriff. He also took the Eske and the Eany into the hands of the people from absent landlords and today as Chairman of the Eske Anglers is guiding the club in negotiations with the Northern Regional Fishery Board (NRFB) who are partners in managing the Eske. The Eany is in the hands of the local people. You may ask why as a Ballyshannon man I fished in Donegal? The reason is that I caught my first salmon on the Eske with the late Jim Thomas and I have been hooked on the Eske ever since. Ballyshannon anglers have their heroes in Paddy Donagher and members of the local club.

Question?

The strange question is when the Fishing Board and the government got the net men off some estuaries in the Northwest the salmon stocks did not increase which is now leading to the closure of not only the Eske but the Lackadh and the Lennon in North Donegal. If this happens, these rivers will also die. My policy and advice is to keep all rivers in Donegal open for salmon fishing and fishing of white and brown trout and impose strict regulations of catching and releasing salmon, and of single and barbless hooks. Only fly fishing and spinning should be allowed with worm and prawn band. Further and most important is that' angling associations and the NRFB cooperate more closely and are not in conflict as is currently the case. The idea of the government and the Fishery Boards is to improve angling tourism to increase revenue and exclude the local fishermen. When I spoke to Harry Lloyd, CEO of the NRFB and a close friend of mine, he informed me that the Eske could be closed for a number of seasons depending on the salmon runs. I don't agree with this on two counts - first the fish counter at the water abstraction point was not in full commission and did not count correctly the number of salmon. Secondly a meeting must be convened between the NFRB and the Eske anglers and other representatives from the Lackagh and Lennon. There is no threat to the Eany which enters the sea at Inver.

With the new developments due to start in Donegal town such as the building of apartments, houses and more services relevant to make the area between Magee's Factory and the Commons a standing town, plus two bridges across the Eske River in such an important area that boosts some of the finest holding and resting pools. The Eske anglers, John Hanna, Chairman; John O'Donnell, Billy Johnston - in fact the whole committee and membership, listed the conditions that would receive their blessing, if agreed. Those conditions are now assured and work can commence – which it will. I am sure the anglers on the Lackagh and the Lennon are fighting their corners.

Finally I call for closer contacts and communication between Eske anglers and NRFB also between others in Donegal. If this friendly communication is continue there is hope. If it is fragile it will be broken and salmon will suffer in the end.

To end, I quote an ancient prophecy of the Cree Indian Nation: "Only after the last tree has been cut down. Only after the last river has been poisoned. Only after the last fish has been caught. Only then will you find that money cannot be eaten."

Yours,

Anthony O'Malley Daly,
Inisfail, College Street,
Ballyshannon

Hugo McGlynn and Raymond McEnhill R.I.P.

Brendan Grace

Bill Doyle was a great angler. Patrick Brown was his ghillee. Bill was in Management in the Royal Bank, Ballyshannon. He was light on his feet for a very robust man.

John Hanna

*First Salmon of 1988 – Caught on the
Drowes – John Hanna (left), the lucky
angler, me, and Thomas Gallagher*

James Cummins with massive sea trout

*Harry Gallagher and
Paddy O'Neill – Pearse O'Neill's
father*

*What can I say about him? An
ordinary man among giants!*

Ed Hanna

*Clockwise from left: Ed Hanna, John Hanna,
Jim Thomas, and Paul Thomas in the foyer of
the National Hotel, Donegal Town*

Sea Angling – Edward Hanna and George Kelly

Seriously Proud

Father John McLoone – "Thumbs Up"

J.P. Hanna with 42 lb King Salmon – his father took him on a fishing trip to the USA for his 18th birthday

John Fletcher – "Say No More"

*Coarse Fishing – A Fine Catch by Harry Halsall,
Manchester*

Brendan O'Kane with 10 sea trout caught while night fishing on the River Finn at Liscooley

Micheal O'Brien

28lb Salmon caught by Pat McGettigan at "Perch Hole", Bundrowes River on Sunday February 1st 1965 at 1:10 pm on "Brown and Gold Devon 2.5 inch"

The Buchers - German Anglers in Belleek

Pauric Daly, brother of James Daly, fishing the Drowes.
See Book 3 for his two stories.

*James Gallagher with a 50 lb bluefish
tuna off Ocean City, USA. Will the real
William Gallagher please stand up?*

Billy Grimes – see his story in Book 3

*Patrick O'Malley - If you want to catch a
fish, wear a Hanna Hat!*

William Gallagher, Jim Mahon, and Jack Drummond (R.I.P.) with one of the last "shots" of salmon from the River Erne

Book Three

Injun Joe

Fishing Stories
Contributed by Family and Friends
– and a few of my own

Bernadette Hanna, me, John Hanna, Freddie Gilroy, JP Hanna

Here's what John Hanna and Freddie Gilroy looked like a few years earlier...

Boxing Legend Fishes in Donegal as Salmon Season Ends

by Anthony O'Malley Daly
The Donegal Democrat, October 8, 1998

Belfast bantamweight (8st-6lbs) boxing legend Freddie Gilroy came to fish in Lough Eske in September, and though he drew a blank, he enjoyed his day out. I finally got to meet my icon and my idol of the art of pugilism from the fifties and sixties.

Freddie Gilroy won a bronze medal at the Melbourne Olympics – when Ronnie Delaney won the gold in the mile. The year was 1956. Turning professional, Freddie Gilroy won the British Empire and European titles, and fought Alphonse Halimi for the world bantamweight crown. Freddie dominated his bout against Halimi, but failed to get the decision. In fact, the referee made a terrible mistake when immediately at the final bell Gilroy went to Halimi's corner to shake gloves with his seconds, while Halimi went to Gilroy's corner, whereupon the confused referee came to Gilroy's corner, raised Halimi's hand in victory, and did not rectify his awful decision that cost Freddie Gilroy the goal of his career to win a world title. This is not generally known.

Freddie Gilroy is still recognised by the older generation of boxing fans, and many came to shake his hand in Donegal where he is remembered. However, if Gilroy had remained in his own corner a few seconds longer, his arm would have been raised in victory – which is worth a million handshakes. Freddie Gilroy won two Lonsdale Belts outright for his defenses of his British titles. His bout in Belfast versus John Caldwell, which Freddie won in the ninth round, is part of boxing lore. (John Caldwell also won a bronze medal in the 1956 Olympics in Melbourne.)

Freddie Gilroy was guest of John and Mary Hanna and family, Donegal Town. Freddie Gilroy carried the boxing banner with pride and honour, and his memories of those past days of glory, now flown, are mostly good.

Anyway, he did not catch a salmon or a trout.

Stories

Tributes

Injun Joe – Boat and Boy - continued

As I said before, I am "Injun Joe," and so is Edward Hanna, and so is the boat, *das Boat,* like the name of a Native American, or the story of a German Submarine.

However, Injun Joe is a simple name. It showed the confidence the crew had in me. John Hanna is the skipper. Edward is the first Mate. And there were others – Raymond McEnhill, Frankie McEnhill (Prince Vince), Hugo McGlynn etc. etc. We fished Lough Eske every Saturday that came and went. We went up the river Eske when the salmon and sea trout were running.

Many thanks to everyone who contributed stories to this Book. Of course they're all true. You have to swear to tell the truth in order to get a Fishing License.

But before we get to the stories:

If you haven't gone fishing for salmon yet, the following story may help you understand how they are found in Irish rivers, and why:

The Life of the Salmon

By Anthony O'Malley Daly

You all know sea lice are on salmon when they arrive back to the river where they will spawn. Then, in their third year, they go to sea after two years in the river. While there, the salmon eat and grow on plankton which are a small "jerkey" thing. Anyway, when the time-clock bells start to ring, all the salmon commence the journey that will end up with them arriving off the mouth of the river they left two or three seasons ago.

Cocks And Hens

The Eske salmon are at the mouth of their river. The Eany salmon are at the "their" river waiting. It is all the same worldwide.

If there is enough water the salmon will run into their river. They will rest in the pools, and the sea lice will fall off, or they will scratch them off against rocks or sand when they run from the sea water into the fresh water. That is basically what occurs. And if you too had lice with tails on them you would want to scratch until you got them off.

The fresh salmon is silver and firm. When the season progresses the body changes colour and the firm freshness changes to a softness. There are variations to this path of life that they take in order that a salmon – say a cock fish, identified by a hook or kype on his lower jaw – meets a hen fish. The hen and the cock salmon go through the changes as summer season changes to autumn and winter. Then both (yes, you need two salmon) get the urge to spawn. Make Love. It is also the same for sea trout.

Redds

The salmon picks the spot. It is the spot comprising shale of sand and small stones. The hen fish goes about digging out the sand and small stones by turning on her side and flipping her tail. The shale rises up, the current takes it away, until there is a bed or Redd dug. The Hen and Cock appear on the redds about two weeks before Christmas. The final act of Love takes place any time both feel that their sojourn or cycle is at its climax.

The hen (don't mind my sometimes capitals or lower case) will go into the redd and will start to lay her eggs. It is because the excitement is building. The eggs scatter about the redd. When the Hen is finished, the Cock fish takes over. He has a climax.

All her eggs are now covered by his ejaculation - his love juices. You will see that "class act" (If you are lucky) on Christmas Eve or Christmas Day.

The favourite viewing platform on the Eske is Lough Eske bridge. You lean over the bridge, the salmon are not there. The next day they are there. You wll get the "thrill of your lifetime." You will witness the most exciting phase of the salmon's "Cycle Of Life."

Do not disturb the salmon spawning. If you want to see the salmon moving it is

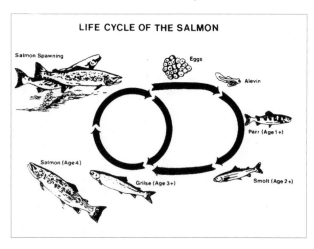

"permissible" to cast a small pebble up or down river. You look up and you will see more salmon "boiling" in the act of spawning. Look down river. Yet more salmon spawning.

The sea or white trout have already spawned. They have spawned end of October to end of November or beginning of December. They spawn up to the left side as you face the lake. (You have everything to get to know the delight of watching and enjoy the spawning of the salmon and sea trout on the Eske system).

Life Cycle Of The Salmon

This chart shows that when the salmon has spawned on the Redds, the Atlantic salmon (there is only the one species) don't normally die, except the salmon has spawned more than once. There are five species of Pacific Salmon. Chinook or King salmon are very large fish, Coho or silver Salmon are the best fighters and resemble the Atlantic salmon in weight and colour, Chum, Sockeye and Pink. They all die after they have spawned.

Back to the Atlantic Salmon. And, in the case of cock fish, the hook or kype eventually pierces the upper jaw and the end comes when the "old "multiwinter-at-sea" salmon chokes or suffocates to death. When I supervised the FAS scheme on the Eske system, I did see a few big salmon dead in the river after they had spawned.

PARR —
AGE: 1 TO 2 YEARS
LENGTH: 9 TO 16 CM

The Cycle Of Life shows the salmon spawning. The fertilised eggs, after a few months, grow into Alevins. This stage is mostly invisible. The next stage is the "growing" – from being a "thing" in the river to the definite shape of a fish – to the Fry, and then the Parr, when the fish can be seen. The Parr makes its way down stream and grows into a Smolt of about 3 to 4 inches. A Smolt will often take a fly or a spinner, proof that he/she is game. The Salmon and Sea Trout is classed as Game Fishing.

After two years the Smolt leaves the river. The Smolt is maximum five inches and is (max) half pound.

The Smolt Migrates

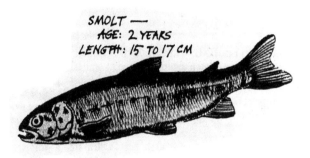

SMOLT —
AGE: 2 YEARS
LENGTH: 15 TO 17 CM

The Smolt migrates (that's the word I was searching for) - yes, migrates to the feeding grounds off Greenland. There he/she meets his /her pals and they shoal. They get into gangs, multitudes. They feed "voraciously" on plankton and eels (called liffogs) – so much so, that after (only) one winter at sea, the Smolt who left the river barely a half pound weight, is now six or seven pounds (weight) and they could grow bigger.

The Springers are the really big Salmon that arrive first back into the river in January, February, March. The first salmon of the season on the Drowes river is a spring salmon. It is ten to twelve pounds weight.

Next comes the Grilse. They are a separate run of salmon, are eagerly awaited, are from three to seven pounds. The Grilse are great takers, fighters, jumpers – in other words, they are as "Game as Hell." They are light eating. A lovely Fish. A Bar of Silver. Bristling with muscles. Streamlined. The Grilse run takes place in May or June.

Springers

The Springers are the big spring Salmon. Grilse, if he/she gets the urge to depart Greenland for his native heath. A Grilse is anything up to seven pound, with a body like Barry McGuigan. Eager to reach his river. He can still change his mind if he sees a nice partner and spends another Winter feeding in Greenland.

Daly Strikes Gold in the Honey Hole

By Edward Hanna, Virginia, USA

Thirty-nine and three quarter pounder... While most of us out here consider this just average, to Anthony "Injun-Joe" Daly it was a monster Salmon. Well, as I told you before, I was arranging another fishing trip back to Oregon to catch these mighty fish, but all I got were three anglers, John Hanna and Anthony O'Malley Daly of Ireland, and Patrick O'Malley Daly of San Francisco. The craic couldn't have been better!

Anthony and John arrived at my place and with just a 24 hour layover, we took a flight to Portland. Arriving at the airport we were picked up by Richard "Dick" Kelly. Remember I told you that George Kelly was the best angler in all of Oregon? Somehow or another, he fell second place to his brother Dick. Well, Dick was on a roll. He was landing fish in the region of 25 to 27 pounds.

After we were taken to our motel at 3:15 p.m., George and Dick had us on the river by 4 o'clock. The skipper of our boat was called Stan Anderson of Irish descent, a good fishing buddy of mine. He had everything laid on - sandwiches, sodas and fishing poles. The skipper says, "Are you ready to go fishing, guys?"

John replied, "Is there something holding you back?"

Down the river we go, the mighty Willamette, famous for huge Sturgeon and Salmon. There is nothing small in Oregon. The cry from the back of the boat came, "Hey, Stan – head for the Honey Hole." John and Anthony thought we were heading for the NEAREST PUB. But, with no pub in sight, we began to fish.

Using smelts, which are small herring, we threw them behind the boat and hoped for the best. George tied on all smelts and lures. The first pole was given to Anthony, the second to John. It didn't matter who grabbed the next pole. Dick hooked and landed the first fish, a nice little fish of 21 pounds.

By now, Anthony was using a downrigger with a rooster tail spinner which Stan had rigged up for him. Claiming it was too bright to use smelts, every angler has "his own." And guess what? Stan, the Man, was right. "Injun-Joe" was stuck in a fish within 20 minutes. What size no-one knew. But, it did not take long for him to realize that he was in for the fight of his life.

The line pulled away from the downrigger. "Reel it in," shouts Dick. "He's a king!" The downrigger is up, all the poles are reeled in, and Daly goes one on one with the great one. The fish never showed for about 25 minutes. All of a sudden, up he comes with a mighty leap into the air. The sun catches his silver side to show us all his beauty. "He's 25," says Dick. "He's 25 and 10 more," says George.

Were you ever third or fourth party in a boat when a fish was hooked? A cry from John - "Hold on to him, Daly!" From Dick - "You are too hard on him!" "Give him line, Anthony!" says George. "Hold your pole up, Anthony!" cries Stan. You think the poor man hadn't a clue about fishing. You could be right. "We're only here for a week, Daly. Get the fish in the boat!" says I.

By now, he was 30 minutes into the fight. And now the great one was fighting Daly. But the old buzzard (me) wouldn't give in. He got him to the boat when he was netted by Stan, the Man. The fish topped the scales at 39 and three-quarter pounds weight and was 37 inches long. His tail tip to tip was 14 inches. I looked over to Daly to congratulate him. He was beat. Holding a can of pop in his hand, he said, "I don't know who beat who."

This trend went for 6 to 8 days – 22 pounders, 29 pounders, and 35 pounders. George, Stan and Dick sure know this lovely river. Without their knowledge, we sure as heck would not know how and where to catch such fish. You have to say they know their stuff.

Taking a day off from fishing, we headed for Bonneville Dam, which supplies electricity for Oregon and California. The fish are counted going up river to spawn. It is manual – three ladies take three 8-hour shifts. In the dam, you can watch fish going past the fish window. The reason I say "fish" is that you can have Chinook, Chinook Jack, Sockeye, Coho, Coho Jack, Steelhead and Shad. Official fish count for 2001 was 4,431,143., minus one for the fish eagle.

Bonneville Dam is bordered by Washington State and Oregon with fantastic scenery on both sides. When you are fishing here it is not uncommon to see eagles swoop down and lift Salmon from the river - quicker than you can say "Tight lines."

Leaving Bonneville, we took a ride west to my favorite fishing village of Garibaldi where we stopped off and had lunch. The Wilson River was nearby, and what a river to fly-fish on – beautiful pools, streams, and deep holes with slow and fast running waters, just an angler's paradise. Our guide, George, took us to the pool about 300 yards long. Everything the fly angler wants is here.

I rigged up my fly rod, and headed for the top part of the pool. With my 13 foot split cane fly rod, hand-made and signed by Mick Rogan, Ballyshannon, I proceeded to peel out the line, when all of a sudden, I heard my brother say "Edward, please give me the first shot at this pool." Well, me being a fair angler, I handed over my rod with deep regret. I stood on his left side as he began to fish.

It wasn't long before a Salmon showed to his fly. John covered the fish again, and up he comes with a fly in his mouth. The cry from the other anglers was "Set the hoooook!" Back into the water, he jumps once, twice, and three times from one end of the pool to the other. To watch an angler take in a Salmon on a fly rod is simply amazing. John Hanna is considered by most of his colleagues in the angling world to be somewhat of an expert with a fly rod. The fish was landed in 25 minutes with him topping the scale at 19 pound weight. John felt as if he just won the Lottery.

With a repeat performance he landed a King Chinook from the same hole 10 minutes later. This fish weighed in at 27 pounds. You want to know the name of the fly he was using? Well, it was a good old Mick Rogan's "Green Peter" in the region of 30 plus. We finished the week with 655 pounds of Salmon. About 30 percent of the fish were released because they were native fish. The rest of the fish were given to the skipper and the gilley, George and Stan.

As I'm writing this story, I'm just after getting a call from George to let me know that Stan, the Man, Anderson caught a king Salmon – 57 pounds weight. From his tail to his nose, he was 59 and a quarter inches and his tail, tip to tip, was 16 inches.

Rivers that produce fish for us were the Willamette, Bonneville, Timothy Lake, Sandy, Hood, Garibaldi, the Klackamas, and my favourite, the Wilson. The cost of our fishing license was $37 per week. As I said before, this entitles you to fish all rivers at no extra charge. If you plan on coming to Oregon next year to catch these mighty fish, you can contact my brother, John at Donegal Town on 074 97 21475. Our fishing guide will be George Kelly because there is no better. The skipper of the boat will be Stan, the Man, Anderson who knows every nook and cranny of every river. I will be seeing Stan and George in August, so until I see you next time, remember that when you hook a fish, to cry, "SET THE HOOOOK!" You will then see how quickly aged men can get to the bank of the river.

Tight lines all,

Edward Hanna, Virginia

Gone Fishing

by Anthony O'Malley Daly

There is a song sung about "Gone Fishing," and I will guarantee it is the most popular notice hung on the knob of the door...

Or the two words which instil envy, and "wish" it was me and not him – scribbled on a blackboard, or whispered in the ear of the one you love...

To get you out of the house, to see your pals. Tell a white lie or even a major "fib," after a friend contacted you to tell you, "I'm in a big one..."

What's keeping you?

I rose another salmon just as you asked about "what fly" they are taking...

I'm going to say it just one more time. Get your rod, and I'll meet you at the Mill Pool, or I will be at the Water Abstraction Falls. Bring a few worms as it is starting to rain, and the water is turning brown...

Now, take your mobile with you. I must cut you off, as the 10 lb fish is ready for the net. See ya – hurry!

This shoal is just off the tide. This salmon is full of sea lice. He has sea lice strings like twine along his back...

Hang out the sign - "Gone Fishing!"

My Granddad Anthony

By Cillian Meehan

My name is Cillian Meehan, I am eight years of age and I live in Ballyshannon, Co. Donegal.

I love fishing however it's only been recently that I've gotten really into it. I first starting playing fishing games on my dad's smart phone and I started to learn about all different kinds of fish, pollock being the main fish I caught.

My Granddad Anthony or as we all call him 'Gaga' was and still is big into fishing, he is the one who inspired me to pick up fishing and ever since then I have loved it. Gaga was out at sea for many years and I love hearing about all the story's and the one that got away that he himself or other family members tell me. In Gaga's house he has two fish, one being a salmon and the other being a brown trout. Many people admire the two fish and I like to pretend that I caught them, which someday I intend on doing.

I have gotten some of my friends into fishing and also my cousin from the USA. When my friend Conor Foy comes over we are usually out in the garage sorting out hooks and our rods. I love fishing that much that if I'm going out with my mum or dad the first thing I ask is, 'Can we go fishing?' You never know where you might end up. The two main places I fish off are our local piers in Ballyshannon.

I thornily enjoy fishing, I find it pass's the time and I get to go out and about and it also lets my mum get some training done while we are at the pier. I have met a lot of different people and have learned a lot from them, like when it's raining the fish swim to the top of the water and when the tide is in it is easier to catch.

One day my Dad, Mum and I went up to Teelin and went deep sea fishing. It was a new experience and I loved it, I had been asking my Dad to take me deep sea fishing for quite some time and when he told me I was ecstatic I couldn't wait. It was a full day's event in which tired me out. I caught give or take seventeen fish, two were horse macrel and the rest were just plane simple macrel. We saw some amazing views while out on the boat, even seeing people up on top of the mounts. We also saw big fishing trawlers. Over all it was an amazing day and I learnt a lot from the other much more experienced fisher men that day.

I have also gone down the estry with my dad and one of his friends who owns a boat. I always love going out on the boat fishing because it's again a day's event. I seem to always catch the most fish, which for me isn't surprising as I fish nearly every day.

I am always learning about fishing and different fish and were and when to catch them. Fishing has become a hobby of mine in which I really enjoy and I want to thank my Granddad for that because I don't think I would have found a love for the sport if it wasn't for him.

Fishing with my Granddad

Fishing with my cousin Ultan from San Francisco

The Sam Maguire Fly, designed by Cillian Meehan. Hook #4. Body in gold. Tail in green, with stripe of silver. Presented by Cillian to Donegal Manager Jim McGuinness.

Fishing or Catching?

By John Meehan

There's a reason why they call it fishing and not catching. Fishing/angling is both a great pass time and a therapeutic way of relaxing even if you never catch a fish. However, for a young eight year old it can also prove a tad frustrating if there is no success. My youngest son Cillian is absolutely crazy about fishing. Needless to say he didn't take it "from the wind." My late father was a regular down the channel here in Ballyshannon, on the Melvin in Co Leitrim, on the Erne in Co Fermanagh, and he made an annual pilgrimage to Cong in Co Mayo. I remember him telling me that there's more to fishing than simply choosing the right bait or learning to properly play a fish. He told me that one of the most important attributes of a true angler is the ability to "stretch the truth" -- from touching your thumb to the scale when you're weighing your "record" catch to delivering a lengthy monologue later in the bar about the giant you nearly reeled in the last time you were out on the water. (You know the one whose proportions bring to mind the protagonist of that 1950s sci-fi flick "The Beast from 20,000 Fathoms.") He believed that when you tell a tall fishing tale, you're following a time-honoured tradition.

How true he was. I remember reading an article in the newspaper when a former U.S. president tells a fish story in the interest of diplomacy, it becomes international news! In 2007, President George W. Bush took Russian President Vladimir Putin fishing on a lake near the Bush family compound in Kennebunkport, Maine. According to The New York Times, Putin caught a bass and was photographed in Bush's boat, holding a fish that to the "experienced fishing eyes" appeared to be about 20 inches long. By the time the leaders had reached the dock, however, Putin's fish miraculously had grown to 31 inches -- or, at least it must have, since that's how big Bush told reporters the fish was. The controversy drew international media attention, with two Russian TV stations openly doubting the size of Putin's haul. Some speculated that Bush's fib was an effort to improve then tense U.S.-Russian relations, but David DiBenedetto, editor of the fishing journal SaltWater Sportsman, sought to put the Presidential prevarication in an everyman context: "We've all had a non-fisherman on the boat and added a few inches or pounds to his or her catch," he explained. This appears to be an international phenomenon and not confined to the north west of Ireland.

Cillian's grandfather (on my wife Sarah's side) is affectionately known as "Ga Ga" (and the force behind this collection of stories) and is a respected angler known the length and breath of the country. Lately his heroics in raising funds for the Parkinson's Disease Society have eclipsed his long love and experience of angling. But Anthony enjoyed nothing more than his excursions on Lough Eske with his buddies John and Edward Hanna on board the "Injun Joe." Many amazing fish were allegedly caught by these men and many a late night was had recalling the "one that got away." So you can see that the genetic angling link has passed on to Cillian.

I am amazed how Cillian is so focused on fishing. He watches fishing programmes on TV and YouTube and even the games he downloads are finshing related. He is the proud owner of three rods and has gone through a number of reels throughout his fishing career to date. He utilises the world wide web for tips and tricks to catch the ultimate fish. His goal is to catch a salmon bigger than the one Ga Ga caught many years ago and which now takes pride of place in a cabinet in his sitting room. I can see that when Cillian looks at this 29lb monster he is determined to go one better and I know that someday he will.

I was reflecting on my first trip down the Erne estuary with Cillian. The skipper of the boat was my council colleague and friend Cllr Billy Grimes the whip of the Fianna Fail grouping within the council (thank God he doesn't have many to whip). Billy for as long as I've known him has been into fishing and angling and I always note the little proud smile on his face when people ask about the picture of his late father holding a 54lb salmon that is proudly displayed in Finn McCool's bar. Billy is respectful of my position as one of the Famous Five blue shirts on the current council but to be honest we always leave politics in the council chamber, and I think that's the place for it.

We departed the Mall Quay (Billy, Cillian and I) one grey summer's day in 2010. It was Cillian's first trip down the channel. Packed lunch and flasks of tea and hot chocolate were on board Billy's boat to keep us going throughout the day. As we passed Inis Saimer we discussed the history behind the island and Cillian surprised me with his knowledge of same. I have to admit that Billy met his match in Cillian when it comes to chatting as we progressed towards the sandhills. We put out our lines and began to trawl towards an area referred to locally as "the bar" (an area where the Erne estuary meets the sea). As we looked at the natural beauty of the sandhills I recalled taking my eldest son Patrick on a similar trip many years previously and pulling up on the beach then climbing to the top of the sand dunes and sliding down. Billy was the captain of the boat that day also and his son B.J. was also along for the spin. Sarah my wife and Fiona my daughter have yet to accompany me on a fishing trip down the channel but I sincerely hope we get around to it. Sarah is more of the sea swimming type and Fiona more of the surfing type (if you know what I mean, dude!).

Cillian (on that day) was more interested in the fishing but we did get to climb the sandhills and enjoy the slide. Anyway by the time we arrived at the "bar" not one "bite" did we get, even though the bait was genuine sand eels. I could sense the frustration on the boat when suddenly Cillian's rod began to bend. He was on a fish. Just to see the excitement and elation on his face was priceless. Billy (as usual) began to shout instructions, and as the silvery shine of the fish could be seen from the boat Billy confirmed, "It's a trout!" Out came the hand net and with the ease of an expert angler Cillian landed his first sea trout, 1/2lb or so in weight but a memory that would never be forgotten. Billy showed us how to gut the fish and as we started back trawling, we could see that one of the other boats also fishing at the bar was also landing fish. For the next few hours we slowly made our way up and down, over and back along the lower end of the channel and our catch for the day (although not substantial) included trout, mackerel and a flat fish caught by yours truly.

I have to admit that at times I forget (and do not appreciate) the natural resources and beauty that is on my doorstep here in Ballyshannon, and I hope that Cillian enjoys and appreciates this as he moves through the different stages of life. No matter what happens the lasting memories of our time fishing will always bring a smile to my face and I can only look forward to future adventures with Cillian.

The Sea in My Blood

by Jim Mahon.

(Jim Mahon was "discovered" by Ann McGowan and me when he was sent to do work experience in Atlantic View, Ballyshannon. He is a great angler, and hunter to boot. I think you will agree with me and Ann.)

Let me take you on a journey, a journey which holds so many fond and cherished memories for me from an early age. We go to the Erne Estuary, a long narrow stretch of the most breath taking scenery you could possibly lay your eyes on. On the Finner or south side a sandy shore dominates the scene with a small island which could tell a thousand tales if it could speak. Not least it being where the Parthalonians landed, the first settlers in Ireland. The rack shore or North side is a mixture of both sand and rack (seaweed) but it holds the same beauty for me.

Dawn slowly peeps through the curtains and the alarm clock sitting on the bedside locker shows little or no regard for the peace and quiet of the morning or for those in deep slumber lost in dreams. The man in question wakes, taking in his surroundings and drags himself away from the warmth and comfort of his bed in anticipation of the days fishing ahead. The plan, now in motion, made and talked over countless times the evening before with his best friend, his Dad, is to catch the early morning tide.

The lads with all the necessary equipment loaded make their way to the Mall Quay, a location well known to every fisherman in the town of Ballyshannon. It's a fine spring morning with all the hallmarks of a dry day ahead. While loading the boat quietly they are greeted with what can only be described as nature's way of saying good morning, the Dawn Chorus is now in full harmony like an orchestra performing.

Slowly, throttle is applied to the engine and the head of the boat is brought round to point in the direction they intend taking along the rocky shoreline known as the Laundry. This is a narrow but deep drain which runs adjacent to the shore and is a safe way down to the open deep water to one of the first fishing spots I was introduced to: "Gibby's Point." Safely through the passage and out of harms way, it's now time to open to full throttle and exert full power. Steaming on past another well known fishing spot "The Chair," I feel the warm morning sun rest on my back, its a powerful sensation and one that makes me feel alive and in great spirits with both life and nature.

Every nook and cranny along the shore brings a total recall of happy times gone by. To the many fishermen I had the pleasure of knowing both young and old, to each and every fishing location which granted a wealth of silver amongst the fishing crews. I am so happy and proud to have been part of it all and I tip my hat in gesture and the highest respect to all.

With our final destination in sight I study the sea-birds lined along the strand feeding on the ebbing tide. The seagull hovering overhead with it's distinctive unmistakable haunting cry, the large multi coloured shell ducks who have become regular sight dotted along the shore line and the cormorant with its wings spread to the maximum, drying out. How could I forget the herring, like the lone fisherman tucked away in his own corner standing tall in his grey coat, like a statue? The seal pup lying on the strand just short of the waters edge basking in the morning sun, no doubt waiting for flood tide to claim its share of the fish. They are all residents of the Erne Estuary with their individual personalities going about their daily life.

The Bar Mouth has now been reached, it's where the Erne Estuary meets the mighty force of the sea. On Tullaghan Strand lies the remains of a ship's boiler, but more to the point it's a grim reminder of the danger that lurks on every unforgiving wave rolling in. The anchor is dropped where a close eye can be kept on the surrounding water. The day's fishing is about to begin. The rods are extended and the bag which holds the bait is now opened for the first time. A fresh packet of sand-eels is the choice of the day for both men. While setting up the equipment they casually talk of the view surrounding them, across Donegal Bay. To their right hand side lie mountains that appear a hazy blue due to the fine weather conditions. Looking out towards the Atlantic a lighthouse can be seen vaguely in the far off distance off St. John's Point. Directly across the bay from this landmark is the small fishing village of Mullaghmore, which at this time of year is a big attraction to those who enjoy the sea and the beauty it has to offer. Running your eye along the coastline back towards Ballyshannon you have to admire the majestic Benbulben Mountains lying in the background. Finally your eye comes to rest on the seaside resort town of Bundoran which is a big attraction to many people longing to experience the summer sunshine and the *craic*.

Flood tide draws near, as every wave coming to rest on the shore now shows strong signs of a light green colour. The forces of nature are about to approach without mercy. Both men grow anxious as the seagulls circle endlessly gathering for the feast of live bait soon to arrive. The distinctive taste of salt sea air is ever present with the slight breeze that slowly begins to blow in from the Atlantic. Without warning the circling seagulls reach a stage or uncontrollable excitement screaming aloud announcing to all parties that the first shoal of sand eel has been spotted. They are on their way up the estuary towards the awaiting fishermen. Lines are double checked and tensions on the fishing reels are set to allow for a running Sea Trout if it takes without warning.

The first strike happens within a split second. The fishing rod bends and hearts start racing with excitement and anticipation. Line is stripped from the fishing reel at a quickening pace as a fresh bar of Atlantic Silver Sea Trout rises to the surface of the water thrashing its head violently in disapproval. The fight continues, the inherent wildness of the Sea Trout demands respect. A fine fish by any standard is soon taken on board to the delight of the fishermen, Without haste the first catch of the day is bagged and a fresh sand eel is quickly applied before being delivered out into the green murky tide once again.

With great pleasure for both fishermen, the day's fishing continues on the same note as it had begun, and a respectable bag of fish has been accounted for from the flood tide. On the journey home they reminisce on the day's fishing with fresh tales now embedded in their memories, and no doubt cherished like countless others. The younger of the two looks towards his Dad sitting at the head of the boat and quietly in his own deep thought thanks him. This is the man who has taught him how to be at one with nature and respect his surroundings. The sea, I know, will call me back again in the very near future. It will send its beckoning message up along the Erne estuary to my home in the town of Ballyshannon. I will always accept that invitation, for the sea has a special place in my heart and runs through the veins in my body.

Dedicated to the fishermen of Ballyshannon present and deceased.

The Salmon and the Pearl

By Anthony O'Malley Daly

In Ireland there are many Salmon rivers and lakes, quite apart from waters that contain Trout and many other sought-after species. To me each amenity could only be described as a "factory" because Anglers arrive to fish and bring employment and business. And the people who come to fish are taking their holidays and escaping from places that are industrialised and have lost their recreational value. Indeed, instead of us seeking to be industrialised, with its attendant pollution, we should be exploiting the natural richness of our land and water to give employment rather than importing dirty industries that will eventually lay waste the nation.

My area of angling embraces Lough Melvin and the River Drowes; Lough Eske and the River Eske; and finally the River Eany. The Melvin is a mighty lake steeped in history. Its connection with the lasting sea is through the Drowes river. Each year the Drowes opens for Salmon fishing on the 1st of January. Whoever catches the Salmon gets a big sale price (if they so choose) from a market eager for the privilege of purchasing the first fish of the incoming year.

Lough Eske has a character all of its own, and the scenery and landscape viewed from a boat is a tribute to our gift of sight. The Eske river, as you might have guessed, flows from the lake and reaches for sea at Donegal Town. I caught my first Salmon on the Eske, so you will forgive me for having a soft spot for it. Now the river Eany is a spate river, which means it does not run from a lake and depends on the rain for its floods. It has a split personality in that it has the Big Eany and the Wee Eany before it runs out of land under Inver Bridge. To know if the Eany is in condition for fishing, the knowledgeable fisherman looks towards the mountain to spot the water cascading down – and if it is, then the river is right, and if it isn't - forget it. This white cascade is called the Grey Mare's Tail. However, don't ask me where the Grey Mare's Tail is, or you might get a funny answer.

The story:

Now of course we come to the story, but for the tale to fit I must tell you that not so many years ago certain people went to the river Eske for something quite different to fishing. That quite different thing was Fresh Water Oysters, and from the Oysters comes the pearl, and the pearl is valuable as an item of jewellery. You are thinking now that you never saw a Salmon wearing a string of pearls, or even a ring with a pearl inset as a birthstone, but the pearl had a use for one particular Salmon.

One May day some years back I went out fishing on Lough Eske. I was heading for the favourite fishing grounds, rowing at a good steady pace, trolling my bait. Suddenly at O'Donnell's Island, where I would not normally expect a fish, my reel began to sing. I didn't drop the oars, but turned away from the proximity of the island, leading the well hooked Salmon out from shore to where I could best play and catch him. The fish was big (aren't they all!). He bored down deep, making long steady runs. Eventually I got him near to the boat, and I was right this time – he was big. I could see him looking at me, then he would turn away into one of his long steady runs yet again. I was beginning to wonder how I was going to land him because I was by myself, and I didn't see this Salmon consenting to the net, such was his bulk. The more I endeavoured, the more he dug in his heels, or words to that effect. I was exhausted, and the Salmon was also weakening, but each time he saw the net he searched into his reserves of fight. His final act was to start shaking his head. This told me that the hooks were loosening, and indeed they were, for suddenly the bait shot out of the water, and my big fish submarined silently back into the deep.

In my frustration and anger I fired the rod to the bottom of the boat, *Damn him*, I thought, and for a time I addressed myself to the mute boat in language that would make a Cape Horn sailor blush. When I settled, I picked up my rod and inspected the hooks. My brave Salmon did not get away scot free – for embedded in one of the treble hooks was one of his eyes.

I of course told my story to my pals, and it was not long before a legend sprung up around the departed Salmon, so much so that when we would be out fishing in the area of O'Donnell Island the subject would crop up, and if a Salmon was caught my pals, John, Edward and Jim would say, "I hope its not Anthony's old one-eyed monster." It was good for a laugh, but I took it seriously, and always hoped no one would catch him, because I had grown quite attached to him. Indeed, I vowed, that if ever again I hooked him, then I would, on recognition, let him loose. It is strange, but I would often wonder just where he had gone, and would I really ever see him again. An imaginary bond held us together, and despite the passage of time I somehow knew he was still alive, and returning my affection.

I didn't fish the lake for some years until fate seemed to draw my back for a days fishing. Edward was with me, and of course, in keeping with the legend and destiny we were passing round by O'Donnell Island. Edward mentioned "Old One-Eye," and I smiled as we glided along. He was rowing and I was relaxing at the back of the boat holding our trolling rods. Suddenly mine went bang. I was in a Salmon. No need to say he was big, for it would be no use saying he was small. Thoughts of my escapades some years previous sprung to my mind, and I was certain sure that if I did see "Old One-Eye" then somehow I would contrive to let him off the hook. I said as much to Edward, and he said, "Don't be daft." This fish reminded me of the titanic struggle I had in the past, and related here, so when I did get the Salmon alongside I was greatly relieved to discover he had no empty socket, nor was the fish wearing a eye patch. I got Edward to verify my findings and he confirmed the Salmon had two eyes. He said, "Old One-Eye really got to you! Well, this isn't him, so haul him in and I'll slip the net under him." I did, and Edward landed the Salmon. The fish kicked around the boat briefly before I grabbed him firmly by the tail, placing him writhing on the seat and began to batter him on the head. The Salmon stopped moving – he was dead. "Give him one more knock to finish the job," said Edward, and this I did.

Something dropped onto the floorboards. "What's that?" said Edward. "What's what?" said I, and Edward picked up something small and round. "It fell out of your fish, and it looks like a pearl. Or glass eye," said he. I froze, the blood ran to my head. I looked at the Salmon. You'll have to say it for me - yes, the Salmon had only one eye, and one vacant socket. I had killed the fish I loved. I was shattered, Edward was admiring the Salmon, guessing his weight, and elated – both at the catch, and my obvious distress. He was saying things like, "The words of the song say that you always hurt the ones you love, but not only did you hurt 'Old One-Eye' – you killed him!" And then his sides shook with laughter. For me, the bottom fell out of fishing for a long time. I don't even remember who ate the Salmon, or what happened to his mortal remains. All I know is that I still have "Old One-Eye's" only worldly possession – a pearl glass eye. And as the boys often say, "We don't know what you're so upset about – you're the only one who got a mention in his will." Scant consolation that is.

You want to see "Old One-Eye's" glass eye, do you? Well, I'd show it to you, only I changed this morning and it's in my other jacket.

Battery Hens

By Anthony O'Malley Daly

I was sitting beside a Corkman on one of our flights. The airline was giving us a meal then – a snack you would not get now. Anyway, we had the meal. We were just settling down when the hostess appeared with another snack. It got the better of my companion who said thus: "We are like a lot of Battery Hens – they are feeding us again!"

A Village Divided

by Noel Carr

There had been great controversy in an un-named Irish village on the difference between a switch-cast and a Spey-cast. Eventually things got so bad that it created a great rift in the village. Friends fell out. Brothers stopped talking to each other. Once-friendly neighbours stopped talking. And sons argued with fathers. So the priest felt it his duty to bring the matter to a head.

He stood up to give his sermon in the Sunday morning Mass. "Now," he said, "you have been falling out over the difference between a Spey-cast and a switch-cast. I will now tell you the difference, and that will he the end of it."

To help in his explanation, he held out his arms as though holding a long salmon fly-rod. "In a Spey-cast, the line and fly hit the water. So!" And he made movements with his arms as though Spey-casting.

"Now, in a switch-cast the line and fly do not hit the water. So!" And he waved his arms about as though to make a switch-cast. "Is that clear?" he demanded as he glared around the congregation.

A voice broke the silence. "And if one of them casts had reached the water, it would have been a miracle!"

Noel Carr is the former Chair of FISSTA (Federation of Irish Salmon and Sea Trout Anglers, *Conaidhm na Slat Iascairi Bradan & Breac Geal*).

Dalmatian Poocher

By Anthony O'Malley Daly

A dalmatian dog and its owner were done for poaching on a river in the west of Ireland.

The owner would "spot" a salmon, "point" the dog in the right direction. The dalmatian jumped into the river, and emerged with the salmon in its mouth. Simple, except the man was caught by the authorities. He is issuing no more orders to the dalmatian, except maybe *Sit* and *Don't Move*.

The Boiler Hole

by Eugene Conway

In 1946 the river Erne was probably the greatest salmon river in Ireland. The Assaroe Falls threw the mighty Erne into its estuary in a mad boiling cauldron of spray and spume. The local population called this "the Boiler Hole." As a child I was terrified of just being near it. To day I am 72 years old, and the falls have long been sacrificed to the demand of commerce = electricity. When I bring my boat up into the now silent Boiler Hole I can still feel fear!!

Only recently I was talking to an engineer who worked on the power station during the years of its construction and he told me that 400,000 tons of water passed through the Boiler Hole in one hour!! At low tide there was a rock wall of 18ft with 6ft of water over a fairly flat bed-rock. When this river was in flood in the springtime, the first run of large spring fish that arrived to go up to spawn in the most beautiful upper reaches of this river was really something to behold. If we had it today, a fortune could be made from putting up a fence and charging people £10 for a 5 minute gawk!

Now, I was only 10 years old at the time my father – Detective Officer Louis Conway – caught the best salmon of a long life of catching good salmon. The previous year (1945) he received a gift from his brother, my Uncle Leo. It was one of the first Mitchell spinning reels to arrive in Ballyshannon, Co Donegal, in Ireland. That reel changed forever my father's approach to fishing. While he was a dedicated angler before, now he became a salmon fishing junkie!

When time allowed (and often when there was no time at all) he lost weight, slept only long enough to be able to get up in the morning without staggering, and he would be off to the river. He discovered that there was a large sewer pipe running along the right hand side of the falls in such a place that he could stand there and reach out to where the fish were jumping up the falls. The problem though was that these big fish were just in from the sea and, when hooked, went ballistic. They headed down stream in the heavy water, and even 25lb nylon couldn't hold them. It always sounded the same over the roar of the falls – "*snnnapp* " the sound of the line parting under heavy stress. *PEESSSSSEEESSSCHRISSSSSTT, the basterd has cleaned me out again!*

He lost a lot of good fish like this, and a lot of nylon too, and only got a few – but they were a bit small, being in the region of 10lbs or so. When one looked for a few minutes at the salmon trying to negotiate the falls, some of them had to be over 50 lbs. (A 60lb one was caught in the nets near the sandhills.)

About this time there happened to appear on the river below a 2-man wooden kayak made in the local technical school by a lovely man, who was the woodwork teacher

– Louie Emerson, RIP. With my brother at the paddles, Dad took the kayak up the side of the white torrent right alongside the big pipe. Rope tied around the pipe provided a good hold for my brother Louis. Dad got out onto the pipe, and with a good solid pipe under his feet he began to catch some great fish.

How he managed it was simple, really – get the boy (Louis) to sit in back of the kayak with paddles ready to go, get out on big pipe, hook into large salmon, open the bale of reel, and hand rod to Louis. Get into kayak – very carefully – and push off, back the kayak down the river, close the bale on the reel, and take up slack from then on.

Dad was boss. Anywhere the salmon went, Dad was there behind him. Many salmon to 29 lbs were taken, plus countless 10 to 20 pounders. Then my Uncle Leo again made the job safer by giving Dad a 13ft aluminium boat, shaped like a duck and safe with air chambers in it. The kayak felt a bid dodgy at times, and I never felt very safe in it. Then, with the boat being more stable, it was much easier to manoeuvre. We had no life jackets in those days, but the call of the salmon was never ending.

Then in the year of 1948 my older brother Tommie and Dad went up to the falls at the pipe as usual. After fishing for a half hour, Dad got a pull on the line, and the line went slack. For a while Dad was reeling in like mad. Eventually the line went taut, and away went the fish down-stream.

This fish felt very heavy and so strong that Dad had to back off the drag, and Tommie had to row the boat faster. The fish was heading for the bar mouth – that's the open sea – about one mile down the estuary. Dad told Tommy to pull ahead of the fish, and he would try and pull the fish towards the ocean. This did the trick, and the fish headed back up into the cauldron of the Boiler Hole, then back down around Inis Saimer Island – and over into Abbey Bay, back out and down towards the ocean again, about 2 miles down near the sand hills.

By this time Dad knew the fish was foul-hooked in the tail. The line in the water was moving from side to side with the motion of the fish's tail. This was war. Dad was getting tired in his arm and wrist. The fish had not been seen yet, but he was tiring and slowing down.

There is an area over on the south shore where kids used to swim. It was a nice sandy bottom and no deep holes. Into this bay he goes, and when they were in about 5 feet of water they saw him. Dad says, "Ch— t, will ye look at that! Get the gaff son, and be careful – if you mess this up, you'll get your arse kicked!"

An old home-made gaff with a wooden handle about 4 feet long. The fish obliges and turns on his side near the boat. Tommie reaches out and down on the outside of the fish and brings the gaff up fast and true. It is very important while the gaff hits the fish, it must be brought through and on into the boat, no stopping...

Well, didn't the old gaff straighten out, and the fish took off like a streak of lightning. Dad had again to get the drag off to save the line from breaking. On the oars again, and the race is on.

By this time Dad is really hurting in the arms. The fish goes back up the river, but Tommie got ahead of him again, and he headed back towards the sandy bay. When they got into about 3 feet of water, Tommie jumped out of the boat. The salmon was about done now. Tommie put his hands into the gills of the fish and was trying to lift it into the boat, but he couldn't quite clear the gunnell. Dad came to his help, and the fish landed in the bottom of the boat. "Jes — Ch— st, son, will you look at that!" The big fiddleback silver and copper spoon was lying alongside the fish's tail, and there wasn't a hook stuck in him. The line had somehow twisted over the treble hook, and the fish was lassoed around the tail. 35 1/2 pounds – 2 hours and 35 minutes – and not a hook stuck in him. Tommie did not get his arse kicked, the fish was taken into Ferguson's pub at the bridge end and was on the sawdust on the floor for 4 hours while half the town came to see the big fish.

My father got plastered, and no one would let him buy one drink.

Specimen Fish

By Anthony O'Malley Daly

I got a 20 lbs 4ozs specimen salmon in 1986, and when I got the results back from the Central Fisheries Board, it said that my specimen fish was a one-winter-at-sea and said also that it was 3 years old – which made it a Grilse. I got it stuffed at £8 punts an inch. My salmon was 36 inches from tip of his nose to the V of his tail. They said in addition that it was cock fish. Look at the picture of the fish and you will see a rare salmon indeed.

I hooked him coming out from Ardnamona, going towards the Tailors Ditch. Edward and John Hanna were with me and I had just said to them that I got a "Dib" - which was my way of saying to them that it was only a trout. I confirmed when I said, "Don't stop the boat. It is only a small trout"

The next thing I got the "Dob." (On the scale we invented, a "Dib" was a small trout. A "Dab" was a sea trout or a brown trout. A "Dob" was a salmon, and a big one at that.)

My rod doubled. My reel started to sing. I knew I had at least a 16-pound-plus. John and Edward started to chide me because I said I had only a trout. Nevertheless, they began to clear the decks. John cut the engine. Edward readied the net. The salmon exploded and leaped 2 to 3 feet into the air. They both knew then that I had hooked a big one.

After my Spring salmon acrobatics I settled down to play my fish. It was a sunny, calm day and John said to me "Daly, you are a very lucky so-and-so." ("So-and-so" is a cover for an expletive.) By jumping, the three of us knew that I was exercising my lucky streak of catching big fish. At the same time, I was not rated or in the same league as both men. The fact that I had hooked a specimen salmon riled both John and Edward.

The salmon had sea-lice upon sea-lice, strings of sea-lice. The fact of the matter, it was a massive fish. My salmon came to the surface and when I saw him I really thought I would lose this fish. The size of this fish was the largest salmon I had ever hooked.

In the clear, calm waters the sea-lice laden salmon settled down. He took about half a dozen runs away from the boat. He took the line out at will. The pride I felt was palpable. The salmon circled the boat four times. Edward put aside the net, bent over and grabbed the salmon by the tail. Landed the big salmon into the boat. The salmon was dispatched. When we looked at my fish, it was like looking at a bar of solid silver. It was the biggest, freshest fish any of us had ever seen.

I was proud as punch, for I had landed a salmon that would turn out to be a one-winter-at-sea cock fish that had fed so voraciously off Greenland. I had him stuffed by Lundy Taxidermists, Tubbercurry, Co Sligo.

As I mentioned earlier, the fish was 36 inches from tip of his nose to the V of his tail. His girth was 22 inches. He was 20 lbs 4 ounces. He was declared a specimen. The dearth of specimen salmon had taken the weight from 25lbs down to 20 lbs. I got presented with a specimen badge in Dublin. I was followed by Derek Davis who caught a specimen Tope in North Donegal. My luck over my ability displayed that my luck was still in Lough Eske.

My specimen salmon was a prized possession. However, a year later John Hanna was holding a Display and Buyers Exhibition, and he asked to borrow my salmon to add to the occasion.

Everything was going great. I got a call. It was John. One of the buyers had pointed out to John that the salmon was gone from view. It could not be seen. The salmon was in a pall of steam. John had put the salmon in the window. The sun shone brightly. John had forgotten about the salmon. The sun got hot. I got hot. The salmon got steamed up. The photo is the proof.

My specimen salmon, slightly cooked.

Doctor Trout

by Anonymous

A local village in the heart of angling country had a development of tourist cottages which were very popular with fishermen from Germany, Holland, and Switzerland.

So popular were they that a major Swiss tour operator installed a courier in one of the chalets each year for the peak fishing season as an organiser of their clients.

The man they chose was a retired Doctor of Engineering, a Swiss man with the unlikely (but real) name of Dr Trout, who may have been most knowledgeable in his field of Engineering, but his knowledge of fishing was scarce. In fact, it was Zero.

He made himself known in the local shops and pubs. He endeavoured to learn about the local lakes and rivers. To put it mildly, he had the local populace plagued with questions about fishing!

"You sink zis is ze good day for Melvin?"

"What you zink is best bait for Drowes?"

These types of questions, day in and day out, year after year, had workers in the local shops annoyed, since the majority of them had absolutely no interest in fishing.

On one occasion Dr Trout was getting some groceries in a village shop when he, as usual, asked Jim (the shop-assistant), "You sink zat today is a good day for my clients to catch ze big pikes on ze Lake McNean?"

To which Jim replied, "Doctor, I've told you many times – I know nothing about fishing. I've no interest in fishing."

At this point Frank, a local wit known for his quick repartee, entered the shop. Jim continued, "Here's a man who lives on the river shore. He probably knows a lot about fishing."

Dr Trout turned to Frank. "Ah! So you are ze fisherman?"

"Oh, no!" Frank quickly replied. "Bird's Eye and Findus do all my fishing!"

"The Bigger the Fly, the Bigger the Fish"

By Anthony O'Malley Daly

Edward Hanna was at home on a visit with his wife, Breege O'Neill, sister of Pearse O'Neill, and daughter of Paddy O'Neill, who married "on to" the Hannas. We went out on Lough Eske. We headed for the Ridge, which is one of the best places to catch a salmon.

The Ridge is at the mouth of the Lowreymore, or Barnesmore river. In the old days, the Lowreys had a post station there with coaches and horses for the mail, on land owned by the Garyelvin family, as I discovered when I was supervising the FÁS scheme. FÁS workers had a hut there, to the west of the Lough Eske bridge.

There is a stretch of Lough Eske, that is "dreamed off " or fished more than The Ridge. That Saturday we loaded "Injun Joe" at our berth, the newly-built offices at the roadside that we share with the Northern Regional Fisheries Board. We crossed the lake, past the outside of O'Donnell's Island where the famous clan had a prison and a cattle corral, and the ruins still have the "watch openings" that allowed them keep watch on the The Ridge only. The "watch-outs" do not permit any other visions but the narrow look-out of The Ridge.

Anyway, we made our way round the Island and headed for a stone or rock, called Salmon Rock, which is 100 (A Hundred) yards west of The Ridge, and is the start of the drift (Fly) or troll (Spoons or Devons or Tobys). Edward Hanna and anyone who got a berth (only temporary) in the same boat, like Raymond McEnhill, his brother Frankie (Prince Vince), and your narrator Injun Joe. (I am also "Captain Pugwash" and any other Captain or Corporal you can think of in your idle mind.)

About the Yanks, about Edward, about Breege, about Ulstermen...

Edward and Breege Hanna went to America to seek their fortune in a foreign land along with a bit of salmon fishing in the North West Territories. David Hanna, Edward's father, was from Belfast, an orphan. He landed in Donegal Town. As you can guess, Edward was in the "rag trade" and in addition to his skills at cutting the cloth, he was an excellent tradesman.

Paddy O'Neill, Breege Hanna's father, was from Irish Street, Dungannon. Frank O'Neill, Joe O'Neill's father, came from Pomeroy, County Tyrone. Joe went to every All Ireland Hurling and Football Final in Croke Park to date. His father Frank always said it took Joe three hours to get to Dublin and three weeks to come home.

Paddy and Frank got jobs in Ballyshannon. It was during the 2nd (Second) Great World War – 1939 to 1945 – Paddy O'Neill bought a Confectionery and Newsagents shop at the Bridge End, Ballyshannon. Frank O'Neill purchased a pub and turned part of the frontage into a Cafe. They made out very well, as Ulstermen usually do. It is called Business Acumen.

Paddy O'Neill was a great angler. He went fishing every Wednesday on Loch Melvin (mostly,) with his great friend Frankie Miller who owned The Royal Millstone Hotel and a Garage next door to repair cars and such like. These premises were situated on Main Street, opposite Dorrian's Hotel. They were razed to the ground and will be developed for the enhancement of Ballyshannon – the oldest town in Ireland.

Paddy O'Neill, the most popular man in Ballyshannon

Edward and his wife Breege were soon working in Boston, as were all the Irish, including myself when I went there on holiday for a month. We went to visit our son Patrick and daughter Orla, who had gone to America and also landed in Boston.

Edward Hanna – A Tasty Worker and Angler – Injun Joe

Edward Hanna took to working and fishing in Boston. He would arrive home with Breege to Ballyshannon. Before I managed to greet him, he was gone to Donegal Town. He stayed there until a "posse" was sent to get him, and he was dragged back to Virginia, USA. One thing John and I knew for sure was that when he was in Donegal the salmon and trout were in grave danger of being caught, and when he was back in U.S. of A., the rest of us stood a chance of a fish.

One morning, when I went with him to gather his wages, the contractor was lauding Edward and how he was worth the money he was getting. He was searching for a single word when I intervened and said Edward was a 'Tasty' worker. Yes, indeed.

The accident he had when he fell from the roof of a house he was painting nearly killed him, and has left him with more iron and steel in his body that would anchor him to the bottom. His sister Margaret, who is a nurse, went to Virginia to bring him back to health.

Dry Humour

by Noel Carr

An old fisherman began to suffer from dribbling. Eventually it got so bad that his wife said to him, "I'm tired up of you coming home with your trousers and waders wet and stinking of the pee. You've got to go and see the doctor."

So he went to the doctor and the doctor said, "You've got the prostate and will have go to the hospital to have an operation." He said to the doctor, "I can't go into the hospital until the fishing season is finished in October." "Fine," said the doctor, "you can have the operation in November."

And he did. And the operation was a complete success. Well, at the start of the next season he went fishing and caught a lovely twelve-pounder – a beautiful silver fish, straight from the sea. And he sent the fish to the hospital with a note that said, *"To the surgeon who did my prostate operation, and the nurses who looked after me, I hope you enjoy this salmon. It's the first I have caught with dry flies for a long time!"*

I Knew My Goose Was Cooked

By Harry Lloyd

Harry Lloyd is from Tippererary. He has retired as Manager of Northern Regional Fisheries Board. He has a boat and is a regular on the Erne Estuary. He has written a story about a Goose, not a fish, but he is bigger than me, and a friend of mine. Hence the dispensation!!!

Ireland in the 1950's was a very rural place to live in and for a boy growing up on a mixed tillage and dairy farm in Co. Tipperary it was a mixture of hard physical farm work and enjoyable outdoor sport. Rivers were used for swimming by large numbers of the rural population before the advent of the swimming pool in the local town. Fishing was very popular but tackle was scarce and of very poor quality, however trout perch and pike were usually caught using a spinning rod and a No 2 and No 3 red spotted brass Mepps bait and when that failed a big lump of lead to hold down a bunch of worms carefully threaded on to a long shanked hook.

However it was the start of the shooting season on the 1st of November each year which brought the most excitement and joy to me. From an early age I had been trained in the art of a game beater by my father. This consisted in positioning oneself on the far side of every fence level with the shooter on the other side while at the same time using a long hazel stick to continuously beat the hedgerow to drive out

the pheasants or woodcock. In large sugar beet crops beaters always remained within a shot of the nearest gunmen which was about 30 yards to his left or right. Gun dogs used in mixed tillage farms were usually English Pointers or Irish Setters which would stand still and set each bird after they had located it by sent. When beaters and gunmen caught up with the dog it was sent forward to flush the bird up.

By the time I was 14 years of age I had seven shooting seasons behind me and knew how to load and fire a double barrel shotgun. One day in early November soon after my 14th Birthday I took my father's double-barrelled shotgun and a pocket of cartridges and "snipe" our Irish red setter up to the sugar beet field. Half way down the field about 60 yards out from the hedge the dog set. I waited to see would the bird rise itself as I knew I would have a far better chance of shooting it rather than flush it up as it could run on the ground and rise in any direction.

The dog moved forward and a large cock pheasant got up almost at my feet. I fired and he fell dead in the beet about 30 yards away. I had shot my first cock pheasant! I picked it up and went home left up the gun and cartridges and waited for my father to return home. I could see even though he gave out to me for taking the gun without his permission that he none the less was happy that I had now managed to shoot my first cock pheasant.

Each year on the 31st of October my home resembled Fort Knox. The kitchen table was cleared and sitting around it would be my father my eldest brother and Johnny Birmingham who worked for my father. Each man was now in the countdown for the start of the shooting season the next day. Three shotguns were cleaned oiled and checked and cartridge belts were carefully filled with a mixture of No 5 and No 7 cartridges. The number fives were used for pheasants which were located in hedgerows, beet crops, potato gardens and stubble cereal fields, the no 7's were used for Partridge which were usually located in fields of turnips especially adjoining wheat stubble fields.

It was on one of these mid winter shooting trips in early December that my father managed to steal up a flock of wild geese that had landed on a bare piece of wet meadow hilltop. Before he was in close range the geese took flight but portion of the flock flew directly over where we lay behind a low sod bank. My father using his shotgun which had a set of 32 inch barrels with one full choke managed to shoot two large geese. Wild goose was a one in ten year shot and it was like a second Christmas or to be more precise a second little Christmas.

At that time most farmers reared both bronzed turkeys and geese in addition to the normal domestic flock of hens and ducks. At Christmas a bronze turkey hen of 10 to 14lbs was cooked for the Christmas dinner while a large goose of 8 to 10lbs was cooked for Little Christmas on the 6th of January. So to have two wild geese in December was like having an early Little Christmas and was a very welcome relief from eating the home cured salty bacon.

Each day I kept a lookout for any more wild geese and to my delight at about dinner time on a snowy winter's day one week later another flock of wild geese had landed on the hill in the wet meadow. This time Johnny who had been foddering the cows with pulped turnips, cotton cake and hay dropped the hay fork as if it was red hot and disappeared into his room. He re-emerged carrying his shotgun wearing his heavy raincoat a pair of heavy leather boots with the tops of old wellingtons cut into leggings which came down over the bottoms of his trousers which he had stuffed inside his heavy wool socks. His heavy rain coat which had seen better days was kept tight around his waist by an old leather belt and his own cartridges belt which he had pulled to the last notch in a vain effort to keep himself warm from the snow and east wind.It was a very cold wet sleety-snowy evening and Johnny was fully aware of the torture that lay ahead of him if he was to creep up on a flock of geese in these conditions. His hands were covered by a pair of old socks and under his hat he had tied a scarf over his head and down over his ears with the end pushed inside his raincoat. As it would soon be dark there was no time to lose and I volunteered to finish foddering the cows and the last I saw of Johnny was of him disappearing into the grey sleety snow on his way to try and shoot the geese.

Johnny knew that if he was to have any chance of shooting the geese he needed to be in position before it got to dark. He arrived at the tillage field adjoining the wet hill meadow where the wild geese had landed after half an hour of hard walking. First he had to locate the flock in the 10acre field, portion of which consisted of a round bare hill surrounded by wet slopes which on that evening were covered by a mixture of snow and slush as it melted in the water coming off the hill. Once he left the tillage field he would have to break cover and as it was at least 300 yards from the boundary fence to where the geese were on the top of the hill he knew he would have to crawl on his hands and knees over the wet rough ground using the line of three low sod banks which were part of this large field. In the field were two ponies and seven cattle which had been foddered earlier that day with hay and turnips at a feeding trough half way up the hill.

All this was taken into account by Johnny before he started his approach to the goose flock. He slipped into the field by crawling on his hands and knees through a small gap in the boundary fence. Once in the field he lay in the wet snow opened the shotgun and inserted two number five cartridges into the barrels and closed the gun with the safety catch on. As he crawled through the wet snow his leggings filled with snow as he moved forward. His sock covered hands due to the wet snow felt like lumps of half frozen bone and flesh. Johnny who was in his mid forties and a veteran of many wet cold hunting trips knew that he would have to suffer for his prize He knew that it would be worth it as he visualised himself next Saturday night in Hilda's O' Connells pub with his back to the counter surrounded by both local neighbouring farmers and their workmen as he would relate how with two well placed shots into the middle of the flock as it rose he had brought down four geese. His mind was suddenly jolted back by the searing pain which was now also affecting his toes as the wet cold snow water has managed to find its way down inside his leather boots guided by the leggings which were now acting like a funnel.

Johnny's favourite books were Irish history books, Kit Carson comic books, Frank Buck "Bring Them Back Alive" hunting stories and above all the stories of Cuchulainn and NaFianne What would all his heroes think if he had to give up the pursuit of the wild geese? What would Cuchulainn and NaFianne who lay out for days in the mountain snow while hunting the great fourteen pointer red stag deer think of him if after just one hundred and fifty yards of crawling through snow he was forced to abandon the task because he was not man enough to endure the pain in order to triumph? No! By God he would show them that he too was made of the stuff of heroes and he would press on even though his fingers and toes fell off one by one.

He had cleared two of the low banks by sliding over them down into the wet shallow drains at their upper side facing the hill. His clothes were now soaking in snow water and all his body ached in pain but still he pressed on. The final bank ran at an angle of sixty degrees up the hill on which the two ponies and four of the cattle were standing in the shallow drain at its side. Johnny now crouching down in the drain proceeded to hunt the cattle and ponies forward up the hill. Now he could hear the sentry geese on the outskirts of the flock cackling nervously and he knew he must be within fifty to sixty yards of the flock. All his body ached his toes and fingers must by this stage be frostbitten or have fallen off as he could not feel any of them. He would not give up now and how was he ever going to get centre stage in Hilda O' Connells pub if all he could report was failure. No', No! God help him he had to continue up this hill of Calvary to be redeemed by one great act of courage and hunting skill.

Now looking out between the legs of the two ponies that had stayed in line up the hill he could see the geese. My God there must be two hundred in this flock which had landed and were now within a shot of him. He nudged the ponies forward one more time and keeping as eye out for the sentry geese he could now see that the lead pony was level with four or five of these geese who had lifted their heads high up and begin to cackle nervously. One of the ponies make a little run in the direction of the geese nearest it. Johnny knew that all hell was going to break loose at any second and he left down the gun in the snow and began to take of the wet socks from his hands. Before he had the second sock off there was what seemed like a moment suspended in time before any action can occur or an escape can take place where both prey and quarry become aware of each other. The geese and Johnny came face to face! In an instant, great clouds of wings beat downward, trailing feet lifted off the ground, a great chorus of fright erupted and the geese were airborne. Johnny grabbed the gun in his frozen hands, he is sure he can not miss at this range; he points it at the rising flock of geese. He pulls the trigger, nothing happens; the geese have gone 20 yards he pulls the second trigger nothing happens; in panic he opens the gun to see are there cartridges in the chamber, there are; he closes the gun and the geese are gone 40 yards into the fading light he must fire now or is it to late, again nothing happens why wont the gun fire he looks down in despair to see that the safety catch was on. It is too late the geese are at 50 yards; he fires in desperation both barrels after the departing flock only to be greeted by their seemingly mocking cackling as they depart warm and uninjured into the grey gloom of the gently falling snow.

Now the cold hits him all over his body as if all his senses which were numbed by the effort of stealing up on the geese had all suddenly returned! He was painfully aware he was cold and wet on the side of a snowy hill over two miles from the warm farmhouse with nothing but failure to report and no wild geese to carry home.

My mother was just approaching the kitchen table with a pan full of salty home cured bacon which she was about to divide between me and my brothers and father all of whom had finished their farm work for the day and at 6pm were glad like the cows to be in out of the weather for the night. The kitchen door opened and Johnny who was a large man stood like a grizzly bear covered in a mixture of clay and brown snow from which sprouted twigs of the fences he had crawled through and bits of grass and hay which had gone down inside his coat and boot leggings. My mother never broke her stride she handed him a towel to dry and clean the barrels of the shot gun which had the same status as a horse after a day's work which had to be bedded and fed before you could eat, so a true huntsman would clean and dry his gun before he removed his wet clothes.

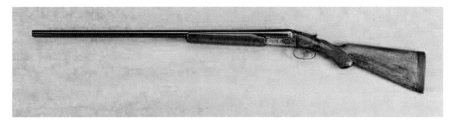

Johnny disappeared into his room and after about half an hour resurfaced in his Sunday clothes clutching his wet boots and clothes held out at arms lengths which were spread out over the frame above the cooker so that he would be able to tog out again in the morning for work. Turning towards us all in the kitchen Johnny told how he had been so close to the flock that he would have shot at least four geese from the flock had things gone to plan. The details of snow, mud. Ponies and cattle together with how his will power had overcome the terrible numbing cold in his hands and feet was told with pride as he crawled through the snow.

There was a silence when he had finished for about two seconds. Then remembering how a half an hour before the picture of Johnny appearing like a grizzly bear covered in brown and white snow was too much to hold in and I started to giggle and as if on cue everyone fell around the kitchen laughing.

That was my fatal mistake, and only a short time would pass before Johnny had the last laugh.

About a week later after three days of heavy rain I was foddering the cows with hay turnips and cotton cake meal. Johnny comes into the yard with a tumbling cart pulled by one of the large draft horses which was full of yellow globe mangolds which he proceeded to trip up against the end of a large pit of mangolds in the yard which was covered with a large sheet of stitched jute manure sacks. I go to the cow house door to salute him and he tells me that on his way down from the tillage fields he saw a wild goose in the island field.

As I now fancy myself as a good shot and I ask Johnny for the loan of his point 22 rifle and a few bullets. He agrees and in less than no time I am cutting access the field at the back of the house towards the island field. I crouch down and there sure enough is a single large goose out in the middle of the field. The middle of the field is like a lake after the heavy rain and in the middle of the lake sits the goose. I take a bullet from the box and pull back the bolt. I can smell the three- in- one oil on my fingers as I insert the bullet and cock the rifle by pulling back the bolt and then push it forward and clamp it down in the firing position. I place the barrel on the lowest bar of the gate of the field lying flat on my stomach to keep out of sight of the goose. I fire and to my amazement all the goose does is to stand up raise his head and open his wings out full span on both sides of his body and then settle back on the small lake. I quickly load again and taking careful aim I fire again. This time the goose stands up and it slowly falls over on its side. I have done it; I have shot the wild goose.

I run forward into the water and pick it up and to my delight the goose is far heavier than I expected, it must be nearly 10lbs in weight. My father, brothers and Johnny are busy in the farmyard when I make my dramatic entrance through the gate from the field adjoining the yard. Everyone gathers round and I proudly tell my story of how I shot the goose.

My father says nothing until I was finished and then leaning forward he picks up the goose by one leg holds it up and informs me that I have just shot Jack Moloughney's Christmas Goose which he had been fattening on boiled potatoes and meal. The goose had come down in the flood and Johnny had set me up. Johnny was back to his old self after that because the next morning as I went out to milk the cows he was marching up the middle of the farmyard with a fork of hay on his shoulder singing "The Wild Colonial Boy."

And I knew my goose was cooked.

"Go On"

By Anthony O'Malley Daly

The Erne Estuary, known as the channel, was full of Salmon from the year dot. Every year fishermen arrived from Inver, St John's Point, Doorin, Bundoran, and Ballyshannon to fish with draft nets from March until September when I was beating the backside of myself crossing the old bridge, making out to be Hopalong Cassidy or Gene Autry and in my bare feet too...

There were fishermen in small flat-bottomed boats, tourists or anglers, fly fishing every available space on land or water. The run of Salmon was unequalled in the whole wide world. The Salmon could be seen jumping Assaroe Falls in their thousands. I took no heed of them. I was the cowboy on the white horse.

When we got bigger, we too went fishing. There were tons of fish for the angler and the net, for commercial use and for fishermen. When we were living in Bishop Street, we used to go into the houses on the south side. June, July and August saw the point-men arrive with their nets, boats and their fishing gear. Their draft nets were made of hemp, which was like cord, but that didn't matter so much as the net was used for surrounding the Salmon quickly and then hauling the catch to the shore. There was plenty for everybody from Belleek, down the river, and up the river, from Cliff right down the River Erne, under the old bridge and the famous falls at the mall quay, round by the Laundry, Port Na Mara, from Gibby across to Black Point...

Then you had the channel, which was where the netting took place. The punts were crewed by five men, four at a pinch. The best time for netting was the last quarter of the ebb tide, the slack, then the first quarter of the incoming tide. There were a number of poles. One was the south pole the other was the north pole, and you were not supposed to shoot the nets below these marker poles. There were two other poles further back. They were set to indicate to the skipper and crew that the next boat could put out his net once the previous boat had reached that pole.

First shot at the limit was the best shot, and the south side was the better side. What usually happened was the boats would made their way down to the limit with the ebbing tide. They would shoot off their net because they would have been out on half-net, with the bud on shore holding the back rope and keeping his eyes wide open into the body of the net and as much of the area as he could see. The half-net would also be held up gently by the man who shot the net, usually the skipper. Three oarsmen made up the five – sometimes two was adequate. They were pulling on the oars to keep the boat and the net fishing properly.

When the boats reached the limit, they shot off the net and boarded it. Sometimes it was first-come-first-served. Mostly it was by rota, as the first boat at the limit went to the back of the queue and worked his way up again. Whoever had the first shot at the limit put out his net when the tide was slack, and then when the tide turned and started to flow in, the net and the boat began to move back. The men on the oars rowed to keep the boat from falling back until a Salmon showed or hit the net. Sometimes a Salmon would show or jump too far down from where they had a chance of catching a run, and the next in line was preparing to shoot off round the Salmon. Suddenly, a Salmon would show, or plough, or touch the net gently, just dipping the corks, and all hell breaks loose.

"Go On!" the bud starts shouting, flapping the rope. The net starts to come out fast, the oars start straining full speed ahead. You hit the beach running, because every second counts. The bud is already coming to meet the rest of the crew. He hands over one of the ropes, and hauling the net begins. The Salmon can do many things, he can jump or hit the net or he can stay still, everyone is giving orders.

The poet William Allingham wrote, "...a silver shoal of Salmon rolls in among the crew," which used to be the case, but sadly not any more. There are no Erne Salmon left. There will be no nets on the channel. Two small but powerful words were shouted by the bud, the man on the net, by anybody who could see a Salmon within catching distance. But *"Go On"* is now extinct. When *"Go On"* was shouted, all hell broke loose. Now *"Go On"* is only a memory.

I was chairman of the Erne Estuary Salmon Fishermen's Association from 21st January 1986 until 16th November 2001. At a meeting prior to our season starting, we got a letter from the Northern Regional Fisheries Board. In effect the Board said that there were no Salmon left in the channel. There was a pause, then up stands one man and utters, "Well, I am going down to get my F****** share out of it."

Largest Sea Trout

by Paddy Clancy

The largest sea trout in the ocean off Ireland has been landed in Co. Donegal.

John Cunningham, of Killybegs, hauled an 11 lbs 1 oz whopper, more than five times the average sea trout in Ireland, from the shore off the Erne estuary in Ballyshannon, Co. Donegal.

A record Irish sea trout, 16 lbs 6 oz, was landed in the Shimna river in Co. Down in 1983, but 48-year-old John reckons his is the biggest one caught at sea, instead of inland in the rivers and lakes.

The trophy trout will be officially branded a specimen fish by the Irish Specimen Fish Committee.

For a sea trout to become a specimen it must weigh over six lbs. Most sea trout caught in Irish waters weigh an average two lbs.

Sea trout visit inland lakes and rivers to spawn and then return to the ocean.

John, a father of four, said the 72-centimetre fish was the catch of a lifetime for him. His prize sea trout was caught at the edge of the Atlantic within sight of old Wardstown Castle outside Ballyshannon.

John said most of the fishermen in the estuary use sand eels as bait for sea trout but he used the white belly of a mackerel and fished with a long beach caster rod.

It took him up to eight minutes to land the fish after hooking it

Size Matters: 58lb Salmon

By Tara McCauley

Tara McCauley is my niece. My Sister, Fidelma, is a nurse. She is 4th (fourth) in line as far as age goes, but I am not telling you her years on this Earth, for there would be a rumpus.

Her name is now Murchie, so you can tell more about her. However, the salmon was caught by her daughter Tara, who is a nurse too. They all reside in Vancouver. The salmon story is a delight to have in my Book. And with all the stories, they all have a "between the lines message."

A couple of years ago I was invited as a guest to go to a floating fishing lodge off the coast of British Columbia. It was at a place called River's Inlet. The lodge was a floating lodge, and I was with a friend and her Mom and Dad.

It was August long weekend here in BC, it was a hot August and apparently the fishing at the lodge had been terrible as the water was very warm, so the salmon were very deep down.

I have enjoyed trout fishing over the years but have never fished for salmon, especially in a little boat in the ocean.

I was the only other female at this lodge besides my friend's Mom. They all knew her as she and her husband were there every year, and she is quite the fisher-woman by what everyone had told me.

On our second morning there, the owner's son decided to take us out in his boat, as he heard it was my first time there. We woke up and headed out at 4:30 am on his boat. After getting to our spot, he set up all the rods and said that the first bite would belong to me. It didn't take long before we got a bite and they all yelled "Keep the tip up!" "Palm the reel!" "Let out the line!" We basically started following the line with boats around us getting out of the way and pulling in their lines.

As the fight continued, the owner's son started saying "It's a monster!" My arms were getting really tired, as was my back and neck. I needed help from the people around me to hold the tip of my rod up, but I held on! It took 45 minutes, and then we saw the salmon. Someone got out the net. We got him in the net and then he got out. The next try we got him in the boat, and thank God, as the hook had come out – so if he had jumped again we would have lost him. I had never salmon fished and had no idea about size. But by the remarks of everyone around me and people on boats nearby I started to realise what a catch this was.

We made our way back to the lodge where I received my "Blackgold Lodge Tyee Club" hat and pin, and we weighed my fish. It was a spring salmon weighing 58 lbs!! I was asked to pose for pictures with my catch so they could use the picture on their website and brochures because it would help bring more women up fishing.

As we walked back to our cabin it really started to sink in what I had caught. Needless to say, none of the fishermen at the lodge were very happy to hear me excitedly tell my tale since they had all paid for an expensive weekend away fishing and had nothing to show for it. I decided I had better keep my story for when I came home.

I received a free trip back to the lodge as I had caught the biggest fish there all season.

The best thing about my fishing story is that I can tell it everyday and it never gets old!! I have my own business and have quite a few clients that reside in longterm care facilities. Most have Alzheimer's Disease. I bring in the picture of my fish whenever I want, and it's always a new and exciting story! Although the nurses and staff are sick of seeing my fish picture over and over again!

Sea Trout Fishing

by Harry Lloyd

Injun Joe

Towards estuary mouth, under sand-dunes, with sand eel in tow we go.

The curlew calls, the swans glide by with redshank and tern quick stepping away.

Overhead the seagulls glide on windy wings; cormorant and seals poke their heads above the   waves observing the oilskin-clad intruders.

Under salty waves sea trout are prey and predator in a watery world of mammal and fish.

All are fishing; all are waiting for a catch.

In shock he's caught by an imitating foe that has infiltrated into the shoal of his sustenance.

Now fishing will continue but without him.

10,000 (Ten Thousand) Salmon

By Anthony O'Malley Daly

Do you keep a record of how many Salmon you catch, and just how many you have landed? Do you keep a record from season to season, and maybe each year to add up to your "lifetime" total?

The mention of 10,00 Salmon in modern day reckoning is a lot of fish. To have it said that 10,000 Salmon were caught commercially would be amazing, but to think of so many Salmon landed by rod and line would be absolutely astonishing.

And further, If I were to tell you that just such a total of Salmon were caught by just one man, then your amazement would be off the board with astonishment.

Well, it's true. One Robert Pashley who fished the river Wye for almost 50 years until his death in 1956, actually landed and recorded 10,237 Salmon – his lifetime total for his endeavours. The rest of us pale by comparison. The river Wye rises in the mountains of Wales, and from what I can gather, crosses an English shire before entering the wide expanse of the Bristol Channel below the racecourse town of Chepstow.

Robert Pashley kept a daily record of his catches. He used an ordinary outfit, and mostly he fished the Fly, but his time consuming persistence and skill netted him what must be a world record, even by those plentiful days. In 1926 he caught 535 Salmon, 1931, 354; 1933, 461; and 1935, 326 until in 1936 he recorded a Salmon catch of 678 for his season. In one week in 1936, Robert's daily totals of 11, 8, 14, 10, 11, 12, and 9 summed up to a grand total of 75 Salmon.

The largest Salmon Robert Pashley recorded was one of 48 1/2 lbs, but he had many fish over the 40 lbs mark, all species. Have you had enough? One last statistic: the 10,000 Salmon landed were calculated to weigh 65 tons. Such an angler and such a river, and it has to be said that while the mortal Robert Pashley has crossed the river, the Wye is still producing Salmon.

Injun Joe

Ten-Year-Olds Go Fishing

by Micheal O'Brien

It was a long journey for the ten-year-olds. For John Likely and I (inseparable friends), one bicycle was the mode of transport.

Me pedalling and John on the Bar, we went out the Knather Road – the back road between Ballyshannon and Belleek past the Hydro Electric Dam (which in my opinion destroyed the fishing in Ballyshannon). Our destination was a Bamboo Grove growing three miles or so out the road on land owned by a man named Doctor Delap from Belleek. Nobody seems to know where this Bamboo originated from, but we didn't care where it came from, as it was our source of material for making fishing rods.

It was a beautiful day close to Bonfire Night. We had spent the previous week gathering fuel for the bonfire which was held in the Fair Green in Ballyshannon each year on the 23rd. That is when we decided to go out to the grove.

I was exhausted by the time we got there, as the chain was coming off the sprocket and the pedal was loose. We were armed with small hacksaws which we borrowed from our fathers' workshops.

We got off our bicycle and went into the wood of bamboo. We were amazed with the sight that met us. It was like being in the Jungle, but there were fishing rods here to no end. We had a large selection to choose from, long and short, big and small, all there right in front of us. We spent some time selecting our material and then started to cut the rods we needed. We cut 20 straight bamboo cane rods perfect for fishing. We tied the rods to the bicycle and headed for home.

The next destination was my mother's sewing box which was like a gold treasure chest to me. It was full of safety pins which made perfect eyes for our rods. We cut them in two and secured them with thread we found in the sewing box.

The next stop was P.J. Fox's fishing tackle shop on Main Street which of course was filled with fishing rods of all descriptions which we couldn't afford (but weren't nearly as good as as the ones we had just made ourselves). We bought a roll of gut, a selection of hooks and two cheap reels. We came back home after our large purchase. We got two tin boxes to hold the tackle and two jam jars to hold worms. We melted down lead pipe for weights. We tied string on the neck of the jars for carrying them. We were two well-equipped anglers, ready for action.

The next destination was our back garden and armed with garden grapes we started to dig for worms, we unearthed dozens of big fat black-headed ones which are perfect bait for all types of fish. We put them in jam jars with some clay to keep them fresh.

Next morning John arrives at our house at 7am. We headed off walking out Bundoran road, past Myles shop and took the steps to the right which led down to the river. We arrived at Port Na Mara, which is on the south side of the river Erne beside Inis Saimer. The tide was coming in, so it was time to bait our hooks and cast out.

The smell of freshly baked bread coming from the Ballyshannon bakery across the river in the Mall was making us hungry as we didn't have any breakfast. The church clock chimed at seven thirty, two swans swam past with five chicks following close behind, the trout were going "plop plop plop," a salmon jumped in the distance, a perfect morning for fishing. We cast out our hooks baited with the big fat wriggly worms we had with us. We were after fluke or flat fish as big as soup plates and as tasty as cod. (We weren't interested in salmon or trout). The sun was beaming down, the water was rippling past, we were eating sandwiches we had packed the night before. We felt like we were in heaven.

Oh my God, What will my mother do when she sees my bed empty and reads my note saying *I have gone fishing?*

NOTE: Micheal O'Brien was a great friend of mine. He could compose a song on local events "At The Drop Of A Hat – yes, a Hanna Hat."

The O'Briens are our neighbours. They were and remain the best of Good Shepherds when we came to College Street.

Micheal O'Brien, Sr, the father; Mrs O'Brien, mother; Sister Kathleen; Margaret, teacher; and Murette, office worker, Dublin, have all passed away. Micheal's sudden death, February 2012, leaves us with "A Gap" that is hard to seal... Still good neighbours, still goods friends, Semper.

The Bag Net

By Anthony O'Malley Daly

Yes, the shares over the years, got smaller and smaller, but the crews, turned out, year after year, season after season, and why? They loved the Channel, and the nights down at the dunes, looking at the lights of Ballyshannon, the Oldest Town in Ireland. Waiting, hope against hope, that the words "Go On" would ring out, just one more time, with feeling.

It has been a long time, since any amount of salmon rolled in into captivity, either in the Channel, or outside. During 1968, when an enormous run of salmon did roll in among the crews, especially, in the Channel, we all took to draft net fishing, and with the introduction of the "Bag Net," a completely New Era in Salmon Fishing burst onto the scene. 1969 onwards, was the beginning, and the start of the end for Salmon Fishing on the once mighty Erne............

The Bag Net had been introduced to the shores of Donegal by a Ballyshannon man who fished it off Mullaghmore. At least that was the rumour. So when a "Gush" of salmon really did roll among the crews, the "Fish Rush" got up in earnest. Men who had never gone down the Channel or wet a line suddenly had some place to go to. There were so many boats on the Channel that the rules had to be enforced. The Bag Net was illegal, but the new net was making its way around the coasts. I invested in a bag net, and bought sheets of drift net, 35 mesh deep, from a small man who had a net shop in Ardara.

My next door neighbour, Derek Doyle, had a half-decker, and we headed off for Arranmore Island. Denis McGuinness, another neighbour, came up to the Island at week-ends. Margaret, Derek's wife, visited us to clean out the caravan we lived in. We were assisted by Charles Gallagher, and by his Mother and Father, and another sister. Derek was fearless, and I was put to the pin of my collar to keep up with him.

Derek had the half-decker which he had purchased a few weeks previous when we went to Rosbeg to "seal the deal." The vendor produced a bottle of whiskey, when we started to deal, "slapping hands," and taking "slugs" of the "raw" whiskey, which made the deal for Derek. After the deal was "clinched," the vendor (well known in Ardara, but dead now) did handstands and other acrobatics before we took off at speed, in the general direction of Ballyshannon. I don't know how the half-decker made its way to Ballintra (yes, *Ballintra*) on Arranmore Island, but I remember it going by sea, and both of us nearly drowning as we tried to tie up Derek's "Pride and Joy" (the half-decker) when we arrived there.

I had about 2000 yards of nylon drift nets, all in one piece, 35 mesh deep. My friends Darby McGroarty and Owen Coyle (both dead now) had hung the nets in my backyard, and taught me the skill of tying on the corks, the back rope, and the lead on the bottom of the net, the sole rope. Later we used nylon net, which meant we had to go out at night, put out our net at dusk, lie down, drift for a few hours, arise, put our noses above the gunwale, pull in the net, take the salmon out of the net. If it was a calm night, we got nothing, but if there was a sea running or a "jobble" (getting rough), the salmon would be bogged in the top of the net, at the back rope, next to the corks. We were moderately successful. Later, drift nets were made of monofilament or clear gut, and the fishermen could put out the net in any kind of sea or weather, but that was not in our time.

We worked very hard. Sometimes, with the volume of boats out in the briney, we got "tided," which was when another boat shot in front of us, close to us, and he got the salmon while we got nothing.

Both of us stayed on the Island until the season ended (in a Caravan). When we got our payment from the Co-Op, it was small indeed. That convinced me (and us) that drift netting was not for me.

Behind the Wheel

By Ruth Swan

Ruth Swan is the daughter of Scott Swan. The Swan family controlled the fishing in Ballyshannon and in Donegal Town. Scott Swan was the brother of Tom Swan.

One day there was a group of fishermen who arrived at the car parking area on the avenue. My Dad was talking to them and suggesting the best places to try for salmon. It was then that the fishermen realised that they did not have a landing-net suitable for salmon.

My Dad turned to my sister Diana, who was about eight years old, and suggested that she run up to the house and bring back a salmon landing-net. The fishermen were horrified at the idea of this little girl running half a mile to the house to get the net and bring it back to them. But then my Dad handed Diana the keys of the car, and she jumped in and sorted herself so that she could see over, or maybe through, the steering wheel. Off she went in full control of the Hillman Minx, returning about fifteen minutes later with the net!

As a family, we all learned to drive at a very early age, either on a tractor, a motor bike, or a car.

North Channel Wrecks

By Anthony O'Malley Daly

A sequel to my story about the wreck "*Athenia*" was provided by Mrs. Patricia O'Reilly, Station Road, Ballyshannon who contacted me to tell me that an Uncle went down with the *Athenia*, which was torpedoed on September 3rd, 1939. His name was John Keown, Roscor, Belleek, Co Fermanagh, and he was the cook aboard the "*Athenia*."

According to Mrs. O'Reilly, all hands were lost in this sinking during the Second World War. A shark had followed the "*Athenia*" when it left port in Scotland for the journey across the very dangerous waters of the North Atlantic, hunted as they were by German U-boats in packs on the day the war broke out. John Keown left behind a grieving widow and three children.

Mrs. O'Reilly had hoped to get a piece of the wreck as tangible memory of her late uncle. However, on speaking to Des Mills, it appears that the wreck of the "*Athenia*" lies some hundred miles west of the original "*Athenia*." I find it strange that there were two ships named the "*Athenia*," and both went down in two world wars. Des Mills indicated that in the second sinking there were some survivors.

I thank Patricia O'Reilly for the sad memory, and Des Mills from Culdaff for the information. Both ships are cradled in the deep, providing wreck fishing for recreational sport anglers, who little know the grief locked in the hulls of the two "*Athenia*," and the pain left in our hearts of the mourning families ashore.

Author's Note: The crews who manned those merchant ships were the bravest of the brave. When the war broke out, the merchantmen crossed the Atlantic in convoys that were prey for the German u-boats. The vessels were mostly Liberty ships and wrecks that were past their prime. However, these brave sailors ventured in convoys. Many of them were torpedoed as soon as they crossed the tide out of the harbour. Their escorts could not give them the protection needed. The old ships broke down, and the convoys had to keep going. How they kept their sanity and kept Britain supplied with food is nothing short of a miracle. Some of the convoys in the early years took 90% casualties. In addition, when these brave men took shore leave, they were attacked by soldiers because they wore no uniforms.

The northwest passage is confirmed as the world's merchant ship graveyard.

Brief History of Creevy & District Community Development Co-operative Society Ltd.

By Molly Reynolds

The destruction of Creevy Pier in an Atlantic Hurricane in the February 1986 was followed by the drowning of three local young married men in August 1988. These were Eddie Donagher and his first cousins, brothers Brendan and Thomas Patton. The search lasted 3 weeks and everybody was traumatized, not to mind, these families who lost their husbands, fathers, sons, brothers, etc. These incidents combined with other local issues lead to the subsequent battle to have the Pier and access road re-instated, so there would always be a safe anchorage for anybody at sea in the locality and led to a group of locals organising themselves to lobby for financial support. Thanks mainly to the good offices of Pat the Cope and some others, a small amount of finance was provided and with voluntary effort and labour this was finally achieved and the pier was back and could again be used for seafaring but also by the hoards of local Ballyshannon people, young and old who see Creevy as their playground, especially when the sun shines favourably on us and many tales of daring emanate from their diving off the nose of the pier, swimming, fishing and just relaxing in a glorious unspoiled location full of character, fresh air and tranquility.

One man featured big in this drive, the now, sorely lamented, Seamus Goan, RIP. had returned with his wife Ita to a small cottage, he had inherited, where his father was born in Cloughbolie; his mother nee Daly was from neighboring Kildoney townland and specifically "the Hill".

Having being with other member of his family involved in community work in Belfast when conditions for many of the population there was far from ideal, and having fought long and hard for help and assistance, for that community's rights and a better quality of life, he was well versed in knowing that people must organize themselves to achieve anything in this life.

Following the restoration of this centuries old facility, Bun a tSruthan Pier, the local community activists went on to form a group who met regularly, brainstormed, argued, trained and finally "Creevy Co-op" was registered in 1995 and Seamus was one of the dedicated bunch who were convinced we could do more to help ourselves and maximize on what this wonderful little corner of Donegal had to offer, while maintaining the local ethos. We sold shares and between voluntary work from many willing souls and some small grant aid we started the Creevy & District Community Development Co-operative Society Ltd. Another to whom great credit must go in those early years is Kevin O'Connor, who facilitated us with a meeting place and willing support.

As part of the initial Business Plan we created a ten mile Shore Walk, between the "foot of the road" on the Erne Estuary and Rossnowlagh with the goodwill and support of local landowners, and I am proud to say that to this day this wonderful scenic walk is much used and loved by many who, thankfully, continue to use it daily but do respect the freedom to so do is with the goodwill of said landowners.

We provided a Deep-Sea Angling & Sightseeing Charter Boat, commissioned and built in Kinsale and launched by President Mary McAleese on a glorious day in Creevy 31st July 1999.

An idea was researched and we restored derelict cottages to let as Self-Catering, complete with Angling facilities to Failte Ireland 4* standard with disabled access, later these were the first in Ireland to qualify for EU Flower standard, a recognized standard in environmental awareness and preservation, and we have literally had visitors from all continents and many return regularly to enjoy the Creevy Experience in these unique "olde world" cottages where we have managed to retain the rustic charm combined with all modern facilities discreetly, in their original locations, even retaining the names of the previous residents.

The first sign of success was when Donegal Local Development Company awarded their only ever Prize for Innovation in 1997. The following year FAS also honoured us for Innovation and Enterprise. We also were recipients of AIB's "Better Ireland Awards" and Teagasc / Farmers Journal Rural Tourism awards in subsequent years. There have been many more over the years.

The original plan included a Boat House to be made available nearby Creevy Pier on land previously part of the Goan property but donated by Malachy Daly & Family, as a base for Deep-Sea Angling, Diving and Sight-Seeing Charters, boat storage and maintenance and all seafaring and allied leisure activities. This was achieved in 2011 just a couple of weeks before Ita Goan RIP passed to her eternal reward, when this building was dedicated to Seamus' memory and a tree planted. As I write the final touches are being put to this so that it will henceforth be the headquarters for the Co-op, with meeting room, offices and other facilities to add to the mix that is Creevy Co-op and the Creevy Experience.

As one of the founding members and first Manager I provided a base at my home in Creevy until my retirement, a few years ago, since then the office is located in town which is not ideal so I look forward to the day it is, once and for all, as near to being under the one roof as possible given the type of operation it is.

Injun Joe

Anthony O'Malley Daly became a shareholder and valued member of our Committee through the good offices of his great friend, Seamus Goan and both have contributed much to life, but Anthony's guts and sheer determination know no bounds and what he has achieved in later years despite much adversity due to declining health has been an inspiration for many. I wish him nothing but the best with his latest efforts in publishing this book. God Speed.

It would be remiss of me not to acknowledge the support of many funders over the years, starting with International Fund for Ireland, FAS, Peace & Reconciliation, and Donegal Local Development Co. with which I have had a long and fruitful association having served as Board Director for approx. 15 years and most of that as Company Secretary. Through my work in Creevy and elsewhere I have been very aware of the needs and concerns of the community of the Northwest of Ireland and have been pleased to give of my time in setting up various organisation and serving on the Board of many of them, which I still do to the best of my ability. I have learned from many good people over the years and hope I have contributed something that will benefit greater Iniatives in the future. We must live in hope.

Molly Reynolds
www.creevyexperience.com

To Our Unforgettable Friend Anthony

Congratulations and Best wishes from your Coarse Fishing Friends from Manchester

John Fletcher
Michael Fletcher
Harry Halsall
Tommy Cribben
and the whole crew

Was It the Major? R.I.P.

By Anthony O'Malley Daly

It's well known, and well worn in fishing circles, that the biggest one gets away, and the monster fish that have won in struggle with anglers are legion and indeed legend, so by the way of a change this is a true story of a big Salmon that was hooked, held, and hauled in – more is the pity, almost!

In my early teens when I wanted to be Hopalong Cassidy because I never saw him doing algebra. And when I was a country Irish lad thinking I was a "Great Fella," the first into long pants, the great pleasure, apart from the cinema, was rambling to the country houses dotted around our famous fishing lake called The Loch. Whist drives, 25-card drives and even a shaky hand of poker or pontoon were mainly popular, with chickens and turkeys as prizes, not forgetting a wee drop of poteen, taken from the turf stack, to put a bit of zump into your Irish dancing, and talk about singers and songs - will ye stop! - verse 56 was nothing out of the ordinary. Then as the night wore on we would all gather about a heaped glowing turf fire and listen to a local sage telling stories.

Most of the stories were sinister and ghostly, like evil neighbours in the past "stealing the butter" or ruining another farmers' crops by witchery, too vivid. I remember haring home as fast as my legs could carry me right along the middle of the country road with all the mad dogs of Hell snapping at my heels. However, the tale I recall for now concerned the Major.

The Major was a retired military gentleman, a keen fisherman, and close friend of the landlord of that era that owned The Loch and all the countryside thereabouts. The Major spent his ageing years visiting for the fishing, and sharing his tobacco throughout the locality. Sure before the end came he was almost a local. His love for The Loch was great, and when the poor man passed away his last request was that his ashes, for he took cremation, be distributed over The Loch – the beautiful haven during the twilight of his life.

Now Sam McGee from Tennessee had a similar request granted, and a man's last request is surely sacred, but the country folk, his friends, were just more than a little disturbed when a small aeroplane scattered the Major far and separate around The Loch. They had sort of expected the Major, their friend, to go to his final resting place in the little estate churchyard overlooking The Loch. His last repose there would have been serene, with a lovely view of the mountains, and he'd be close to the spot where The Loch feeds the river to hear the the spiritful splash of the Spring Salmon. About him would grow the mayflower, sprinkled with dew and sparkling in the fresh early morn, or that profuse gypsy flower the daffodil. And even in the wintertime someone visiting the church would keep the weeds away and his memory fresh. But when the Major allowed himself to be scattered, the folk could frankly not see him getting much rest. The wise ones said there would be happenings.

Since that fateful day, down the years, the manifestations attributed to being the searching restless Major were many – a monster cannibal fish that had menaced cattle and sheep along the shoreline – a huge hound that late-night travellers had seen about The Loch and mountainside with sparks coming from its tail as it wagged (indication of friendliness, but none had waited to be licked). And, most sinister, footprints coming out of The Loch in the dead of winter that had burned through the hard snow and ice (suggestions of someone backing up into The Loch discounted). Many a prayer was sent upwards for the poor man to be granted a compact final resting place.

One evening in the late season a few years back I took a friend, John, onto The Loch for a spot of fishing. As I rowed to the best area, The Loch was so calm it resembled a sheet of glass. Tired birds were gliding to the tree tops of a small island, a tractor was labouring in a distant field to win a late crop for its owner, and I could see why the Major and others had found a lifetime of happiness and tranquillity here. The only chance of a fish was to put the rods out at the back of the boat and do a slow, deep troll down the centre of The Loch.

Going down we spoke in subdued tones, the calmness and quiet was so marked. Suddenly I pierced the stillness and John jerked in fright - "You're in a fish!" was the shout. The rod was bent and tugging, the gut was screaming as it paid out under tension. John grabbed up the rod, I reeled in the other, and the battle began. The Salmon didn't show for a while, but moved strongly about deep down as if thinking the action to take. Swiftly then he shot to the surface and broke angrily, fully twice his shinning length into the air, only to crash writhing, like those early rocket attempts, back into the water again. I said he was surely a 20 pounder, but John said he felt Moby Dick as his arms ached under the campaign, and so the struggle continued with me having to relieve John with the near cramp he took. A show of spirit induces admiration, and this Salmon gained our respect as he leafed every trick in the book – furious jump, gut snapping roll, running deep for rock or weed, and diving under the boat – but he was well hooked, expertly held, and after nearly an hour was hauled into the boat and dispatched on the road to the salad.

It was with pride that we gazed at the biggest Salmon either of us had seen taken from The Loch as I pulled for the jetty. All was quiet again and yet, oddly some new sound was reaching my ears, and John felt the same, I stopped rowing and listened – breathing! Well I was breathing and John was breathing too, but another was breathing just didn't fit. "Am I hearing things?" I said. "Like breathing or something?" replied John. Then something did click inside me that said - *The Major?* I must have paled like a white loaf because John's mouth fell open as he watched me. Our eyes forced our heads around to look at the fish which I picked up reverently and placed on the seat between us - Believe me or believe me not, if I never have another hot dinner, the Salmon, The Major, the anybody, your man was breathing – No! – *gasping* more, but even and distinct, and him as stiff as a poker so I couldn't throw him back. I don't know how long we stared numbed, listening to the breathing, but eventually I was rowing again towards the jetty. The complexion of all things had changed - the mountains seemed as the bows of a supertanker hurtling upon us to destroy us, the birds on the island were all watching us - a thousand eyes focussed as one hypnotic stabbing glare. The silence was such it equalled a howling gale, and if Alfred Hitchcock had turned the island carrying a 'cello or walking some poodles upon the water, the drama would have been completed. And I would have not been surprised.

When the boat touched the jetty, the breathing had stopped – indeed, I thought my own was faltering a bit too. Anyway and every-way, to make the long and short story – THE MAJOR had a quiet funeral. We buried him deep in the dusk of that calm evening in a nice wee shaded place overlooking the jetty where he will have a good view of the catches and catchers. To tell the truth I couldn't see him in a salad. He'd travelled enough, and after that spirited fight he put up, I reckoned he deserved a long lasting rest-in-peace.

Note: I wrote this story in 1963, when I was the Radio Officer in the Merchant Navy, on board an oil tanker called "The Border Chieftain," entering the Persian Gulf or Arabian Gulf, with orders for Mina Al Amadi, Kuwait. We were going through - "The Gates Of Hell." It was so hot that I fried an egg on the deck.

The editor of the company magazine wrote me saying I had a "great turn of phrase," such as "the Spiritful Splash" of the salmon, and she liked my story. (She was a lady.)

Note: "Stealing The Butter." Farmers used to churn and make country butter, which they took great pride in. So, if a bad neighbour took exception to the good butter being in demand, they used put a "spell" on the butter. When the butter was churned it did not set, and the farmer was humiliated.

Country butter was made, and was in great demand, by housewives who only took the country butter made by the farmer. Some farmers did not have hygienic methods. Country butter tasted a bit salty, which suited some people. My mother would only take country butter from her regular source, Jenny O'Reilly, from Mulleek, near Belleek. If the butter got stale, did not set, had a hair in it or a bad taste, the farmer lost his good reputation. The bad deed done, it ruined many farmers, who stopped churning.

"If You Snooze, You Lose..."

By Billy Grimes

The picture tells the tale. It is a famous 1933 picture. It is of the Grimes family, who fished mainly in Bullia Thomas, the Channel, Ballyshannon. Bullia Thomas was the "shot" before you entered the Abbey Bay, and because the Abbey River runs into the bay it was the last "shot" (shot was where you put out your net). The Grimes family lived close to where they worked (so to speak), and they never had to spend money on travel.

One day, when they were having a bad day, they shot-off their net. Nothing moved as the net was being hauled in. It was only when they about to throw down the last of the net that one of them noticed this big salmon. It was still, as if it was asleep.

The salmon was hit and dispatched before it "woke up." The salmon was alone in the net. The surprise was great. But not when the crew observed the size of the fish. As it turned out the salmon weighted 55 lbs. It was the largest recorded salmon ever landed in the Erne. The Grimes family had to get a special box made for the salmon, by the Gallaghers of Lareen, who worked a timber Mill. It was sold in the Billingsgate Fish Market, London – without even knowing where it came from. So "If You Snooze You Lose"!

1968 was the best year, and before that, and afterwards. the decline of the salmon continued, until now we have reached the "Hell" – that all there is down in the channel is water. The last recorded "fullest net" was taken 1968 when Charlie Gillespie landed 180 salmon at the South Pole. That year 22 boats fished the Channel, and men went "hoarse" shouting, "Go On!" After that it was all downhill.

I Remember a Great Angler

by Charlie O'Doherty

I remember a great angler here, who was always fishing. When not fishing he was telling tall stories.

He hooked a great fish just below the Wooden Bridge. He played the fish for a week. His wife brought him his four meals each day.

When the fish was played out, he started to haul it in. When the fish's head was half way up the river walls, his tail was coming up under the Iron Bridge, a quarter of a mile downstream.

Then the line snapped, and the fish escaped.

He said he didn't know the weight of the biggest fish that he caught. He said that when he pulled it out, the river fell half a metre.

He said he was using a worm soaked in whiskey, and the worm had the fish by the throat.

Charlie O'Doherty
Doherty's Fishing Tackle Shop
Donegal Town
Member of the Eske Anglers Association

Angling Battle

By Anthony O'Malley Daly

This is a story I wrote in 1991 to lift your morale.

Charlie O'Doherty, the well known Eske angler and fishing tackle retailer from Donegal town, is usually watching the trends of the river. When the Eske is ready for fishing and fish arrive, then Charlie is equally ready to head to the river, and search them out – usually with a 4am start.

Anyway, Charlie had been stalking a big Salmon. It had moved upstream to the dam pool, and he spotted it there. Another fisherman came, hooked a Salmon, and landed it, but it was not the big one Charlie was after. Charlie fished on without success, and thinking to give up angling and take up golf. Suddenly he noticed his line going upstream against the flow. Charlie struck, and after 3 days was into his Salmon. This fish did not surface, but went up and down, and over and back. The fish then breached out of the depths and went polaris like into the air. Matters hotted up. The Salmon, held only by a No. 8 hook, left the dam pool, and headed seawards, peeling out Charlie's line. There was nothing for it, so Charlie jumped into the river after the retreating Salmon. The fish took McCauleys's turn at speed, but was held. Next came the rapids called The Carry, and fish and man fought on.

Charlie, clad in full fishing gear and waders, was as game as the Salmon. Both swam beneath the old railway bridge and finally, all hands floundering, and in a heap, into the broad Mill Hole – up to half a mile downstream. Here Charlie got below the Salmon and blocked his exit from the pool. Eventually, the brave and persistent Charlie O'Doherty landed his brave, persistent but exhausted opponent, and the battle was over.

The statistics of the struggle show the Salmon weighed 14 lbs not 34 lbs as the telling of the tale increased it; play lasted from 6 am to 8 am; and Charlie was bruised and sore all over, wet and cold, but proud to have encountered such a Titan. After that, Charlie, how could you take up such a mundane sport as golf? Stick to the fishing.

Injun Joe

The End is Nigh

By Anthony O'Malley Daly

Now is it the End, or the beginning of the End.
Is it the Start of the Finish,
or is it Finished, before it Started?
Maybe it is the End of the Start.
And is it Fatally wounded.
Possibly it was Mortally Wounded.
I Think it was Dead all the while we
were Searching for Life to Stir In It.

After We Searched in Vain.
And We Read the Minutes Of The Last Meeting,
We came to the Conclusion,
That because the Meeting Ended
Without a proposal to End the Meeting,
That the proposal to Start the Meeting was Invalid.
That it was deemed So because,
There were only 4 (four) Fully Paid members,
although there were 5 (five) in attendance.

By The Powers vested in me as Joint Secretary.
I also Hold a second Casting, as Chairman.
Therefore I declare the meeting Invalid.
There is neither an End or a Beginning, A Start or a Finish.
End thus Tuesday And Hold Also,
By The Powers vested in me, Go on Home.
For that is where we all Belong.
Like the World Wars - After all the damage we have "wrought,"
The End is Nigh.

"Pack Up Your Troubles in Your Old Kit Bag,
And Smile, Boys, Smile.
You Had Your Fun,
And, Now is the Time,
The Wolf is at the Door (the Bailiffs),
You Had Your Chance.
The Swans are now an Emigrant Species.
And So are You (Plural),

Good Night Irene, Good Bye Irene...
We, Might see You (Singular),
In Our Dreams, but Every Thing Else
Is Gone, Gone, Gone.

Now is the Time,
To Burn the Boats, the Nets, the LOT.
Go to Bed, Sleep, and Get Used to the
NIGHTMARE / SKIPPER.
(That is All You Have Left.)
P.S. WHO GOT MY F......... SHARE?!!

Alaskan Halibut

By Patrick O'Malley Daly

This story comes from San Francisco, where four intrepid Donegal and Tyrone anglers took a trip of a lifetime when they flew to Anchorage, Alaska. They transferred to a small aircraft. The pilot dropped them off, with rations, at a cabin in the wilds – to fish. Part of their stores was a canister of Mace, to ward off bears – should they (the bears) wish to embrace them.

They shivered at night, fished all day, without success, until Tyroneman Johnny McConnell hooked a monster Halibut. Between fear and excitement, it took the four to land the fish, which weighed 165 lbs. It was the only bite they got. They returned to San Francisco without sighting a single bear.

The Irish record for Halibut is 156 lbs caught in Belmullet, Co Mayo, in 1972.

Super or Supernatural Salmon?

By Anthony O'Malley Daly
Illustrations by Vera Cave

I am a Salmon fisherman, and although I certainly fish for other species, it is the Salmon that arouses the fervour in me. Each year as the season opens I vow that it will be more successful than the previous one. However, despite my efforts, last year was my worst Salmon season ever, but when the 1st of January arrived, away I was again searching for the now exclusive and elusive King of Fish the Salmon.

To catch a Salmon is a great thrill and honour, and I don't just see it as that alone. I see this beautiful and brave water creature struggling against all the elements from the time of his spawning in some turbulent river until he or she arrives back to the same place in the same river to complete one cycle of life and start another.

Because the Salmon is such a vaunted sport fish and also much sought after for the table, he is harried and hunted where ever he goes, and if he had countless predators in the past he has an addition to the chasers in the form of the mink. Man of course is the main hunter, and man too is producing the scourge of pollution, but make sure one thing – if the Salmon ceases to visit our coasts, leap our falls, splash in out lakes, and reproduce in our rivers, then the waters of life will slowly cease too, and man will surely follow into extinction. History tells us of the external wisdom of the Salmon, and the story I have to tell really emphasises this quality, but in the telling of this fishing tale (not fishy, mind you), maybe you too will come to the realisation that somewhere in his run through life, sometime in his struggle for survival, some place out of the great alone, this Salmon encounters the power of the supernatural. Embraced the occult. *Crazy*, you are now saying. Well, you'll see.

Setting and Strike

Of an August Saturday two years ago, I went with old fishing friends John and Edward onto our favourite Lough. I never called this expanse of water anything other than a "Lough" for it has islands, rivers, forests, mountains and a great character about it. The wind was gentle from the west and the sun was getting through the clouds now and again. By the afternoon we had seen one or two Salmon showing and had landed a number of white Trout. John was on the oars. Edward was fishing from the stern and I was casting up front. Our John knew the Lough well, so we were into the best grounds, but no Salmon, and by now it was late in the afternoon.

At this point John said the real killing time was 5pm. He used to say it was 7pm. It was five minutes to five. He began to encourage us to keep casting with intention, and you might say he got us sort of "psyched-up," for we set into our angling with real vigour and confidence. Well, lo and behold, on what seemed the very dot of 5pm didn't Edward get stuck in a very big Salmon. Indeed, I thought I was in a fish myself until the bare flies proved otherwise. In the meantime, Edward was shouting orders to John, and John was using some of his select words reserved for anybody not bending a fly rod in a Salmon or threatening to tumble the boat by standing and tramping about such a fragile craft in excitement.

Struggle

The Salmon headed out into the Lough. "Pull after him!" shouted Edward to John. "Just you keep your rod bent in him.You have tons of line," cautioned John. I was watching the Salmon, and while I was glad to see Edward playing his fish, I had some envy because it was him rather than me.

The three of us ventured our guesses as to the weight of the Salmon was until, after about five minutes' play. he struck the surface and jumped clear out of the water. "A 16 pounder and up a long time," said John, and that was agreed by Edward and myself. Indeed he was up a long time from the sea because he was losing his silvery hue and getting reddish around the body. The way he jumped would win him no prizes for height or grace, such was his bulk, but the splashback was mightily impressive.

Checked my clock; it was 5:15. "Come on, Edward," I said, "He's no way played out – bend the rod in him." I always maintain that an angler should not be afraid to use his rod to the utmost in tiring a Salmon, whether on a river or lake. So the time went on with our Salmon twisting and turning, tugging and running in his vain quest for a freedom that was fast slipping away - or was it?

The time moved to 5:20, then 5:25 and then onto 5:30, until I saw it was 5:45, and the struggle was not over, or even near it. John kept saying what I was beginning to think – "Edward, you're nearly an hour in him, and that time is now on the Salmon's side." He was right because the hook must have been wearing loose with the fish pulling one way and Edward pulling another. "Edward" I said, "keel haul him if you have to, but get him to the side of the boat and I'll net him" You see, I fancied myself a bit with a net – you might say a "netspert" – and I was poised to make the one decisive move as soon as the Salmon came along side.

Edward worked hard on the fish and got him to the boat where he still strained stoutly on the line. "Rise him to the surface, and he'll be in the boat before you know it" said I, and with the rod bending double, Edward slowly began to get the better of the brave Salmon. Up he came, his off-white belly turning towards the surface in final surrender.

I remember saying confidently and deliberately, "I see him," and preparing to dip the net under him for the final swoop. I remember that because John and Edward have told me often enough that this is what I said, but just when I was poised "matador-like" to do my expert thing, a glare of light swiftly split through the high trees from a nearby island, hit the water with the effect of a mirror, and stopped me for a second or two in my tracks. Quickly, my vision returned and, with the line and gut as my guide, I deftly netted the prize in one staggered action and into the boat.

Shock and Supernatural

I don't know how long I stared at what I had in the net, but the harsh words from Edward, as he clamoured across John, restored my senses. "Where's my Salmon? What have you done with my fish?!" And of course, other unprintables followed. I was dumbfounded and unbelieving as I identified and picked up exactly what I had netted - a slimy, water soaked and dripping heavy lump of bark with the golden olive fly embedded in it. John was pop-eyed, and protesting that it wasn't much use him breaking his arms rowing both of us about the Lough for a piece of wood. And Edward - well, he had by now turned crazed customs official, frantically searching and demanding to know where I had hidden his monster Salmon. I tied to reason with him saying that I had not the fish on me or in me, but he was not amused. Indeed, I didn't see anything hilarious in it myself, but I had what I had, and that appeared to be that – or was it?

Edward eventually sat back in the boat staring at me in anger and awful doubt. John started moving again for land. I was left holding a sinister stick which I scrutinised and examined, but no matter how I viewed it, it did not remind me of a Salmon, but only of a branch of a tree too long in water, and covered in a dripping red-brown slime.

Foolishly I asked "What'll I do with it?," and you know the answer.

Art work by Vera Cave.

Anyway, I leaned out of the boat and placed the heavy thing I had in my hands in the water. The sunlight split through the trees on the island again, and it's glare that made me blink. Something strong and alive stirred out of my grip. My vision returned. My God, there was Edward's Salmon again – belly up, but with one slap of his tail he was gone.

I gasped and jerked upright in astonishment. I was blubbering and pointing, but what could I say or do – nothing. Then I looked down at my hands - the hands that had held the sodden piece of wood, and before my tortured pupils, there were scales on both my palms, and the red-brown slime had turned more red, say like blood. You will realise that I could not relate the latter events at the time to either John or Edward. John had his back to me as he rowed, and Edward was more or less in the same state of shock as myself, only not so far through with anguish. I mutely reasoned that I had taken enough stick for netting a piece of wood for a Salmon in the first place, never mind the lad who played it, so what would happen to me if I told my pals what they had not seen? Sure wouldn't they heap more scorn upon me in double dose for throwing the Salmon back. Do you get my meaning?

Summary

Whatever happened on that fateful day I will leave you to puzzle out from the vantage point of hindsight. John and Edward often recall the incident with me over a drink with never the same conclusion. As for myself – I sometimes wonder just where out in the great alone, where the moon is awful clear, where is my super, or supernatural, Salmon?

The illustrations for this story were done by Vera Cave, who is the daughter of Reverend Cave. She was a journalist for the Donegal Democrat, covering anglers' meetings and commissioners' meetings.

The author displaying three salmon caught in the Columbia river – 35 lbs of fish. I won the first derby of the season on the Columbia river...

John A. McGee
B&B
Carrickboy House
Belleek Road
Ballyshannon

Ph: 071 9851744

John A. McGee & Sons
Funeral Directors
Belleek Road
Ballyshannon

Ph: 071 9851744

24 Hour Service
Funeral Home Available

The Pope's Blessing !!!!!!!!!!!!!!!

By Anthony O'Malley Daly

We were sheltering in the lee side of the Mall Quay one very stormy day. The tide was full out. We had tried every fly in the book, along with every spinner, without success.

Arrived onto the quay side – a car, spotless... Maurice gets out of the vehicle. His wife remains in the car. She never gets out of the car. Maurice goes to the boot, and with great pride, puts on his waders, then his fishing jacket... As he is a small man, the waders reach to his chest. He puts up his rod (fishing). History is being made in front of our eyes, and we know it – it just has not hit us yet.

Maurice turns to face us, and his story begins to unfold. "I got my rod back, and fixed, from Mick Rogan," Maurice tells us the story as he pulls out the line. He enters the river. Soon he is up to his knees. He is about to cast. Then he turns, and says the following (which is written in the History Books of the Angling Club): "Willie, give me The Pope's Blessing." Willie, who is the Willie Miller who resided in the house at the front of the Handball Alley, cringed visibly.

The Crack was Awful

Maurice, with the admiring eyes of his wife on him, began to pay out the line. Just as Maurice was setting himself to take the first real cast on his shining "Newly-Repaired-by-the-Master" fishing rod, there was a loud cracking sound. And whatwas to be a graceful cast turned into a disgraceful break – the top half of the rod was in the water. The bottom half of the rod was like a stick to prod cattle at the mart. There was a deathly silence. Willie said nothing, but there was just the hint of a grin. The Pope must have owed Willie a favour, and Willie had called it in.

It is near the end of the story, but not quite. The care with which Maurice had mounted the rod was now abandoned. He chucked the rod, flies and all into the boot. Got into the car, waders and all. Drove off. I cannot say if he said anything bad, but his lips were moving. One thing is for sure. Mick Rogan received no plaudits. Did he care?

Fishing Stories and Memories

By John Hanna

Lough Eske has always been a very special place for me, and not just because of the wonderful Salmon and Sea Trout fishery it has always been, but also the great memories that keep flooding back – drifting down the Ridge from Salmon Rock, or drifting into the Dog's Head at Corraber.

On one of those days, my cousin Jim Thomas (of The National Hotel fame, Donegal Town) decided to join myself, brother Edward, and Injun Joe himself, Anthony O'Malley Daly. We all arrived at the Shore Road on a very warm June morning with Jim accompanied by his son Paul. With Jim's years of experience and knowledge of the lake, he directed us straight to the lower end of the lake (Dogs Head).

Jim's son Paul watched his father's every move, as we were in the presence of a very special person who taught all of us that wonderful art of fly fishing. Jim had not fished for many years, and most of his gear was here and there. Let me say for an expert he was a bit upside down, but he had the tools to improvise when it counted most.

Jim was fishing his old Hardy fly rod and, as normal, one size eight Black Doctor fly, at the end of one yard of Maxima 10 lbs gut. The four of us watched Jim grace the west wind that took us drifting towards the shore. Jim said, "Old Spencer never left this place," and at that moment the reel started to sing. "Jim, you're in a salmon. Take him easy" – so Jim eased it, and then the expert became the advised when all of a sudden Jim's fly reel fell into the lake. "Hold on to him, Jim," said Anto. "Grab the loose line," said Edward, "and feed it to Jim." And all this while son Paul could only watch in bewilderment at all the goings-on while Anto guided Jim, and the boat.

Edward started to retrieve the reel from the bottom of the lake, while keeping a loose hand on the line, which I fed to Jim. After God knows how long, the reel appeared in the boat, and then Edward started to reel in the loose Kingfisher line that lay around his feet. Anto was doing a great job on Jim, because the nerves were shattered, and a calm air was in it.

Eventually, Edward reeled up all the line back onto the reel, but unfortunately the pin holder on the rod had broken, so up pops Jim with an idea – Take off my shoe lace, and tie the bloody thing on – which Edward duly obliged and left the expert to his own means as Paul, Anto, Edward and myself sat, watched, and admired a true expert at work. Jim Thomas was our best friend, and will always be remembered, whenever we make our own way to The Dog's Head in Corraber.

"A Modest Day's Fishing"

I always wanted to do a book review. Now I have done that.
This book was a joy to review and read – Anthony.

"A Modest Day's Fishing" is written by John L. Dudgeon, who resides in Ballinderry, Co Antrim. John Dudgeon is a retired lecturer in textile technology, and once ran a textiles factory in Co Fermanagh. Since his childhood he has spent many holidays in South Donegal. Indeed, being in textiles, and tweed being one textile, and tweed being of the land and its surroundings, then I think the author has a grasp of its subject. For angling is the basic starting point in the fullest appreciation of water, land, air and sky and all the creatures who fill the environs.

The book is some eighty-six pages in duration. The print is large and readable to all eye visions, and is dedicated to his wife, family and friends "...whose company brightened many blank days on the water." I know what he means. John Dudgeon may have spent many blank days out fishing with his wife Sally and his sons Colin and Tim, but he blended into the local surrounds in that while he was out in the boat, his wife, and maybe one of his sons, would be nearby on land doing some bird watching, and staying in the vicinity of contact. An example of family outings.

However, not all days were blank, and John Dudgeon, I suspect, is quite an accomplished fisherman. In these reminiscences the family registered good fish catches of Salmon and Sea Trout on such diverse locations as Lough Sheelin, Melvin, the Eany and the Eske. On Lough Erne he landed a pike of 22 lbs weight. The Dudgeons fished Lareen Bay in one of Thomas Gallagher's boats, and despite very windy conditions brought back a bag of three-quarter pound Sonaghan, two Gilaroo and three Brown Trout,

On Lough Eske, in one of Scott Swan's reliable boats, John and son Colin row to the famous Ridge where they proceed, to their joy, to catch eleven good Sea Trout ranging from three-quarters of a pound to great specimens of three pounds weight - more than a modest days fishing by any standards. On the Eske also, John had other stories to relate - like catching a small Brown Trout, and it in turn was devoured by a cannibal Trout, and both played at one time; or spotting a rare osprey eagle, and catching the mighty little Char. Of course there is much, much more, and very descriptive. I liked John's description of a fish rising to the Fly as "a sweeping swirl."

The final chapter is a story about the mystical factor that every angler encounters sometime in his/her life. John's friend, Michael, goes fishing on the Erne river at a point called The Wings – now underwater as part of the hydro scheme. He gets stuck in a heavy fish which "fights furiously and silently in the dark water." Suddenly, he

(Michael) is not alone, and a tall, strangely clad figure deftly lands the fish. Michael is puzzled, and relates the tale when he returns home. Anyway, it turns out to be the spirit of a monk long departed this life. "A nice, quiet man, with a great way of landing Trout without a net," are the final lines of this simple book, which should be contemplated for a quick and easy read.

Nicely illustrated by the author's son, "A Modest Day's Fishing" is priced at £3.95, published by Excalibur press of London, 13 Knightsbridge Green, London SW1X 7QL, and is available from the publishers or from the Four Masters Bookshop, Donegal Town, the regional tourist office, Sligo, and other outlets upon enquiry. – Anthony O'Malley Daly

Daly Will Drink It

By Anthony O'Malley Daly

About the same time as Lorraine Thomas caught the 9lbs salmon on Lough Eske in 1963, John Hanna, Edward Hanna, Patrick Hanna, Paddy Clancy, and (of course), myself, after a good days fishing on Lough Eske, and a steak meal – the lot of us arrived into The National Hotel, where we started drinking, from where we had left off to have a meal. We were boisterous, (a little rowdy) to say the least. Jim Thomas was serving us. The "measure" had not been used all evening, so with "cousin" Jim in a generous mood, we were "full."

At about 2am, or 3am, we just didn't know what time it really was. At this point not only did we not know the "time a day" it was but we did not know our "own" names. Jim's mother arrived on the scene. Anyway, between the"pulling and dragging," she got us to make a "promise." I immediately thought (if I was able to make a promise or have a coherent thought at all), that if Annie or Aunt Annie gave each of us a full glass of brandy – we would "Throw it back in one gulp, and walk out." End of Story. We all agreed. John Hanna was the first "in the Barrel." Next came Edward, then it was Patrick's turn, then it was my turn. No problem. Paddy was the last.

"Houston we have a problem!" Paddy was saying. He was getting served a smaller "glass" of brandy than the rest of us "bums" got. Well, before Paddy could measure the brandy, Aunt Annie (or just plain Annie) uttered the famous words – "Well if you (Paddy) don't drink it, Daly will!" I reached over quietly, lifted the brandy, put it to my head, "dumped" it down, and headed at speed for the exit, closely followed by Clancy, saying things – "rude things" – and screaming what he was going to do to me if he ever got his hands on me. It was the perfect ending to our day's fishing on Lough Eske.

Dorrian's Pharmacy
The Diamond
Ballyshannon

071 985 1444

The staff of Dorrian's Pharmacy
send our best wishes to
Anthony O'Malley Daly
on the launch of his book
Trilogy

A Bottle of Raspberry Ripper

by Albert Johnson

The following is an account of an incident which occurred in the 1970's as recounted to me by the late Willie McGowan of Donegal Town – a very skilled and experienced fisherman. Fly fishing was his passion – and he did not hold spinning in the same regard.

Willie was a former postman, and the bag he used was an old canvas post bag which was much bigger than a normal fishing bag, but was perfect for carrying tackle and salmon. A gaff was the normal landing method back then, and much easier to carry than a landing net.

Albert Johnson

Willie was a very good fishing companion and was very generous with his advice on tackle and river craft. He would have known the Eany, the Wee Eany and the River Eske. He would have grown up fishing on the River Eske, but he also became an expert on the Eany, and in particular the Wee Eany, which was probably his favourite river of all. In fact, we could only imagine that he would have been pleased when it was on the banks of the Wee Eany that he passed away a number of years after this event took place.

The Eany is a spate river, and because of this it is difficult to hit the right conditions. A falling flood after rain, when the river is clearing, is ideal. On this particular day there had been rain during the night, and when Willie arrived on the banks of the Eany, conditions were perfect. He tied on his favourite cast, which was a Curry Red Tail Fly and a Fiery Brown and Donegal Blue on the droppers.

Willie had been fishing for about half an hour without rising a salmon when he got to one of his favourite pools. He started fishing the pool from the top. He thought he noticed the movement of a fish some yards below. As he approached the spot with growing excitement, he cast over the lie anticipating a rise. As the Curry Red Tail fly covered the lie there was a swirl in the water and after the normal couple of seconds Willie struck hard, which would normally give the salmon time to take the fly and turn to back to his lie.

What happened next shocked Willie. To his complete amazement what appeared to be a huge dark bird burst from the water and took to the air above Willie's head with the Red Curry stuck on his neck. Fortunately, after rising about fifty feet in the air, the fly became dislodged.

Willie sat down on the river bank and lit up a John Player to settle his nerves, realising that he had hooked a cormorant. This bird had a wing span of three feet.

What had appeared to be a fish's head was in fact the head of the cormorant coming up for air.

Willie went on to land two salmon that day, but the bird that got away was probably the most exciting part of that day's fishing.

As a footnote it should be added that at that time the Ballyshannon Fishery Board paid a bounty of five shillings for a cormorant's head and, incidentally, £5 for a seal's nose, which is a far cry from today's conservation measures.

A shorter version of this story was submitted to *Trout and Salmon*, receiving a letter of thanks and a bottle of raspberry liquor called "Raspberry Ripper" on publication, which is yet to be consumed in memory of one of the most likeable and modest anglers I had the pleasure to know and fish with.

Mill Hole

By John Hanna

The Drimeany River meets and flows into the main Eske, situated above the old Railway bridge and the pool below the Railway bridge. Next comes the Mill Hole, my favourite pool, so called because there used to be a working Mill, providing work, and working from the diversion of the water that was put through a Mill Race to turn the stones that made the grain into flour.

The diverted water served a triple purpose. One was turning a mill. Two was draining the lake into the sea at Donegal Town. Three was allow safe passage to the butty salmon that arrived each year to run the river, jumping its falls, cascading down the length of the this famous river from Lough Eske, six miles upstream from the sea. It was a working river in the past, now it's recreational only. Its past is behind it, but still visible by the stillness of the many mills and flax pits that are dotted about the banks and surrounds.

Fishing with Friends

by Hugo McGlynn

You know the saying – "If you are in the company of friends, the joy is in the mix." Well, I just made that up. However, in truth, when you share the fun and the *craic* with real friends, then these are moments to treasure all your life.

My sojourns with John Hanna, Anthony O'Malley Daly, and Raymond McEnhill (R.I.P), and our fishing exploits on our own Lough Eske have been truly magical.

I confess to be something of a part-time fisherman. I suppose I have never allowed myself the freedom to commit on account of other obligations.

Quality time for all of us can be elusive. So whenever I get the call to go fishing with the lads, I seize the opportunity for much needed therapy.

They tell me that a true fisherman is a combatant, wily, someone who studied his foe in all matters, with all the skills and tricks he can muster to finally land the prize. Me however, I'm more of the dedicated optimist, believing if your luck is in, then you're on a roll. Technique is for the birds – "The Bigger the Fly, the Bigger the Fish."

It's the in-betweens I love the best. The Banter, the Jokes, The Stories, The Tall Tales often Recounted. Perhaps even a Song or Two. "It's The Way I Tell Them." Laughter is a tonic even in small doses. These Tales never lose their mystique.

The half lies never cease to amuse.

The jokes couched in different language have stood the test of time.

"Ah – The Friendship"

Then there's the ever-changing landscape. The backdrop: the historic Blue Stacks. Celebrated in legend and song. (Older than the Himalayas and the mighty Everest). The people, the generations who have settled (!) these awesome beauties.

The splendour of the fauna and flora.- who needs therapists when you have God's creation at your beck and call?

I sometimes think we don't deserve all this as we seem intent on destroying and polluting the very treasure that will restore our sanity.

The fire on the lake shore is an occasion for innovation, come hail rain or shine. Mr. Hanna extols the art of cooking a freshly caught trout – this succulent dish washed down with a little vino/beer or a cuppa and served in God's own restaurant, what a privilege, I feel truly blessed.

"The Camaraderie."

Every outing is an occasion for adding to the long list of folklore, but most of all for consolidating the friendships that will endure long after we have served over time – and not forgetting, of course, "There's the Fish..." that grows a pace each time. The master tells the story of "The Wan that Got Away."

Thanks for the memories, Lads. God bless you always Hugo McGylnn is married to Anne McEnhill. Both retired lately – he from An Post, the Post Office. I might as well speak the – <u>Cupla Focal</u> – Gaelic for "few words." After all, the Queen of England said a few words on her recent Historical State visit to Ireland.

Anne McEnhill was a Head Teacher in a National School in Donegal Town, neighbour of the Hannas, and from a large family. Hugo is from Letterkenny. He is musical, a great singer, and breeds Bull. His father-in-law Jim McEnhill, was a motor mechanic who worked in Killybegs. Therefore he worked odd hours. He was off Mondays, and mostly when he came Home, everyone else was gone up the Eske River. I got to fishing with him about three or four times, and he went to the Eany river each time, the Wee Eany and the Big Eany.

Jim McEnhill was a great fisherman. Every time he went to the same stretch. He drove an old Austin car out the Mountcharles road, turned right, drove past Ballydevitt school, up the hill, turned right, crossed the "Dummies Bridge," and after driving another mile, he stopped. We made up our gear in silence. Jim always took the upper pool, and I fished the rest of the river. He invariably struck a salmon or a large sea trout. He had a 12 foot rod, and without too much ado Jim beached the salmon when he felt the fish was played out, or he called me if there was a chance of losing the salmon.

On one occasion Jim was fishing three flies – Silver Doctor on the tail, Green Peter in the middle and a yellow fly on the top dropper. All were single hooked.

I had a 9 ft rod, with two double hooked flies. Size eight on the tail, (Black Pendel), and a shrimp, size ten, on the dropper. Both of us would score. We seldom left the bank the Wee Eany without a salmon or a good trout. Jim had it all "sussed" before he wet a line. He looked for the Grey Mare's Tail. By the way – (question) – Where is the Grey Mare's Tail????

A Very Fishy Story

by Austin O'Malley

The story concerns a salmon fisherman who hooked a decent sized grilse and was just about to tap it on the head to kill it, when the fish said "Don't kill me! My name is Rusty and I am very young, with hopefully a long life before me." The astonished fisherman relented and slipped the fish back in the water.

Three years later the same fisherman was fishing in the same spot when he hooked a much larger fish. Once again he was about to kill it when the fish said "Don't you recognise your old friend Rusty?"

The fisherman said "I didn't recognise you because you are much bigger. Where have you been for the past three years?"

The fish replied "I have been living in the Titanic, writing poetry – and I am just about to publish a book of verse."

The fisherman said "What are you going to call the book of verse?"

The salmon replied "Salmon Rusty's Titanic Verses."

Slob Trout – given to me by John Merrifield of
Portnason, Ballyshannon

"Wan for You, and Wan for United"

By Anthony O'Malley Daly

One Saturday, John, Edward, and myself were out on Lough Eske. We were fishing at Corraber, on the North side of the lake. At the side of the Lake was a single man from Derry, fishing a worm, sitting very contentedly. At three o'clock the FA cup final started from Wembley. It was between Man United and Aston Villa. The opposition does not matter. "*Injun Joe,*" our boat, was trolling two rods, while Edward was casting his flies. Suddenly, my rod shot back. At the same time, your man on the shore "leaped" skywards. My reel was "singing."

I am a long time Manchester United supporter. I remember when Johnny Carey was Captain of Man U, when they won the FA Cup in 1948. I had cuttings from that great occasion, of Johnny Carey accepting the FA Cup. That is when I gauge my support of Man United as having started. Born in 1935, now it was 1948, when Johnny Carey captained United to victory in the FA Cup. That made me 13 years old when I became a fan of Man U.

Now I am a supporter for 63 years. The only time I saw them was when I was travelling through Manchester the Sunday after they had lost in (yes, you've guessed it) the FA Cup final, against Aston Villa. That was the occasion when Ray Woods had his jaw broken in a goalmouth clash with McParland. Munich was 1958. This was the year afterwards, 1959. McParland was not put off, nor did Woods go off with such a bad injury. Woods was sent to the wing.

I think he went off before the finish, but Man U lost the final. They were team building. Anyway, the man from Derry and I got our "just desserts" that Saturday.

I landed my salmon, and the Derryman got his goal too. He shouted, "Wan for You, and Wan for United!"

Erne Anglers Win Law Case

by Michael McGrath, Belleek Angling Centre

"The Erne is the best Fisherman's River in Ireland and can be equalled by few anywhere in the world!"

There are many writings about the Erne – The Vikings, the legends, the ships, the fishing, the people. There is one little known story about a Belleek man "Eddie" Alexander Thornhill in the 1870's. His brother George Thornhill then owned the Thatch Coffee Shop & Fishing Centre property on Main Street, Belleek.

Eddie Alexander Thornhill individually caused major upset to the fishing rights of the Erne. The case lasted for years and eventually made him a local hero.

The Erne Fishery Company has suffered severely at the law. In its first experience they were worsted after litigation which ran into four figures, and the second, though it has won so far, it cannot hope to recover costs from the poor fisherman if it wins – which seems probable.

If, during the end of the seventies or beginning of the eighties Alexander Thornhill, a Belleek shoemaker, had not noticed that one evening looked promising for fish and had taken himself to the river with his rod, the Erne Fishery Company would have remained possessed of every fish in Lough Erne.

And an important point of law would have remained undecided, and incidentally the company would have saved much money. Thornhill went a-fishing, and as he pulled in a trout a water, a bailiff came up and asked for a permit. Alex didn't happen to have one, and as he continued to fish, he was summoned to the next petty sessions and fined.

The late Mr. Robert Macredy, a Ballyshannon solicitor, happened to have a case in court (I cannot recollect if he defended Thornhill). And knowing that Honest Tom Connolly, as he was called, and from whom the company purchased the fishery for £45,000, had not as much property in County Fermanagh as would sod a lark, he communicated with the solicitors of the Marquis of Ely or Mr. Maurice Maude, of Lenaghan, his agent, as the Marquis was owner of the fishery in the river Erne above Belleek Bridge.

As a result, an application to quash the conviction was made in the King's Bench on the grounds that the Marquis had never parted with his fishery, and therefore that he, and not the company, was the owner of the fishery in that part of the Erne. Now a landed Estates Court title was in those days considered indisputable, and R.L. Moore and S. Alexander (the principals of the Erne, Foyle and Bann Fishery) produced their deed from the court giving them every fin and tail from Lough Oughter in Cavan to the Sea at Finner in Donegal Bay. And the Kings Bench decided that the title given was indisputable.

Best Regards to
Anthony O'Malley Daly

from Michael McGrath

and everyone at the

Belleek Angling Centre
/ The Thatch

Belleek, Co Fermanagh

NI (++44)28 6865 8181, ROI 048 6865 8181

The Marquis appealed to the Court of Appeal and, needless to say, the case was watched with great intent by the riparian proprietors of Lough Erne who had not before known of the extent of the deed in question. If the company's title were good, trout or other fish could not be fished for the 52 miles of the Erne without payment to them.

The Court of Appeal decided against the company on the ground that Tom Connelly never possessed any property in County Fermanagh, and that the Landed Estates Court had given the Company a title to what Connelly had never possessed. It was argued that notice had been given that Connelly's Fishery was to be sold, and the Marquis had not objected, but the court answered that he had no necessity to do so as Connelly's Fishery ended below Belleek Bridge and therefore, the Marquis had no interest in what was to be sold. If the Company's argument held good, the Landed Estates Court could have given the Company half of County Fermanagh, without a penny of compensation to the owners.

The decision was a blow to the company, and the evening that the news came to Belleek there were more fishing rods on the river than had ever been seen before, and water bailiffs were boldly told to go to Jericho or elsewhere. Thornhill on his return was acclaimed a hero. Then the company appealed to the House of Lords, but here to their dismay, they were again defeated, and left with what Connelly really owned – the several fishery from the sea to Belleek Bridge.

Though this recital is short, it by no means describes the protracted litigation over years, for there were continuous applications to the courts by both parties for discovery and documents and demurrers and heaven knows what. But it ended that whilst fishing for salmon in the Erne below Belleek bridge would cost £6 or more a week, one could fish for a day above it for 10s. I knew one man in Ballyshannon sent each of his friends each summer a fine salmon, and these he secured in one day (up to a dozen or more) with a boiled prawn. It was not sport, or course, for he pulled them in, but he said in extenuation that it was the cheapest way of sending salmon presents. If I recall aright, the Marquis has now handed over his rights to the Erne conservators.

We wonder who they are today, and could we ever have the whole beautiful Erne system from Cavan to the sea under one dedicated management?

Anyhow, there is a photograph of Eddie Alexander Thornhill's son Bill and a Greenhart salmon fly rod from his niece's husband on display in the Thatch Coffee Shop Belleek.

Did "GONE FISHING" Kill General Custer?

By Anthony O'Malley Daly

History tells us of leaders who made war, and also fished. Martin McGuinness, the Deputy First Minister in the Northern Assembly has been seen taking a few casts prior to his "going to work." I am sure Martin would rather be "Gone Fishing" than having to go to "Heavy" meetings, but a leader like Martin McGuinness has to put his "Gone Fishing" on hold.

Generalissimo Franco was an angler. He was the war leader in the Spanish Civil conflict that took many Irishmen and women to Spain to fight on both sides, and give their blood and lives for the *Communistas* or Socialists, against Franco's "*Fascistas*." This war was a prelude to the Second World War, a practice session for what was to come.

As I wrote, my father was a "Blue Shirt," which meant he was a follower of General Eoin O'Duffy, the Garda Commissioner who was sacked by the Government of Eamonn DeValera. Eoin O'Duffy went to Spain. Franco won the civil war, so he had the best pools and rivers to fish. But the General didn't get much time for "Gone Fishing."

The Story

(*At Last,* I hear you say)

When I was at Blackrock College, we got a test of three compositions. I picked the one about General Custer. I wrote General Custard instead of General Custer, and when I handed up my finished article for correction, I didn't even notice the mistake. In fact, I was quite pleased with my finished article. Let's not dwell on Custard or Custer, let me tell you the story.

George Armstrong Custer

General Custer was a reckless soldier, and leader of men in the Indian Wars on the American plains of the 1870s. He was an adventurer and, being Irish, a good Ulster Protestant. He was the product of West Point, but apart from drinking liquor he was straight laced, and he observed the Sabbath. He was handsome, and had a blond full head of hair. He was married, childless, and even though he could have had all women or ladies. He cut a dashing figure, and was a great horseman and hunter. He was a reckless leader and an avid fisherman, as was his boss and superior General George Crook.

The Indians of the Sioux and Cheyenne tribes had been granted reservation to fertile lands in Montana. Things were going rightly until gold was found, and miners began to encroach on the land granted to the Indians,who defended their territory under the leadership of Sitting Bull and Crazy Horse, and had not much interest in gold.

Generals Custer and Crook were sent to quell the skirmishes, and where possible quell the that little bit more. General Crook brushed with the Sioux and Cheyenne, took casualties, took to his heels and took his troops to a safe distance.

General Custer wanted to press the Indians into submission, and he planned to surround them in their hunting grounds in the Black Hills. The Indians were that bit quicker than Custer, and they surrounded Custer at Little Big Horn. The beleaguered officer sent a message to General Crook, asking for assistance ASAP, but none arrived. The rest is history. General Custer's famous "Last Stand" occurred. The Sioux killed all the soldiers, except Custer's horse and his dog.

Débâcle Enquiry

The inquiry into the defeat and the débâcle, and the hindsight of intimate knowledge showed that the reason why General Crook failed to come to the aid of General Custer was that the big trout were taking on the Tongue River. General Crook was a keen angler, he hung out the sign – "Gone Fishing" – and sat on the bank of the river, fishing to his heart's content. Custer's Last Stand at the Little Big Horn was written into history. The true facts are only made known now, and exclusively to us – me and you – US.

So beware the consequences off getting the adrenalin surge of "Gone Fishing."

Ah, what the heck, the story is done. I have a lot more to do, but (this last time, I'll slip away) "Gone Fishing" will explain everything.

After the battle of Little Big Horn was over, the Indians had departed. All that was left alive of Custer's Force were wandering back to camp, were his dog and his horse. Custer's horse never got over the battle, but his dog did. Dog Gone...

What ever happened to General Crook? He lost his General's Stars, was reduced to the rank of Major, for the major mistake he made of not going to the assistance of Custer. However, there was another survivor: the trooper sent with the message, He was an Irishman, just enrolled in the army, His name was Kelly from Westport, County Mayo. He was selected because he was the youngest soldier there – his father was a long term soldier. He volunteered his son, and the command agreed. No one opposed his selection, and so George Michael Kelly, survived the battle of the Little Big Horn, and went on to become Governor of California.

In the film of the life and times of General Custer, he is pictured as rash. And he was indeed rash, but his men loved him, for Custer was an adventurer, and most of the soldiers were adventures too. They adored Custer, and all of them would give their lives for him, and as it turned out, they did give their lives for Custer.

So the Battle of the Little Big Horn was the beginning of the end of the suppression of the Indians. The cavalry, and interference of civilians in the Wild West was starting to take a new course. Civilian influence put the brakes on an unregulated cavalry, and the Wild days of the Wild West were at an end. Recognition of the Indians' rights had to be accepted. The means of communication were far better than previously. The newspapers and their editorials were landing on the desks of Washington, and they could not be ignored.

General Custer's days were over anyway. The high command of his superiors could not any longer accept the newspaper columns and the fact that Custer was a young blond maverick and tear-away. Private Kelly and his father were the last of the adventurers, and that had attracted them to Custer's command.

The influx of civilians began to put the Indians on the back foot, and their way of life was under threat. The Wild West did not last more than fifty years. The battle of the Little Big Horn took place in the year 1870.

Specifications

by Billy Johnston

Photo taken in July 1982

Photographer: John Hanna – eminent fisherman, not photographer.

Child: Robbie Johnston, Donegal Town. Aged 1. Billy Johnston's son. Now much older.

Fish: 21 lb 4 oz, caught by Billy Johnston at McKelvey's Pool, upper stretch of the Eany Mor.

Fishing Fly: Caught on a size 10 Fiery Brown.

Fisherman: Billy Johnston, Donegal Town. Who had a sore back for weeks.

Author's Note: Billy, I get the joke. Your salmon was never weighed, and now you're claiming it is 21 lb 4 oz, which is one pound above my specimen fish.

Was it a Salmon or a Tree Trunk?

By Billy Johnston

It was 6:30 am, the last week in August 1980. I collected "Wee Willie" McGowan at Marian Villas in Donegal Town. It was getting clear when we arrived at Ballymacahill Bridge on the Eany River. As usual we looked at the water level to discuss our fly size, we both agreed size 10's for the droppers and no 8 for the tail fly. My favourite casts on my 15" Hardy Salmon Rod have always been on three flies, even today – Donegal Blue, Fiery Brown and Size 8 Curry Red Shrimp, in that order.

Wee Willie McGowan, with his An Post bag over his shoulder. He and Billy Johnston were constant companions, and Billy never went fishing without him. Willie imparted all of his knowledge to Billy.

Willie decided to fish the "Wee" Eany as he felt that the flood which came down that morning came from the Wee Eany. Now the sun had not appeared yet, but was trying to climb over the distant hills behind me. I was in a rush as usual for two reasons. One, because I wanted to cover as much water as possible before the sun came out, which would brighten up the river and limit my chances of catching a salmon. And secondly, I had to be back for work at 9 am and it was now 7:30 am.

I was delighted to fish "The Devlin Pool" all on my own, a super pool. (Well, not first that morning because Willie and I left that same pool at 1am, having arrived that night fishing for sea trout. We left in a hurry on hearing the rattle of tins, cans and debris. Anyone who has fished the Eany, a spate river, knows exactly what I mean. A flood can come like a tidal wave starting from "The Grey Mare's Tail." You just reel in and leave.)

To get back to "The Devlin Pool" and the excitement of the first few casts into excellent water...

Now to fish these waters was not as easy back in 1980. This was before Anthony and his FÁS team arrived to clear the river banks. The Devlin was then overgrown, as were most of the river banks, with only a few gaps to fish.

As can happen, there was nothing to be seen, even after fishing this wonderful pool from top to tail twice.

I headed off fishing down towards "The Flag Hole," thinking in my mind that Wee Willie, knowing the fishing skills he was endowed with, would probably wander down after me and land one or even two salmon, fishing the very same water.

I covered some nice water in perfect conditions with no reward, when just suddenly, in the corner of my eye, something moved in the water – no splash, just a sparkle, a silver flash – and the slightest touch on my fingers came through the line. I was in a fish, now, where I stood there was only enough room to cast and no more. Anthony's FÁS team had not reached this pool. A beautiful looking fish, at least 8lbs as I could see as he took off into the air with tail flapping, trying to dislodge my Curry Red Shrimp.

When he plunged back into the deep, this fish did of course what any sensible fish would do – he ran like hell downstream. And he did run. This fish had no regard for my thumb, which was almost dislocated when the reel went singing.

Now I had one big problem – this lovely specimen of a fish took off and around the bend below me about 50 yards to my left. I was in trouble. No sign of Willie, just when I needed him. I had an idea!! I fixed my rod safely on the bank and ran like hell to the bend on the river. Down on my hands and knees, using the long extension of my landing net, I found the line just under the water. I gently pulled on the line, and sure enough – this fish was under the bank, hidden under a large stump of a tree which was showing itself just below water level.

As one can imagine I still had a problem: a fish, a line and no rod. Now, one must believe me, this is not a fishy tale. I gently pulled the line in until I reached the knot on my line, looped the cast around my index finger on my left hand and untied the double loop attached to the knot, tied the double loop to a Hawthorn Branch just beside my head, and almost submerged in the water. I smiled as the pressure on the cast was taken by the branch.

I tried to get to my feet but was prevented by a sudden bout of cramp, possibly caused by the tension and excitement of my experience. Well, I jumped and hopped back to my rod, reeling the line in like mad, hopping and jumping back to the bend on the river and to my horror the branch was gone. Down again with my head almost submerged in the water, rolling up my sleeves and managed to find the end of the branch which had moved down into the deep. I slowly pulled the branch to eye level, looped the cast around my index finger once again and untied the double loop from the branch. For a split second I had a salmon – or at least it was a salmon – or a tree trunk – looped around my index finger.

Please, I thought, *whatever is down there – don't run for just a few seconds*. I tied the double loop onto the knot on my line, scrambled to my feet – and now was the telling moment. Did I have that beautiful salmon which I previously saw climbing into the air? Was it still on? I lifted my rod and put slight pressure on the line. The line moved. Was it a fish or a tree trunk? To my delight, I knew that tree trunks don't usually take off downstream.

I played this beauty for a few exciting moments and safely landed probably the unluckiest Salmon to ever enter the Eany River.

In the corner of my eye something moved to my right, yes, it was Willie McGowan casting and whistling in a world of his own. I said, "Willie, where were you when I needed you?" Willie said, "Billy, I had to go back to the car. I caught a 10 lb fish at the top of the Devlin Pool and an 8 lb fish at the tail of the pool. They were too heavy to carry. How did you get on, Billy?"

I had to take a deep breath before I answered. Had I not fished that pool twice before him? "Willie, you might not believe this, but wait until I tell you how I caught and landed this fish."

I dedicate this fishing story to my true fishing friend and to his memory – Willie McGowan or "Wee Willie" as he was fondly named...

Billy Johnston, Donegal Town, is now a successful Auctioneer, Estate Agent, Investment Broker. He was once a new and used car salesman, and auto repair garage owner..

He is married to Audrey. They have four of a family – two boys and two girls, who are all grown. Robbie works in the business, with his father. Billy is a brilliant golfer and a single handicapper, which rates him as a "near" professional. He is a member of Murvagh Golf Club, as is wife Audrey, who can "whack" a golf ball into the distance.

He is a member of several Angling Clubs, and was a director of the FÁS scheme (under my supervision for three years) that made improvements to the Eske and Eany systems.

£32 Boat, Long Shaft Seagull Engine, Change of Scenery

By Anthony O'Malley Daly

I was not content with fishing the Eske, river and lake, the Eany and Wee Eany. I wanted to fish the Drowes and Lough Melvin. It was easy to fish the Drowes. All was required was to get there. The Melvin, being a lake, meant that I had to have a boat.

One day I got advice a boat was for sale from Canise McCreery, the Manager of the Bank of Ireland. Off I go, and bought the boat – a 19 foot punt, but it had one fault... It had been fished on the channel, it was old, without paint or care, and as you will hear, the vendor, Canice McCreary, "took the arm off me" when I agreed on £32.

I was glad to get the boat. First place I landed looking for a berth was Jimmy Connolly's, across the far side of Lough Melvin. I am not sure how I got there. Maybe it was due to me going to Bernard Connolly to ask him to make a pair of oars for my "New" boat. Bernard Connolly was a boat builder, and he made me a pair of oars that have lasted me for thirty years. They are now on "as stand by" in case the engine fails on *"Injun Joe,"* John's boat.

Anyway, I drove each evening after work to get a few hours' trout fishing at Jimmy's house. And, yes, I opened and closed the gate. And when I arrived at Jimmy's abode, his wife, Teresa, who was from Garrison area, would get me tea and things. And if she knew I was coming, she (Teresa) had a table prepared for me, and if I arrived unannounced, Teresa did not let me out of her house without a mug of tea. Mostly, she gave me the best cutlery in the house.

There was a ridge of rock, not showing even at low water, but if there was a breeze blowing, you could see the "jobble" of restless water, and there I fished for brown, sonaghan, and Gilaroo trout. Jimmy was always threatening to come out and fish with me, but I think he only ventured once to put his "life at risk," and that evening we did "quite well." Teresa had a wonderful table prepared for us upon our return.

Teresa is now a resident of the Rock Welfare Home, here in Ballyshannon.. Jimmy died suddenly when he was putting his herd of cattle into the byre, where they were to be examined by the vet. That was the end of my trout fishing in that area. Not quite...

Confrontation

I was fishing west of Rooskay Point. So one day I decided to row down and fish the two rivers, the Glan and the the other river. As I approached the two rivers I saw a "lump" of men fishing from the shore.

All was going handy until I spotted a boat rounding the headland, and at speed. I "looked front," and when I turned back, the crowd of anglers had disappeared. (Magic!) The boat went a different course. I looked again. Lo and behold, all the rods were back in the rivers. (Magic!) When I asked them about "disappearing and appearing" they told me that the two rivers "were" owned by a Landlord. They did not recognise him, nor did they pay him a permit. For that evening there was a flood, quite a few of the men got grilse. (Any salmon that is less than seven pounds (7lb), and has spent but one season at sea is a grilse.)

Later on when I went back and back, I met the owner and we had a verbal set-to. But I remained fishing the two rivers, and got my share out of them.

Looking back at the incidents there was one that stands out in my mind. I was fishing the two rivers when along came the owner and another person in the middle of the boat. I spotted as they drew near that the man in the middle of the boat caught a trout of about 3lbs, a lovely fish. When the trout was landed, I saw them heading my way, and they drew alongside me. The boss said to me "beach your boat," and he pointed to a spot nearby. The usual sentences were exchanged, but I pulled out to drift in.

I was getting the better of the exchanges when my line started "singing," which meant I was on a salmon, and a big too. The Boss, whom I recognise as a true angler, left me tons of space to play my salmon. He even offered to play the fish for me, but I declined (politely) when I had the 8 lbs salmon (like a true angler, for in truth it was a 6 lbs grilse) in my boat, and despatched there.

The Lure of the Erne Estuary

By John Sweeney

John Sweeney and I are friends. When my father came to Ballyshannon in the early thirties, Bernard – John's father – sent my father up to the lounge to fit on a pair of trousers he had just purchased. After a short time, a domestic was asked to get an item from the lounge. Imagine the shock both of them got.

I remember the very first time I heard the term Lure. I would have been about seven years of age, and an American family had come to stay at my father's hotel, the Commercial, 1 East Port, Ballyshannon. One of the family was around my age, so like all good hospitable hosts, I took him fishing at the bottom of our garden, the house where Dr Vera Lang now lives. His query to me was, "What lure are you going to use to catch the very small trout that to us were Specimen Abbey River fish." I had never heard the term before and was so embarrassed that I couldn't answer. Its amazing how a child can become anxious about such things. My Dad Bernard for ages later got great smiles when he recalled the *lure* term. Imagine – well over fifty years later, I still remember that day.

Whether I had a keen interest in fishing from those days or whether I became very "hooked" on it from the day I caught my first trout at Port Na Mara when I was nine years of age, I'm not sure. That day in the company of my Dad I caught a 2lb 10oz trout, and it was Brother Fidelis, who was fishing nearby, who insisted I land it myself. The other possibility that got me "hooked" on fishing the Erne may have been an old 1927 'photo that I still have – of my grandfather, my father and two other men displaying the day's catch by rod and line on the channel. It consisted of a total of 15 fish, 52 lbs weight, two of which were salmon and one of the trout was six-and-three-quarter lbs weight. All I know is that the lure of the Erne is a very powerful force as far as I'm concerned.

Rearing a family while working in the hospitality industry takes up a lot of time and commitment. The fishing had to take a back seat for a good number of years, but I still kept a small boat in the back, knowing that one day I'd have more time to spend down the channel. That opportunity came when I retired and made up for "lost" time. I joined the Ballyshannon and District Anglers Association, and I spend as much time as anyone now down enjoying the wonderful facility that generations of fishermen and women before me enjoyed.

Ballyshannon is a wonderful hub for fishing with its lakes and rivers, but it's the lure of the Erne that does it for me. Long may I continue to enjoy it.

"Injun Joe" Down Donegal Bay from Donegal Town

By Anthony O'Malley Daly

John Hanna used to take "Injun Joe" down the Bay from Donegal Town when there was no water in the River Eske or Lake. When this occurred, it was no good going out on to the lake, because the salmon and trout had no water to run, and the fish already in the lake were by his time gone stale – which means that they had come into the lake off a flood earlier. This must be explained. I will explain the story about the "runs" of salmon and sea trout in a story I have in mind.

Three Bridges - Salmon and Sea Trout Trapped

They (salmon and sea trout) would be seen swimming in shoals up to the 3rd bridge, adjacent to Club rooms. The 1st bridge takes you to Mountcharles. The 2nd bridge is the Red Bridge – it connects you into Tirconnail Street. Then you go down onto Castle Street, where the Hannas live.

During the summer, when there is no rain, a shoal of salmon (and, to a lesser extent, sea trout) arrive in the estuary of the Eske river. They are blocked, or facilitated, by the amount of water in the river. In the event there is no water, the salmon cannot proceed up river into the lake, so they must stay in the estuary until there is sufficient water to entice them to "run" into the lake, and fulfil their destiny of spawning in the pool or place they first saw the light of day.

Pooching

However, you have a " lovely shining silvery salmon" arriving, and departing, each day. Two full tides. In the Eske, a shoal of mullet break the surface and, with all this activity, your will to resist temptation is sorely tested.

In many cases the sight of a "bar of silver," breaks a man's resistance. He has a bit of net in the house – hidden in the turf stack. Next thing he, and a dear friend (a man never goes to the river to pooch – alone) are in the river at dead of night, fumbling and fearful. The net is across the river. Suddenly, a salmon bounces off the net, another one sticks. The excitement of a salmon hitting your net in the full moon is a sensation seldom equalled. And when you end up in court is another sensation seldom equalled – charged with "pooching."

But there is a shoal of salmon, sea trout, and even mullet shoals coming upriver with the tide. They even go as far as the Ash Hole, which is half mile or more up the river.

When the tide turns, the salmon and sea trout sense this, and they would turn and head down river, and out to sea again (if they are allowed). This exercise was repeated until prayers for rain, said in secret, were answered. I say "secret" because people did not take too "kindly" to anglers or fishermen Praying for Rain. Donegal Town is a tourist town, and there is a Waterbus stationed there. Nobody likes rain, but without rain, the salmon and white or sea trout are captured in the Estuary, right down to the Hassens, or as far back as the Mountcharles pier.

When there were commercial fishermen operating, they took all the "falling back" salmon and the bigger trout in their nets, gladly. The when you saw people or individuals of a dubious character looking over the Red Bridge, the 3rd bridge, and strolling up the river to the "several" other pools, like Timoneys Turn, The Clubrooms Pool, the Sandpit Pool, the Ash Hole, the Hospital Pool, or the pool where the two rivers meet. I took salmon and sea trout out of all these pools.

Sentiment and Memory

By Anthony O'Malley Daly

Sentiment and memory from the past. (Nothing to do with Fishing, but everything to do with – Music and Memory!)

My mother was a sweet singer. I was a sweet whistler. Long ago, when only the two of us (or at most the family) were in the house, I was always in a different room. Mammy would start to sing and play the piano upstairs. I would whistle, and between both of us we made wonderful sounds.

Now my mother is long dead. I have Parkinson's and can't get a decent sound. So when the Bingo caller shouts, "Legs Eleven" (11), the men whistle. It is then I remember my mother, and the loss of melody. In those days I could whistle for Ireland. Now I could not even "Turn" a dog.

I fished the Drowes, Erne, Eske, Eany, and Lough Eske. I reckon I have about 600 salmon on my record. Enjoyed every strike. I would gladly go through "the same again," but time marches on.

Glenade Lake – The Story of the Dobhar Chu

By Mary B. McEnroy

Here is how Mary B. McEnroy describes herself:

Kicking and squealing, Mary McEnroy arrived in Aughalative, Glenade betwixt the 7th and 8th of October, 1928. Practically unaware of the hardships of the '30s she enjoyed her pre-teen years there, surviving the rigours of Loughmarron N.S.

The Sligo Ursulines and University College, Galway took up the cudgels after which she tried her hand at teaching, mainly as Gaeilge, a variety of Science subjects, first in her Alma Mater, then Balla, Co Mayo, and finally Dublin.

Currently she's contentedly depleting, chiefly in Glenade, the diminishing Retirement Fund.

Career highlights were literary awards in both high and less high profile competitions.

Claims that a Great Tragedy occurred in Glenade Lake, Co Leitrim circa 1720 A.D. are ridiculed by some, firmly believed by others.

Many versions of the story exist, and vary but slightly from each other.

One states that around this time a man called McLoughlin and his wife, Grace Connolly, lived by the Northern shore of the lake. One day she went to wash clothes or bathe. When she did not return within a reasonable time her husband went to investigate. He found her dead, bleeding, half eaten by the monster, the dreaded *Dobhar Chu*, reputed to dwell in the lake and which was now asleep beside his victim.

The appalled husband killed the beast with his dagger, but as the otter, crocodile or water dog was dying it whistled. This was the signal for its mate to come and avenge its death...

It was believed locally that humans could neither outwit nor outrun the *Dobhar Chu,* so McLoughlin was advised that his only hope lay in fast and immediate flight. He and his Brother mounted their horses and galloped as never before along a road through the middle of the parish which has since disappeared from view

This would have led them towards the ancient road, still in use, from Royal Tara to the seat of Queen Maeve on Knocknarea. Along this route the chase continued, entering County Sligo at Achamore.

The animal, screaming and whistling, was catching upon them, so in a field about eight or nine miles from Sligo town, they sought refuge in a walled enclosure and placed the two horses across the doorway. As they had already been warned, the monster bored through the outer horse's belly and was about to repeat the action on the second gelding. The brothers knew that it was imperative that they cut off its head at this juncture...

This they accomplished and having buried the dead, both men returned home...

Grace's body was interred in Conwal cemetery in Drummonds, Glenade, and a small plaque erected over the grave. This slightly raised stone, with its now almost-eroded carving of the *Dobhar Chu*, is the strongest evidence of the possible veracity of the story A further point in its favour is the place name – Cashelgarron. The "*caiseal*," a stone circular shelter for cattle and /or fodder, is still clearly visible from the Bundoran-Sligo main road. These structures are widespread throughout the country but "*gearran*" - the mildly vulgar Gaeilge for gelding – is unique to this Sligo locality.

Mary B. McEnroy is the sister of John Fahey, Garda Sergeant. The story of the Dobhar Chu puts the Loch Ness Monster in the shade.

Four Salmon in the Garden

By Anthony O'Malley Daly

April ended with an angler's dream story. Albert Johnston, Strabane, fishing the Foyle from the bottom of his garden, got four salmon on the Flying C – one each at four to five lbs, and two scaling nine big ones. How lucky can a fisherman get?

Fishing the Columbia River with the Kellys

by Edward Hanna, May 2001

In my youth I watched television about Alaska, Canada, and the Oregon River. Fishing for salmon, like coho, steelheads. Chinooks. and jacks - that was my dream to get there and catch them. Well, that dream came true - all thanks to Richard (Dick) Kelly.

Dick was born in Portland, Oregon along with his brother, George. The family produced some of the greatest salmon fishermen in Portland. George can boast about catching fish in the weight range of 47 to 58 pounds. The 5H pounder was caught on a spinner, using only a 15-pound test line. Using a fly rod and 10 pound test line. Dick landed fish in the range of 20 to 50 pounds. His biggest fish land on fly was a giant "hog" – a name given to a fish over forty pounds. It weighed in at an amazing 57 pounds. These fish tales were told to me prior to the trip, time and time again.

On hearing these stories, I grew more excited with each passing day. That day finally came on 30 March 2001 when Dick picked me up at quarter past seven. We flew to Seattle and caught a connector to Portland. We were met at the airport by our guide, George Kelly, who took us to his home where we made base for the nine days fishing. Our guide, who actually makes all his own lures, supplied all the fishing gear. We were shown to our bedrooms and told to go to bed at 10pm. "Why, George?" asked Dick. George replied, "Fishing time to rise is 5am – starting time is 6am."

Five am. we are at Sauvic Island just west of the city on the Columbia River. Giant ships were passing up and down carrying (heir cargo of grain, cars, trucks, etc. Sauvic Island is also known as "Social Security" Island. This island is a refuge for birds and animals. Out here, Dick produced a fantastic 27-pound steelhead salmon, which was netted by George, our guide. We were informed that we could fish for sturgeon in the Willamete River using smelts, which are small herring, on a barbless hook, so we would not harm the fish. There are strict regulations for proper catch and release guidelines for species, location, length, month and day. If you catch a fish and put your line back in the water before you fill in the "tag card", you are at risk of receiving a hefty fine and loss of license - and fishing gear.

Going back to the sturgeon – I never fished for these. They have been recorded to weigh over 1,000 pounds. How do you gel a 1,000-pound sturgeon out of the river? Quite easy – you fish with a very, very strong line – and not from a rod. This line is attached to your 4x4 truck (got the gist of it, right?) and you drag it out of the river. What a way to fish!

Well, I was the first one to catch a fish, a small 30 pounder, and then Dick landed two fish at about 30 pounds. Of course, our guide did the trick – a brilliant fish, 62 pounds. All fish were released unharmed. The first day was over.

The second day took us to Bonneville Dam, which produces most of the electricity for California and Oregon. We arrived there at quarter to 5 am. The gales opened at 6am. We were the 28th car in line. Probably another 28 cars behind us. When the gates opened, it was drive like hell to the river and get your spot, which we did. I was given a spin glow (green and gold - no lie!) and told where to cast it and hold on. At 6.30am I landed my first salmon on the Columbia River. At 7, Dick landed two bodacious salmon. All the fish caught had sea lice on them. Bonneville Dam is 150 miles west of the coast. So how fast were these fish travelling? I'll let you figure that one out.

At 11 our guide asked me if I wanted to see the dam and the fish window. What a sight for a fisherman's eyes – thousands upon thousands of fish going through the dam and me with only one fish for that day!

That day, 4,298 fish passed through the dam and 5,702 fish the next day. This was the pattern for 3 days until 10,000 fish were recorded. Including another consecutive three day period, a total of 20,000 fish passed. The fish were mostly Chinook and steelhead. The only problem about fishing there were the rocks about the size of footballs, they were hard to walk on and required us to wear sturdy boots up our ankles to keep from breaking a leg.

A lot of these fish must be released because they are wild fish. The reason for releasing them is the game and wildlife authorities want to bring these fish back to the way they were in the rivers 40 years ago (7 to 8 million fish). The only difference between the native fish and the wild is the native fish's portal fin being clipped. Otherwise, the native fish are the exact same fish as the wild. All the fish we caught and kept were gutted on the river's edge by our guide George. They were then taken to his home, filleted, vacuum-packed, and made ready to ship home.

Rivers that we fished with great results were; the Nehlem and Wilson Rivers famous for 40-50 pound Timothy Lake trout; the Hood River for 4-6 pound steelheads; and the Garibaldi and the Clackamas Rivers for 28-35 pound Chinook. The Elk River was famous for bald eagles, beavers, mountains lions, bears, timber wolves, and coyotes.

So now our trip of a lifetime has come to an end. Sunday we went sightseeing on Mount Hood. What a beautiful place! The native trees are fir and cedar, reaching up 200 or more feet to the heavens.

Well, I fulfilled that dream of my youth about fishing for the mighty salmon on the Columbia River – and I shall return. I would like to extend a very special thanks to Dick Kelly. Thank you, Dick and to George, the best guide Portland has to offer - the best there was, the best there is, and the best there ever will be, and to Stan

Anderson, thank you for a lovely dinner - the Andersons and the Kellys are both Irish, and thank you Cindy for the lovely cabbage and bacon.

So the total catch and release for our 9 days was 21 keepers and 49 released. The total weight of the keepers was 447 pounds and the released fish averaged 21 to 27 pounds. The cost of the fishing license was $34 for 5 days, entitling you to fish all public rivers at no extra charge. The cost of the guide was about $1,200 for 7 days, all meals included. I will be arranging a fishing dream trip 2002 with my brother, John Hanna. Cars and trucks can be arranged on your arrival. So once again, thank you, Kelly brothers. I will see you next year.

Tight lines all.

Salmon

By Paddy Clancy

Funny thing! Google the Internet with the words Paddy Clancy and Salmon and you will find a host of stories by me about other people catching the first salmon of the year, usually on the Drowes between Bundoran and Kinlough.

But there's no report of my own first salmon in what was, for me, a very special summer in 1994.

Special, because the salmon was the only one I ever landed.

It was a beauty, a little over 10 lbs caught on Lough Eske outside Donegal town in a boat called Injun Joe with my brothers-in-law John Hanna and Anthony O'Malley-Daly.

So far as I can remember it was the only salmon caught by us that day, and, of course, there was a celebratory drink in the bar of Harvey's Point Hotel when we landed.

Catching the salmon was relatively easy – well, by comparison with trying to observe the repeated instructions of John Hanna how to stand in the boat to ensure that it didn't topple and with Anthony's

John Hanna, Paddy Clancy, and me

directions on slacking, loosening, "Play it, Paddy!" and similar commands that had me totally perplexed.

Anyway, we got it in, and I realised that the one person missing who had fished several weeks until the day before on the lake was another brother-in-law Edward Hanna.

Edward would spend his life fishing on Lough Eske if he could. I mean that. He would be there twenty-four-seven, 365 days a year.

But like the rest of us he had to earn a living – and he does it in distant Washington. The very moment I hooked my only salmon, Edward was in a car on the way to Dublin Airport to return to Washington.

We just had to tell him. His brother John was less than impressed when I extracted my mobile phone from my jacket and promptly started moving about in the boat to get a signal to phone Edward.

We got through, and Edward, as only he can, wanted a minute-by-minute description of how it was done. Then, as only he can, he expressed his regret at missing my great moment in such exuberance that, really, it would be unfair to repeat the language here.

Let's say, it seemed he was very pleased for me!!

Much as I love the patience of salmon fishers, I am afraid I lack sufficient of it myself. Which is why, when I'm on the water these days, it's occasionally at sea seeking mackerel! Now I just love the way they practically jump into the boat!!

9 lb Coho Salmon, caught by the author in October
1968 at Tahsis, British Columbia on bait "Deadly Dick"

Congratulations, Anthony
from

Razor Sharp Barbers

Upper Main Street
Ballyshannon

087 95 88491

Michelle O'Doherty

Men and Women Dry Cuts from €10
Kids €8

The Gadget Story

by Eugene Conway

In the spring of 1950 my father, Detective Officer Louis Conway, was addicted to fishing. Trout and Salmon were his primary target.

It was no accident that he was posted to the Garda station in Ballyshannon, Co Donegal, Ireland. A few strings were pulled to get transferred to this angler's paradise, with the mighty Erne river famous for its tremendous runs of Atlantic salmon, sea trout in the estuary, and many smaller salmon rivers in the area – the famous Lough Melvin with it's own run of grilse, Brown trout, and the rare and famous "Gillaroo" golden trout. Arctic char still roam the deep waters of this beautiful Lough. The hills of Donegal held dozens of small lakes, all of which held a good stock of native wild trout.

My father was a very competent Angler and believed that the most sporting way to catch a fish was to do so using the best fly rods and flies available. If you have ever had the time to observe an Angler enjoying his sport, you would wonder why he spends so much time gazing into the small boxes and lamb's wool wallets he carries in his fishing bag. He is trying to make up his mind on what fly he will use next to deceive a trout or salmon. This has gone on since man first tied a line to a stick to catch a fish. There must be millions of trout and salmon flies in the world today, and yet men still sit and wonder: "What could I use that would be more productive than all the others?"

Such were the thoughts running through my father's head one afternoon while having a cigarette during a pause in his fishing for the beautiful sea trout in the Erne River. He was sitting on the south bank of the river at me location known as "Port Na Mara" which is where the river is divided by the Island known historically as "Inis Saimer." His oldest son Tommie was his companion for the day. He was wondering out loud when he said, "I wonder what the smell of fish would do on a fly..."

He decided there and then to experiment with what he had on hand, which was a pack of "fags" with a silver wrapper inside, a salmon fly, a penknife and two trout, a box of matches, and some "gut" which we now call nylon. He started by burning off the dressing on the salmon fly to get a bare hook. He then rolled some of the silver paper around the shank of the hook, cut a piece of the dorsal fin from the trout he had just caught earlier in the day and, with the help of Tommie to hold the hook, tied the piece of the dorsal fin to the hook behind the eye – and tied again just before the bend of the hook, to hold the whole thing together. By any judgement it was a very crude device – which promptly caught 2 fish.

The fly/lure was damaged by the trout's sharp teeth, and a second attempt was made to make a second fly. The good news was that he now had two more dorsal fins to remake the fly/lure, and by the time the tide came in too far and the fishing stopped, he had a total of 7 trout in the bag.

In Ballyshannon at this time there was a fishing tackle shop named "Rogan's Fly Shop." Michael Rogan was world famous for his Salmon flies, and he and my Father had many glasses of Guinness together, so Dad took the fly/lure to Michael and told him the account of the day's fishing. He asked if Michael could tie a fly to resemble this "GADGET," and he showed Michael the remains of his latest experiment. (I might add here that the word "gadget" often refers to a small mechanical or electronic device with a practical use, or to describe an object which one has forgotten the name of. It is also amusing to think that the scientists who developed the ATOMIC BOMB nicknamed the bomb "the gadget.") Of course for Michael, being the great tier of magnificent flies, this was no problem.

A week later, Dad went in to see if the "GADGET" was finished yet. It was, and Dad was delighted to see that it did resemble a sprat, or a sand eel. Not an exact likeness, you understand, but close enough to confuse a trout in a feeding mood. When you examine a "GADGET" today, hold it up and look at it and you can easily see how I have described this very successful fly/lure, tied at the front and at the bend of the hook, the hump of its "back." It's light, it's well balanced, it travels through the water with the hook down (like a keel) and IT WORKS.

It is without a doubt the finest most successful fly/lure used in Ireland and England today to catch sea trout. There are many different versions of this Fly, with different colours, sizes, etc. But it is always identified as "THE GADGET."

Author's Note: This story puts the ownership of Rogan's Gadget in doubt. I knew the Conway family very well. Detective Officer Louis Conway and Michael Rogan frequented Ferguson's Pub, and both were drinkers "par excellence." Mick Rogan was "a Rogan by name and by nature." He could down the Guinness just by opening his mouth. And Louis Conway was a "rogue" as well. The Garda were the "law and order," but sometimes they had to take the law into their own hands. Ballyshannon was booming, and arresting them meant that the cells would be full. Law and order was meted out on the spot. The Guards were tough men, but Detective Conway was a tough man, and so was Rogan.

The Gadget might well have been "invented" by Conway, but Rogan made it famous.

A Priest and Annette

by Vincent O'Donnell

Some years ago a newly ordained priest arrived in our parish as a curate. Within a few weeks he had employed my wife, Annette, as his house keeper. Soon, he and I became great friends.

The salmon season had arrived and the fishing was great. One morning I invited the curate to accompany me to the river. I pulled up at Ballymacahill Bridge and began to don my angling gear. The river bank from the bridge to the head of Devlin (*Dubh Linn* = Black Pool), where I intended to begin, was very muddy. Many anglers took a round-about way through the fields to avoid the mud.

Right now I noticed two anglers doing just that. They were ambling along deep in conversation. There was no-one else about. I decided that I was going to be at Devlin ahead of them, thus ensuring a better chance of hooking a 'taking' fish. And so I pushed on through the mud. My friend, the priest, followed me but at a more cautious pace.

On my third cast I hooked a salmon. The priest was soon by my side and was amazed that I had hooked a fish so soon. Now the bank at this spot was about four feet above the water level and there was a tree to the left and one to the right. It was obvious I was going to have difficulties landing my salmon. I rarely bring anything other than my fishing rod and a few spare lures.

Finally the salmon was well played out and splashing about in front of us. Next thing I knew the two anglers who had taken the long dry route were by our side. One of them on seeing my predicament handed me his landing net. I landed the salmon. The other handed me a 'priest' (a short heavy bar of metal or wood for killing fish) with which I quickly administered the 'last rites.'

I then handed the 'priest' back to it's owner and thanked him, and as I did, I looked at my friend, the curate, and said jokingly, "Next time I come fishing I'm going to bring a *priest*."

Then I washed the net, folded it and handed it back to its owner and thanked him. As I did I heard the curate say, in the same tone of voice as I had just used, "Next time you come fishing, maybe you should bring *Annette*."

And with that the other two were moving away to find a spot where they could fish. I doubt if they understood the puns.

"Mark My Words"

by Darren Rooney

A wee man, never quiet or shy,
Wit sayings – he would draw fast like a gun.
"Driver her, baby!" "Did ya miss the boat?"
An action man – having harmless bundles of fun.

Generous, hardworkin', respected and loved.
I hope they were ready for you up above.
"There'll be no sailing to-night!" "I say – I say!"
With yer motorbike revving, and you on yer way.

You touched lots of hearts – like a deck of cards.
Left a legacy of memories with everyone you met.
"Does my hair look big in this?" "I said – I said!"

"Ride her, baby!" That music's not loud.
It's time for the craic, waken the crowd.
"When yer good, yer good!" Handbag is in,
That's when we found the party begins.

A Bar Man's Knightmare – and him one hisself
From table to counter and up on the shelf,
"Don't 'B' at it, I say!" "You'll find that an ill knot."
The enjoyment, atmosphere, it just couldn't 'B' bought.

Of all of our friends – people we knew,
There'll never 'B' a character as lively as you.
Yer batteries were charged – START button set,
So 'R' our hearts with this Mark of Respect.

As the song says – and I say –

It's not wat you take when you leave this world behind you,
It's wat you leave behind you when yer gone...

"Cheers"

Shark Stories

By Anthony O'Malley Daly

I have a shark story Ballyshannon man Brendan Merrifield, who charters from Mullaghmore. The story is –

Shark One 22722

Brendan caught a Blue Shark, which he returned alive. It had a tag number 22722. It was captured in Donegal Bay, 11th August, 1995.

The same shark was re-captured 600 miles south west of the Azores, by Spanish longliner. The date was 28th February 1997. I will leave you to calculate how long the shark had been at liberty, but it had travelled 1400 miles. When Brendan Merrifield caught the shark, it weighed 31 lbs and was 53" long, but when it was recaptured, the detail of its weight and length was not recorded.

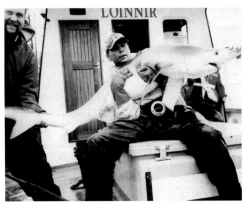

A 102lb Blue Shark, Caught off Arranmore,
Tagged and Returned

Shark Two 24926

The second Blue Shark was captured in Donegal Bay. 21st September 1997, weighed 47 lbs, was 60 inches long, and had a girth of 25 inches . The same tag number (24926) was recaptured on the 3rd October 1997. I hope you are taking all this in. The second shark was taken 400 miles north east of the Azores, 12 days on. This shark swam 900 miles, which works out at 76 miles per day.

Thank you Brendan Merrifield. (I think this is fantastic.) Big Brother is watching, even the sharks!!!!!

Eske Angling Association

My Dear Friend Anto:

I think the time is due when I should put pen to paper, and let you know the role that you have played in helping me enjoy and experience all these wonderful days on Lough Eske.

Perhaps the book you are writing will in some way let your readers know the true companion you are, and your enduring love and passion for the great sport of fishing.

Edward, you, and I were honoured and and privileged to befriend all these great Anglers over the past sixty years, and I know if they were here today, their sentiments would only re-enumerate what feeling there is for you God Bless all our friends, including Edwin and Lexy, Jim Thomas, Howard Temple, Peter Kennedy, Jack Barry, Thomas Harvey, Jim McKeever, Colm O'Donnell, Willie McGowan, Paddy Padraig Martin, and all those who still give us great pleasure to remember and reminisce about while drifting down The Ridge with that killer fly The Green Peter. Lighting the fire on a stormy, wet day, just to light my cigarette from a smouldering whyne branch, and then watch Edward devour a couple of small trout (bones and all), cooked over the roasting ash on a cold day. Far cry from Jim of the National Hotel, who in the late fifties brought out his smoker and treated us all to a decent feed.

God Bless the memories, Anto, and when I set the boat at full speed ahead for Corraber, you jumped in over the bow. Edward turned around and said, "Where's Anthony?" And just like a big seal, your head surfaced behind the boat, well back may I say.

And the day after the Wedding, when we forgot take our breakfast (I wonder why). Edward caught a salmon, and we decided to light a fire and eat him – the salmon. And, on that day there was an American fishing from The Ridge, and when he witnessed what we were doing to the salmon, with a pair of scissors, he could not believe it. Well, when we cooked the salmon over the fire, the American said, "What does it taste like?" as he had only seen films of Native Americans Indians cooking fish like this in Washington State. "Have a wee bit," and Edward handed him a "junt" of Smoked Wild Salmon on a pure warm flat stone, and his remarks embedded all that Mother Nature can provide on the wonderful of our Lough Eske.

The "Breathing Salmon" – well, we will leave that for another time. And the day we launched our boat on the road, and when you told Alex to be careful with the engine, and Alex said, "Anthony, I know every stone in the lake," and then BANG, with Big Walter with one leg out and one leg in.

The memories go on and on, and I only hope that John Patrick and his friends will experience all that is good on this "Special Lake," not forgetting all those wonderful families in Townawilly and Lough Eske who let us rest on their shoreline after a hard day's work.

Both of you are my dearest friends. Edward and Anto, and I Love you. Both very much. Thanks for the Memories.

Your Loving Brother, and Brother-In-Law,

John Joseph Hanna
(Longtime Chairman of Eske Anglers)

John Hanna - Not Lucky, Just Good...

Our First Eurovision Song Contest Winner – Dana

By Anthony O'Malley Daly

"All Kinds of Everything" won the Eurovision Song Contest in 1970. It was such a simple plain song, yet it took the title for Ireland. Of course it was the way Dana sang the song. "The Singer – Not the Song" was the title of a movie, but this was the singer *and* the song. "All Kinds of Everything" and the *real* Dana, not the Israeli Dana that took the winner's prize a few years ago. Nevertheless the Israeli song deserved its win, though there was some confusion over the gender of the person who sang the song at the time. Well done.

Jim Thomas got us to stop at Given's Pub, Ballybofey, where we had something to eat. Then the 'whole plant' adjourned upstairs where we sat around a large TV to watch the contest. Our party was Jim Thomas, his first cousin Edward Hanna, John Daly, my first cousin who was a doctor in Ballygawley outside Sligo. There was a senior politician visiting Mrs Annie Given and later we were joined by Annie herself. The craic was good and we stayed until the very end.

During the voting Annie fell asleep and rolled over, pinning Edward Hanna to the end of the sofa. Annie was a fine large woman and we could not waken her. It was a crucial part of the contest, so we had to leave Edward with Annie Given in such an uncomfortable position until well after the result was over.

Getting back to the Eurovision! The pub has changed hands more than a couple of times. Annie has gone to her eternal reward. Jim Thomas died a few years ago. Dana Rosemary Scallon from Derry was innocent, remains innocent but streetwise, was and is an inspiration. She married one of the Scallons from Irvinestown and was an MEP for a number of years. In 1970 she roused our spirits, and I thank her for being the real deal and for being Ireland's first winner of the Eurovision Song Contest. That night in Given's Pub we were all happy with the performance and the victory of "All Kinds of Everything."

I was in Given's Pub in 1970. Where were YOU?

Like a Fish out of Water

by Vincent O'Donnell

The river was fishing well. I fished mornings and evenings when possible. One day I missed my morning session. It was two o'clock when I arrived at '*Poll Garbh.*' The river was quite low but '*Poll Garbh*' always had a good flow, even in low water conditions.

I had just settled down to a rhythm of casting and stripping when I noticed something unusual. A salmon swam from the tail of the pool to the top along the opposite bank with its head out of the water. This took about six seconds. 'Most unusual,' I thought.

I continued fishing. About half a minute later a fish, I took it to be the same one, swam across the tail of the pool from the far side to the near side almost totally out of the water. In order to keep its body above water it had to swim at a very fast pace. It reminded me of salmon moving upstream through shallow water.

A few seconds later it sped up towards the top of the pool, passing within a few yards of where I was standing. I couldn't resist the temptation – I cast across its back and, yes, foul-hooked it. Like a torpedo, it took off towards the far bank and somewhere en route the fly lost its hold.

At this stage I put away my fly rod and stood watching in amazement. At the tail of the pool is an 'island' and from it to the far bank are stones and gravel that have been washed in there by successive floods. Actually, the last two yards near the bank is similar to a sandy beach. Onto this 'beach' swam the salmon. It wriggled about for four to five seconds before making its way back into the water and continuing swimming about on the surface.

It then made its way onto the gravelly patch, wriggled along until it entered the pool below, a distance of about two yards. Now for me to get to the pool below, I would have to clamber up the bank behind me, make my way through long grass and rushes, cross a bridge, make my way along the river bank through trees and briars, climb over a few fences etc. But my fish was very accommodating, it wriggled back up over the gravel patch and back into '*Poll Garbh.*'

It swam up along the far bank, with its head above water, until it came to a tree that grew out from the bank-side. The trunk, about six inches in diameter, was roughly at 45° to the water surface. Three times it jumped up along that three trunk, its body clearing the water by about six inches. It was the first time I got a good look at its entire body and satisfied myself that there was nothing attached to it that might be aggravating it.

After some more 'running around' on the surface it made it's way back again to the gravel patch at the tail and crossed it once more into the lower pool. But this time it didn't come back. Actually, it seemed to be getting weak and was finding it difficult to keep it's body in an horizontal position on top of the water.

I decided to follow. I negotiated the route already mentioned and after a few minutes, during which it was hidden from my view, I got to where I thought it should be. But now it was being carried downstream by the flow of the water and had already entered the next pool down.

The fish, by now, seemed quite exhausted and its movements were following a regular pattern. Using its energy it would 'push' itself into an horizontal position on the surface, then gradually its tail would drop until it was in a vertical position and only its head above water. This pattern was being repeated while its body was being carried downstream

At the tail of that pool was an extensive stony/gravelly patch, now dry due to the low water conditions, with a narrow channel through which the water flowed to the next pool. Towards this gravelly patch, my fish was being carried. Again I scurried up banks, slid down banks and made my way till I was above the gravelly patch. The fish had about twenty feet to go to the dry gravel unless it was sucked through the narrow channel to the next pool.

I slithered down the bank onto the gravel, walked across and there about eight feet away in about twelve inches of water was my exhausted fish. I lifted it by the tail and carried it onto the gravel. I wasn't sure what to do now that I had it in my hands. Thoughts ran through my head – would it survive if I returned it, should it not be examined, could it be eaten, etc. Eventually I lifted a stone and ended its agony.

I phoned two angling friends who were quite familiar with salmon and their antics, one of which worked on a salmon farm and had had some training in salmon and their behaviour, and asked them to come to meet me. When all three of us were together we had a good look at the fish. Seven and a half pounds, reasonably fresh, possibly three weeks in the river, had a few scars as if attacked by some predator but already quite well healed. We then opened and examined each organ but could find nothing that would explain its behaviour.

The salmon was eaten, enjoyed and, to the best of my knowledge, no one suffered as a result. I have asked many people, surfed the 'net,' consulted books, but so far have found no plausible explanation to the fish's behaviour. Maybe somebody reading this might have one.

Rogan of Donegal

by Anonymous

An era came to an end when the new Ballyshannon Credit Union Building replaced the shop where Michael Rogan and his family created and sold their famous fishing flies. Rogan flies were admired and sold worldwide. Since 1830, the Rogan family and their employees had created superb flies the old-fashioned way – by hand, without any of the paraphernalia usually associated with the craft: hackle pliers, vices, etc.

There are many memorable stories about the Rogan dynasty. Grandfather Rogan used natural dyes in his dressings because the acid peat-rich water of local rivers tended to bleach artificial dyes. Tradition has it that he used ass urine (that from a stallion was said to be the best) as the basis of his dying process. The urine was kept in a big barrel in the garden until it smelled so bad that the sanitary authorities demanded its removal. But it was only at that stage that old Michael Rogan reckoned it was ready for use as a detergent which left his materials in a good condition to accept the dyes and maintain their unfading qualities.

His grandson Michael Rogan tells a lovely story of his grandfather. A titled gentleman (said to have been the grandfather of the present Duke of Devonshire) visited his grandfather, and old Michael Rogan offered his visitor a customary draw of his clay pipe. Before putting the pipe in his mouth, however, the illustrious visitor wiped the stem with a silk handkerchief. Grandfather Rogan, who could be equally fastidious if he saw fit, promptly broke off the mouthpiece and continued to smoke from the shortened stem for the rest of the evening.

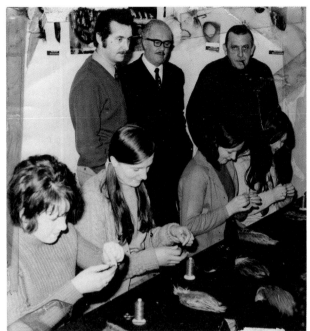

Hand-Tying Flies at Rogan's — Mick Rogan, with pipe, upper right; Noleen McGonigle, daughter of Gussie McGonigle, lower left

Rita Rogan

Ballyshannon and District Anglers Association

By Paddy Donagher

From my point of view, I have always been associated with Angling here in Ballyshannon and I have found that through organisation we tend to get things done, admittedly slowly, but at least it gets done. On a winters day during 1993 I felt that we needed to resurrect the old Ballyshannon Angling club, a club that my late brother Eddie was very much involved in, so I made a few phone calls to see if there was interest in setting up the club again and the response I got was overwhelming especially from my late friend Gerry McNamara and a few others.

A meeting was held in the Day Centre on the 12th of October 1993 and from that meeting there was a committee elected with Gerry taking the chair, myself as Secretary and PJ Coughlin and P O'Malley as joint Treasurers, the meeting agreed that we made every effort to bring on board as many Junior Anglers as was possible, and to this day that situation prevails.

Handover of new boat to Ballyshannon Anglers Association, 1997

But sadly the 2007 season started with a draconian licence increase, with the result that it had a particularly costly effect on all Anglers. Many just packed their fishing gear away and to this day some of those people have refused to return to angling. From a junior membership of up to 20 anglers prior to 2007 we now see a deflated membership down to 4 anglers. While we in the association have lobbied year after year to have licence fees reduced and in the case of the Erne Estuary Special Licence we would wish to have this 1934 act abolished. We have appealed to the minister that there should be no licence fee for junior anglers, but sadly this lobbying has fallen on deaf ears. Where there is faith there is hope, we in the association will keep trying to have a common sense situation prevail and hope that the minister will have another look at the ludicrous angling licence fees that are applied to junior anglers.

We wish Anthony O'Malley Daly all the best in his endeavour to promote and publicize angling here in the North West of the country.

Is Mise,

Paddy Donagher
President and Treasurer
Ballyshannon and District Anglers Association

Jim McGuinness, Manager of Donegal All-Ireland Championship Donegal Gaelic Football Team

By Anthony O'Malley Daly

The 1992 All-Ireland senior was Donegal's very first senior championship. Jim McGuinness was part of that 1992 set-up. And afterwards when the senior team came close to taking a second All-Ireland senior, Jim McGuinness was on the team. I saw him playing senior during the league campaign in 1993, and while he was very energetic, in the end Jim McGuinness failed to impress. He used to throw himself at the ball, and do more damage to his own players at mid-field.

However, it was as a team manager that Jim McGuinness brought glory to Donegal. In the space of two years Jim McGuinness has won three major titles, beginning with the 2011 Ulster title. He repeated the Ulster 2012 championship. The repeat of the Ulster title almost went unheeded. But he did it.

Jim McGuinness has a management team made up of his assistant manager Rory Gallagher, who played for Fermanagh. Jim McGuinness formed his own sterling training regime that took two years of strict training that even intruded into the players' private lives. Not all of the players took to the strict routine. You had some defections like Steven Cassity, the all-star, but also on field and during training. McGuinness struggled through 2010. When we won the 2011 Ulster title he overcame a twenty year gap since 1992 when silverware last appeared on the shelf.

The year 2011 was the year that made things began to happen. We won Ulster title playing "The McGuinness Way." People began to look up. When Dublin beat us in Croke park and went on to win the All-Ireland, the critics started up again… and when Donegal lost, they were naturally enough back on track…

Jimmy's Winning Games

Suddenly there was a song about *"Jimmy's Winning Matches"*. We all sat up. Donegal had won back-to-back Ulster titles – a feat never done before, and that was the beginning of end of our doubts in Jimmy McGuinness. I have been serious about Jimmy McGuinness but this was the start of our belief, and belief too in Donegal as a a football team. For they never lost a game.

The first test of our team was versus Kerry under the watchful eye of the "troika" of Francie Brolly, Derry; Pat Spillane, a Kerry man with All-Ireland medals to beat the band – and the third member was Colm O'Rourke of Meath. Michael Lister, the RTE anchorman, was "in the middle." We will make a long story short. When the half time arrived their story had changed. All four of them were changed and were 100 per cent in the Donegal camp. And there they stayed. Period.

Congratulations to Jim McGuinness on his appointment to the Celtics, and to Neil Lennon as manager of the Celtics for their 2012 victory over Bardcelona.

Fishermen of Kildoney in Inquisition

By James G. Daly

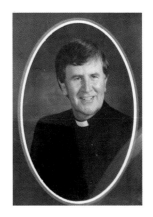

I have been asked to write a bit, so I will write, as I feel
      comfortable with,
Upon the topic fishing, fishermen, and what happened on
      the Erne,
For a stranger, a great little river, this flows from prow to
      stern,
Through ancient Ballyshannon town, where is that, you
      may brazen frown?

In Donegal south, where at the mouth, the Erne reaches the sea,
After a journey long, through lakes, round inlets, all the way from Cavan,
From Cavan to the sea, often scoured by fishermen, and as we shall see,
Those, of other lands, who valued, our prized treasured salmon, eel, appeal,
Not for pleasure, for which many a line is cast, but rather to take, on the make,
Upon this natural source of wealth, which belongs to all, common food and sport.

Not too many know, we had an inquisition in Ballyshannon, many years ago.
An inquisition like in Spain, you might inquire, no, not the same, different bench,
Of faithful, we are told, fifteen local men, stalwart, called in after dissolution,
The legal minds, which fought against Kildoney men, in the battle for rights to fish,
Their estuary, ascendancy minds convoluted, even claimed King Henry the second,
      (two)
Knew of Ballyshannon, and of its salmon, and eels, estuaries, when Strongbow
Trod these shores, tongue in cheek, neck well stiff, lawyers trod on rights, to
      wrench.

In fifteen eighty-eight, at the town, and monastery of Assaroe in death's stench,
The queen, Elizabeth by name, the First of course, sent to dissolve the fishing rights
      of local men,
All over the place, property, lakes and rivers claimed, in name of crown, upon her
      head
Which lay in bed, unlike her mother's. She got the crown, from Bloody Mary, who
Contrary, well known, put Protestants to the sword. But now Elizabeth as Catholic –
But back to dissolution, and resolution, of inquisition, on a mission, to take and
      take,
Waters were up for grabs and fishing rights.

The monks of St. Bernard of Assaroe,
Had to go, for they, after four hundred years, were regarded as foreigners, in Co –
With Clairveaux in France, now lands and all were claimed, for the Elizabethan
     crowned,
To give Foliates, who sound, very Irish and not French, regarded enemies, astound.
Twelve weirs upon the river, for catching fish and eels, the Abbey's by right, lost,
In the night. Of fright, the inquisition, made up of jurors, settle in name of the
     crown,
Many monks in graves at Ballyhanna found, product of settlement, if not then,
     when?
Ten shillings worth, the lot, for Assaroe, as named a season's fishing, then was
     worth,
In money of the day, three and four pence sterling of the crown, of England, which
     in its turn, took The entire "Abbey, all the castles, lands, tenements, tithes,
     and other profits of every kind"

Not very refined, when on the grab, or plunder, claimed for the queen, by right of
     her crown,
The livelihoods, by hoods on heads, Robert Florence, servant of the Es-cheator, as
     the name
Suggests, cheated the rest, a Mr Scaife, and makes it absolutely clear as water that
     the tidal waters, From the sea to the Erne, now the free flowing Erne, for the
     first time was of Property matters,
With a money value imbued, in fifteen ninety-eight, someone owned the river,
     rights of people,
Gone the steeple, which had built the weirs, for salmon eels, and fed the locals, with
     creels,
To fish, good bye to freedom, enjoyed with the monks, since eleven eight four, now
     crown vested,
One could be arrested, like the waters of the Erne; Mammon took from God, yet not
     clear, suggested,

How do you arrest water, you may ask, will it slip through your fingers as the rights
     of monks,
Watered down by the crown in inquisition mode, the rivers of all Donegal, to the
     crown belonged.
And Fermanagh, Cavan, all the way to Dublin, wherever a Monastery could be
     dissolved, faith,
Liberty under threat?

Thank God we're surrounded by water, held no more, for the poor, in debt.
King James, of Scottish stock, took up the disillusioned flock, which government in
     Dublin, mock.

Then fishing on the Erne, from the bar of sand and sea, to salmon leap, changed
    hands regularly.
A chap called Binglie, not of the crooning kind, in October fourteenth, sixteen
    hundred and three, Benefitted for twenty years of lease, on churches, castle,
    town and water, even soil beneath, and a thousand scores of land surrounding,
    for the princely sum of ten shillings, of English sterling, *fiat.*

So by sixteen hundred and three, from flow of sea, all fishing rights, and all that
    bites, once free,
Belong to the king by right of crown, all the fishing weirs, lake, pool, and river,
    comely pleasant sites,
So-called Lough Erne, eels, salmon, herrings belonged to the king, a stout fellow by
    now,
Anything bites, who ignored Elizabeth's grant of the same, to Rorie O' Donnell,
    Earl of Tyrconnell, who must bow out.

Freedom of the waters disappeared as fifteen jurors of inquisition secured the flow
    of water about, for rent, owned, setting precedent for the future, when waters
    free salmon eel, would harness be.

For electricity, and beautiful, winding river, fall would disappear, as North, South
    conspire, in choir, Later we will come to see, when salmon, all fish spree, has
    virtually disappeared, from waters, dire,

Of the Assaroe, I wonder if anyone told the inquisition, in the ports and quays of
    Ballyshannon, lock, where fish is to be caught, as Binglie, tell lie, or not,
    elated, took possession of entire fishing stock.

The social Catastrophe had begun, not just in Ireland but in Britain too, dissolution
    of a way of life, Monasteries provided, for all the people, would lead to the
    famine, in later year, Dickensian days, But this is later, of the mast, pull sail
    to sea, in wind of change, and quickly change again came, stays.

Binglie made way for Foliate, whose descendant, I have in acquaintance, secured,
    Sir Henry,
For Twenty one years, the whole of Assaroe, Including monk's claim, but for five
    measly shillings, It was granted to Henry Crofton also, in between, as Dublin
    and London conspired, and on chilling Twentieth of July, sixteen hundred and
    nine, for six pounds, thirteen shillings, and four pence
Sterling, the creek, bay, river stream, at Ballyshannon, from the sea to the salmon
    leap, curling.

To Mary Baroness Devlin, and her son, Robert Nugent, the catching all kind of fish,
    and salmon,

River Erne was a most desirable catch, for one who desired salmon, investment, and
value going up.
Right over fish had begun, while confusion over ownership, now in three sets of
hands, hiccups,
And now the new, Church of Ireland, stepped in, to stake its claim to fishing rights,
Bishops, of Clougher, and Raphoe, on monastic claim of Assaroe, seeing it as
church possession, in regression.
But Foliate held to his rights, new acquired, not to be taken by the choired, frocked,
and mocked.

November thirtieth, sixteen hundred and twelve, James, King of London, knew of
the little town,
Granted it lock, stock and barrel, with its castle to Foliate, all had sold out to him,
stem the rot.
In the "Manor of Ballyshannon" now Foliate was the peer, who had no peers, but he
soon died,
And in his pride, he left a son of nine, Thomas as his heir. Whom Charles the king
made a lord,
At the grand old age of twenty six, releasing him from conditions, regulations of
plantation, afford.

Thomas left the rights to Henry, which brought it with much strife to the century of
eighteen,
And died, no heir provide, river Erne sighed, so it followed the distaff line, to the
honourable, Connolly, or Thomas Packenham, to give him his rightful name,
in Thomas Connolly Packenham, by name and arms, took possession of the
Erne, fisheries, as of many years before, which the Abbey Ashroe, or
Ashrach, as pronounced in eighteen hundred and ninety seven, This confusion
of who owned the rights, met the fishermen of church on Sunday,

Kildowney in high courts of Dublin, in later years, when Derry consortium claimed
the vacant claim, but in time mean Foliate sold out to William Connolly, price
had gone down, again.
But the download trend goes right back, to Henry II, between me and you, and he
passed it on,
To Charles and James, not to mention Elizabeth, presumes, the legal minds, which
decides, or con, That fifteen good men from Ballyshannon, made up a panel,
to claim the rights, at inquisition, in fifteen eighty eight, but who needs facts,
when you have plantation, the locals gave away, their monastery and their
fishing rights, imagination flights, for lawyers, dramatic barristers.

More dramatic than Shakespeare of Elizabeth's day, dramatic licence, crowned
claims, reigns, on waters of the Erne, returned to local ownership, when there
were no fish, to catch, oil stains,

A shock, electrified the flock, of Abbey Assaroe plantation, replaced by implementation.

New state, new rate, for salmon, herring eel, weirs gone, immigrants flown, fishermen,
Church of Sunday, or Kildowney, men went out in twenty nine, eighteenth of February, to be Precise, reversing history, as written by the crown. Also flown – Elizabeth, James and Charles.
But never Saimer again would see, winding backs, dogs bark, but he is gone, like fishing barrels.
Only on anecdote and stories of the past, can glory days be recounted, salmon of pounds fifty,
And two, caught along the Erne shore, asleep under bank, as now Abbey Assaroe, once thrifty.

Sailing ships to grace the Erne, with embracing sail, obstructed natural channel, and blinded men. Wild geese rise with swan, nature carries on, while men their games play, claims, never pretend.

The Winding Banks

by James G. Daly

I remember as a small boy, getting into a motor boat at the mall quay, and spending a glorious summer's day, with the fishermen, down along the shore, eating homemade bread, and drinking strong sweet tea. And coming home in the evening with a string of fish, as big as myself, to the Rock. Fish were so plentiful then – trout, and flat fish, and salmon – I could hardly carry the load up the steps. The camaraderie was great, men full of stories. These were real people, not just pawns in a political and financial game.

So when the opportunity was given to review, a little, the events which took place in the inquisition which began over Ballyshannon waters, I took the plunge, one might say. It is difficult, in so short a time, to do justice to all these events, of the years between fifteen eighty-eight, and nineteen twenty-eight, when judgement was given. But this judgement, to dissolve the monasteries and transfer the rights over the produce, made a massive difference in the lives of people, not just in Ballyshannon and throughout Ireland, but in Britain too. It was breakdown of a social system, which would have paved the way for the famine in Ireland, and deprivation in Dickensian England.

I do apologise to anyone, who will read this piece of poetry, if one could call it such. The events, which reached from Henry II of England coming to Ireland, were in the minds of lawyers. Also, the idea that he showed great interest in Ballyshannon waters was the dramatics of barristers. When in the sixteenth century Elizabeth I also came to claim the rights over Ballyshannon waters, with the dissolution of the monastery of Assaroe on the winding banks of Erne, she began the process which would eventually evoke the claim of the fishermen of Kildoney. They set out to reclaim what they regarded as their own waters and fish. But in reality, no one can really own the waters, or the fish, but both are a common gift, which we can appreciate to feed ourselves, and to enjoy the sport.

As we see, there were many people representing the crown involved in the process, from those who made up the inquisition, to the final owner Connolly Packenham. The mind of the lawyers made the inquisitors "local men" who dissolved the monastery and transferred the water rights. This ploy to make it more palatable causes one to smile. Again, these minds of lawyers saw the monks of Assaroe as foreigners after four hundred years, with no rights, but beneficiaries of the good will of Henry II. Because the monks were of the order of St. Bernard of Clairveaux, they were regarded as French, and so disposable, as Catholic France was supporting Mary – Queen of Scots, and Elizabeth's enemy. The waters passed from hand to hand as the government in Dublin was in conflict with the London government. Old Irish claims were lost, even those given to Rory O'Donnell by Elizabeth.

There is also some insight given into the Plantation of Ulster, with the choice of Scottish Presbyterians, a thorn in the side of the established church and supporters of the Scottish claims to the English throne. I mentioned "Bloody Mary" (as she was named), and Elizabeth the first. These two half sisters had grown up with the same experience of their mothers being scorned, and one killed. They grew up in fear, and their zeal as Catholic or Protestant left them open to be manipulated. But this is another question, for another day. The relationship between the Follett's and the Stuart kings is again opening up a whole bag of questions. The events of the inquisition at Assaroe, Ballyshannon, as elsewhere in Ireland, had much wider consequences, as I have indicated, not just in these isles, but in the new world too. I spoke with the lawyer who represented the fishermen in ninety twenty nine. He is now deceased. I also have a friend among the Folletts, so it makes it all more interesting, and personal.

The central issue for myself is that waters, and their fish, now became a commodity, and then the beauty of the river was destroyed by the new independent state to serve a commodity. But as always nature has the final say, and it goes freely, despite the "best laid plans of mice and men." Don't let us pretend. No one can now return to the winding banks of Erne, but the water flows proudly from Cavan to the sea. The meanderings of the inquisition still linger on.

James G. Daly is a retired priest.

Congratulations and Best Wishes to
Anthony O'Malley Daly
from the

Ballyshannon Shoe Company
Main Street, Ballyshannon

071 98 51231

TRIBUTES

By Anthony O'Malley Daly

Eddie Barron

Eddie Barron from College Street, looked after all the Irish who left for America when the recession struck. Eddie was a keen net fisherman and has many relations who fished the Channel and outside (in the sea) with drift nets and bag nets. Eddie and his brother Willie married two American sisters. Willie was in the catering business. Eddie was an Auctioneer or Realtor with Geraghty for years and years. Pat McNeely, a cousin, worked and helped Eddie. He bought and sold and invested in property. He did not drink. He was well "got" in Boston.

Eddie Barron will never be forgotten. I promise you that. His remains are buried in Abbey Assaroe, just where he would have wished for. Thank You, Eddie Barron, from all the O'Malley Dalys, especially Orla and Patrick, who now reside in San Francisco, and from all the others. "Go On" to your reward...Eddie.

Gussie McGonigle

Gussie McGonigle, Corry, Belleek, a popular person and well known game angler, died in the early days of February. Appreciations of Gussie's pathway through life have already been written.

He organised completely the annual Keenaghan Lake Trout Fly competition and presented the proceeds yearly to the Ulster Cancer Foundation. He was a master fisherman, and staunch friend. There is some talk a while of me and thee, and then no more of me and thee. Goodbye, Gussie.

"Anthony, They're a HHHHore to Ketch" was Gussie's favourite saying.

He was never shy in standing up for his family. His son Gerry got the first salmon of the 1997, but not before there was "an imposter" put forward by some

Late Gussie McGonigle, Belleek with 26lbs. and 18lbs. Salmon caught using Shrimp on the Duff River

Gussie McGonigle, R.I.P.

"rogues" who pooched a salmon in the night. The two salmon were compared, and at the crucial time when a final decision had to made. Gussie broke the silence, with these words: "The Devon (blue and silver) must have had 'Tail Lights' for the salmon to see it." That was end of story. Gerry got the verdict. Rightly so.

Jim and Lorraine Thomas

The death occurred of Jim Thomas, a great angler and fishing companion, late of The National Hotel, Donegal Town. In fact, Jim got me my first Salmon on the River Eske many years ago, when he instructed me where to cast the bait at Stephenson's Pool. I landed an 8lb fresh fish that day and got the bug for life as a result.

Jim Thomas, R.I.P.

The last occasion John and Edward Hanna were fishing on Lough Eske (some years back) with Jim Thomas, he caught three massive salmon using a silver and copper spoon called the Kerry Boy. At the catching of one of these three salmon Jim's reel fell off and into the lake, but not only did Jim Thomas retrieve the gut tangled reel, but he eventually landed the Salmon – such was his patience and skill.

On Saturday John Hanna and I were preparing to set out on the lake. John was going through his box to select a lure when he came up with the very same Kerry Boy. "Put it on in memory of Jim," I said, and John did. Well, the rest is destined history. John got the only salmon landed off the Eske for such a long while.

Fond memories of past days come flooding back, when we all held the sweet bird of youth in our ambitious grasp. May Jim Thomas rest in everlasting peace.

Jim Thomas died many moons ago. Apart from being a great Angler, Jim married Lorraine McGettigan from Kilmacrennen, who was a dedicated, well-qualified Nurse.

It was the time I had Asthma, and (repeating myself), the time before Inhalers. I still have Asthma, but now it is controllable. Back then I had to struggle about, wheezing. I often say to people – you can suffer from any illness, but not being able to breathe, where breathing is an essential for life, is very distressing. Many can vouch for this. Lorraine nursed me, in Donegal, and I never forgot her for it, and never will.

Thanks Lorraine. A few weeks ago in a column written by Peter Campbell for the "Donegal Democrat" a photo appeared of Lorraine Thomas holding a 9lbs salmon she caught in Lough Eske in 1963. Jim and Lorraine are dead now. They adopted a boy and a girl. Paul, their son, works for John Hanna making the best hats for your head. Laura resides in Galway.

Seamus and Ita Goan

Seamus Goan was the man who started up the Creevy Co-Op and got the the fishing vessel, calling it *"An Dunai Mara."* It is widely used, along with the cottages. Seamus Goan was one of the most popular people to come about the place. Himself and Mandy Goan, his brother, were actually like the sage salmon, coming Home.

When they landed, there they stayed, until first Mandy died, and then Seamus, and then Ita...

Seamus Goan, R.I.P.

They were neighbours of President Mary McAleese, and one sunny day the President arrived to officially launch the boat. We all saw her. She was very nice and spoke to everybody. Seamus was in his element.

I worked with Seamus for many years. We started the Friday Club in Sean Og's pub. We met there every Friday at 3:30, and we had a glass or bottle of beer and a glass of Irish Whiskey twice. Sometimes Freddie Grimes would join us. We used to watch the young people sucking down the expensive drinks. "Anthony," Freddie would ask, "where do they get their money from?"

Ita, Seamus's wife, was from Cootehill, Co Cavan. They had ten children, I think. They are all successful, and I see them in the summer.

The story goes that Seamus and Ita were going to visit Ita's sister, who resided in that metropolis. The snag was that there was a heavy fog, and they were late. In the middle of all this Seamus saw a man standing in the doorway of (where else?) a pub. He was typically attired in a typically black coat that had so many soakings that it was nearly in shreds, a well worn summer cap that had two drooping flaps, and there was a dirt mark where he had taken it off when he was dunging out the duggle, saving the hay, swiping at the midges, alone in the bog – or taking it off when he pretended to say the Angelus. There were many many more occasions when he had to doff his cap. Finally, like most old single farmers, he had a belt around his waist (tied in the middle). He hadn't shaved in a week.

All Seamus wanted to know was "Where is Cootehill," so he said, "Where are we?" To which the figure in the doorway replied, "F - - - g Cootehill." Seamus, Ita, and the third party had finally reached their Happy Abode. Cootehill.

Mandy Goan

Mandy was Seamus's brother. He had a distinctive Belfast accent. Mandy lived in a mobile home, sheltered at the gable of the house. The road to Creevy Pier was narrow when it cut off the main road to Rossnowlagh beach. Cars, as per usual, did not go slow. This worried Mandy. One day he stood out on the verge, to stop any car speeding. First man he encountered was Cecil King, Boss of the provincial newspaper, The Donegal Democrat. Mandy spoke to Cecil, who after the lecture took off. Mandy shouted after Cecil King, "F - - - g Tourist!"

Ita and Seamus Goan had a big family. All are high respected in the area, and they have many relations in the area. Seamus, Mandy and Ita are with God now...

Seamus Goan was one of my Best Friends, and worked for The Democrat newspaper...

The official opening of new Hanger was performed by Cathal Goan, son of Seamus, who was for number years Director General of R.T.E., the National Broadcaster, in Dublin. On the day of the opening I saw my dear friend Ita at a distance. That was the last time I saw her alive.

All the Goan family were lovers of fish. And had a fishing trip each year.

Malachy Daly, who was a great friend of the Goans, donated property to the Creevy Co-Op. He often took Seamus out for a drink. When Seamus died, Malachy Daly was on hand to take Ita to town (Ballyshannon). He called religiously (pardon the pun) to daily mass and Sunday mass in the Friary.

Seamus was an angler, and had a very wide cast. Down at Creevy Pier when Seamus took a cast, the way had to be cleared for him. He had a very expansive cast, not an expensive cast.

One time I heard the Goans and Tommy Cleary (Bishop Street, Ballyshannon) discussing how they fried Mackerel. The method was described (well, nearly) – the cleaning out of the fish, etc, etc, etc, was an art. The final chef act was to slice ravines along its body, fill them with garlic, put the mackerel on a hot pan, and fry the buck (meaning *"f--k"*) out of the fish. Four of them were friends for life. Now they are together in Heaven, where it matters.

Pat and Mary Gallagher

I made friends with all the people around Askill. Pat Gallagher (rate collector) who lived along the road was married to a great lady, Mary. She was co-opted to Leitrim County Council. Mary did a great job as a councillor. Mary had a sister who was married to a Thornton from the West of Ireland. He was a far-out relation of mine.

John and Mary Hill

John and Mary Hill and a large family resided in Leitrim, with a shallow harbour, a line of boats, easy access, and the kindest hearts and friendship that I found in the county. There was Big John, the father, Mrs Mary Hill, then the kids – William, an engineer with Monaghan County Council, Patrick, a bus driver, Martin, Mary, Bernadette, Lawrence, an electrician, and I think that is the lot. But there is more...

Mary Hill, the mother, worked in Hemmings Hotel, which was a hotel in the long ago. It was anglers who frequented the hotel. I am guessing the story, because, because, because... Only a very few can recall the hotel's existence. The reason being is that NOW, yes NOW, you would not find a stone upon a stone. In fact, you would find it difficult to locate the site. Even the slates are gone, gone, gone... What occurred, I have never found out so far.

Anyway, I was told Mary worked there. She married John and reared her family. There was no road in to their house. You either had to do the journey on foot – sliding – or go to the pier at Derrinasceer and take the boat into the house. Eventually, they got a nice tarmac road the whole way. It was very impressive, and she got her wish. It was a miracle. But dear friend Mary died, and to see her coffin being taken out of the Home on the new road was equally sad.

Peter Kennedy

Peter Kennedy and his brother Francis are well known in Donegal Town. Peter was single. At the back end of last year Peter died. When I got to the morgue where Peter was laid out, I found Albert Johnston sitting in mourning. Albert and Peter and Francis were friends for years. When Peter died his friend was beside him. They had fished the Eske for years. Albert Johnston was a friend indeed.

Francis Kennedy

Francis Kennedy, the younger brother of Peter, is married to a Ballyshannon lady, Carmel McGloin, who comes from a large and respected Lisahully family on the Belleek. Road. They have a boy (Joe) and a girl (Ann).

Peter Kennedy, R.I.P.

Francis Kennedy is seen on the next page with a fine salmon that he landed on the fly from the Foxes Pool above Miss Jenny's Bridge on the River Eske. In fact I never saw Francis Kennedy with anything other than a fine salmon. He is a long-time member of the Eske Angling Association. He is a painter and decorator by trade, but can turn his hand to anything. Francis is great community person. The death of Peter, his brother, was a great loss to the community and a severe blow to the Eske Angling Association.

Francis still retains the glass that the late Jim Reeves drank from when he had a "shot" of Irish whiskey with Francis in the National Hotel when the singer was fulfilling an engagement in Donegal Town as part of his Irish tour. Jim Reeves died in plane crash shortly afterwards.

Francis Kennedy is a self-taught Master Mariner (not an Ancient Mariner). He still spends much of his spare time down the Donegal estuary, where he is a tourist attraction recalling memories of the time when his ancestors (and mine from Lahardane, Co Mayo) left Ireland from the Hassans. Emigrants boarded the ships at "The Hassans" – the point of departure from the estuary near Donegal Town. People walked great distances to get to The Hassans.

From the Old World into the New World, they carried the unwelcome baggage of hate, the result of the potato famine and hunger that spread within this nation's people. From the evictions in 1840, carried on until the complete failure of the potato crop in 1845, our starving Kennedys in Donegal and Dalys in Lahardane in Mayo joined in missions of death through 1880 and right into 1900. The stench of death from famine, eviction, and emigration in some shape or form left us as a people and a nation so weakened that we could not resist onset of TB and other illnesses .

We gave to the Americas and Europe our strength of the names and causes we fought for including our own struggle for freedom. Now we are a strong nation of Irishmen and Irishwomen. We help each other the same way that Albert Johnston stayed with his friend Peter Kennedy until his breath left his body for the last time.

Francis Kennedy – Master Mariner (not Ancient)

That is what the meaning of the Angling Association means to me. And Francis Kennedy is the soul of the meaning within that body. So was John Doherty, so is Jody Gysling. the Swiss owner of Harvey s Point. So too is Ben Gallagher and Hans Peter Michele and Charlie McGinty. God bless you "Injun Joes" where-ever you roam. Thanks for the memories. Yes, "...the time will come when you will leave the lake and it will be for the last time."

Edward Quinn

A visitor once described Eddie Quinn of being possessed with "Trans-Multi-Location." This is what TML means.

Edward Quinn,
R.I.P.

The visitor was a Bundoran man, from the diaspora, and he knew Edward Quinn very well. He wrote this story in the "Donegal Democrat" about Edward Quinn. Every word is true.

"Upon arrival in Bundoran I was met at the famous train by Edward Quinn. He opened the carriage door. Got me on to the platform safely. He then got me a taxi. (Michael Carty would be waiting for me.) Edward Quinn got me a porter. He issued orders to the taxi about where I was to be taken.

"Later I went down to the picture house. Eddie Quinn sold me the ticket and took the ticket from me. Later again he was on the door at O'Carroll's Ballroom, keeping order.

"When I went to mass on Sunday, the same man escorted me to my seat, then took up the collection, then directed me to communion. When we were going out of the chapel, Edward Quinn was standing with the charity collection.

"And at the football match on Sunday, Edward Quinn was playing. After doing the gate."

The owner of a caravan park in Bundoran sold his propertyuand purchased a caravan park in Wales. He owed £15 (Irish punts) to the Donegal Democrat. One night he was closing up his windows when he saw Edward Quinn standing just outside. Edward handed a statement through the window and said, "You owe the Democrat £15." The man was so startled that he gave Edward £50. Edward went on to the Chepstow Races where he invested the surplus cash and won a fortune.

Edward Quinn was involved in every aspect of life in Bundoran. He died in 1981. He was driving from Sligo to Manorhamilton collecting accounts for the Donegal Democrat when he took ill. He was found dead at the wheel of his car. He was 71 years old. Eddie did not drink.

He told the story of a GAA game between Ballyshannon and Bundoran. The rivalry was such that both teams wanted to win the game. Eddie Quinn was centre fullback for Bundoran. He was marking the best player on the Ballyshannon team, who was Terry McDermott, alias "the Grunch."

The game started and McDermott got the ball. Terry McDermott was in the army. Eddie Quinn tackled McDermott and called him "Grunch" and fouled. The referee let the game go on. Terry McDermott "lost his rag" with the attention he was getting from Eddie. The ref gave a foul against Terry, who lost his temper. The upshot was that Terry turned and aimed a kick at Eddie. The ref blew his whistle and put Terry McDermott off the pitch.

Bundoran won the game. Edward Quinn was the hero. He recalled the incident and recalled what he had said to Terry. He said, "You are a Free State bastard!" – whereupon Terry McDermott turned around and aimed a kick at Eddie. Terry's boot just shaved past Eddie's nose. Terry McDermott was sent off.

Edward Quinn was the mightiest Quinn... He said, "If you tell a lie, it will take 20 lies to keep that first lie down."

Jack Grimes

Jack Grimes is dead and gone, but he is not forgotten.

He will not be forgotten by the North West Parkinson's Association. He was one of the first members to join up when I started to think of the beginning of the fight for recognition of our plight and our illness. The result is that we now have a specialist neurologist in Sligo, and we are now "hot on the heels" of a Parkinson's nurse. The last meeting we held in Dorrian's Hotel was our AGM. Jack was there to support me for the chair. He was not in good health himself, yet when I saw Jack Grimes I took heart. The Cause was still strong when I had Jack Grimes by my side...

I saw Jack most days, and I was sad that he could not shake off the decline in his health.

Jack Grimes died on Christmas Day. He was a hard worker, and a great ideas man. He was respected in the Community. The Grimes Bakery Cup is played for each year. It is an honour that teams (under-age) play their hearts out for victory.

When news of his passing became known, he was mourned by me and by a host of individuals and groups like the G.A.A., the golf club, and angling and fishing associations where the name of Grimes is respected, and their deeds are legend, and legion. Jack Grimes was the son of Vincent Grimes, who founded the Grimes bakery and provided employment for at least six decades. The Grimes product was a guarantee of an excellent bakery. When he took over in his turn, Jack carried on where his father had left off.

The North West Parkinson's Association extend sympathy to Nora, and to all his Family. Adios, Amigo!!!!

Gerry McNamara

Gerry McNamara was a robust character. He was an international angler, and he represented Ireland on many occasions. He was mainly a trout angler, and he did not stray off his love of trout fishing. He developed his own art of fly fishing that made him stand out. His own style was the short cast. Gerry used a 9ft rod, and when those of us who liked his style observed Gerry use another technique in competitions – namely the quick cast – we knew why Gerry was picked time and again for international duties.

Gerry was always seen (well for a good few years) out on 1st January. After fishing for the first salmon of the year for a while, he would man the soup kitchen. He liked the craic and fun that fishermen enjoyed. If they were cold or fed up, Gerry was always there to lend a

Gerry McNamara, R.I.P.

helping hand or to join in the jokes that anglers always had among themselves, or mostly, on the day that was in it, warm them up with a bowl of soup and send them back into battle again...

He was at the first meeting of the Sheil Hospital Action Committee in 1974.

Gerry later joined the pensioners at the Day Centre, in College Street. He was ALWAYS In the thick of things there. If Marian (the supervisor) wanted anything done, like chairs shifted or the bingo numbers called, Gerry was there to lend a helping hand. And the year he was asked to dress up as St. Patrick was special. When we the pensioners of Ballyshannon entered the parade and sang "Hail Glorious St. Patrick," we made Gerry, with his sceptre and orb, very proud and happy.

His wife Mary and his family can be very proud and happy too. For he was a good friend of mine, even during the period he served on the town council, 1974 to 1979. He was a good public representative. He was a good person. He was a good St. Patrick.

May Gerry McNamara rest in peace.

Francis McGloin

He was, like all the McGloins from The Achers, Ballyshannon, well made, well drilled, well mannered, and well good to stand beside in a pub – for you never got into trouble, and you enjoyed yourself. He was the brother of Benny McGloin. They caught fish in the Monk's Garden, a man-made lagoon that was built by the Cistercian monks.

Francis McGloin, R.I.P.

He was one of the original Abbey Shamrocks. I used to play against him. I used to call him "Elbows and Knees" or "Knees and Elbows," etc, etc. When he tackled you, you got elbows and knees, or knees and elbows – take your pick, you got them.

Francis was one of a very large family, and now even the most respected gets carried. To Anna McLaughlan, Benny, Vincent, Allo, Mary Egan, all the McGloins of the Acres, my deepest sympathy. Good Bye, Francis. *Adios*, My Friend.

Others

Sean Murray, who fished the Duff. He took half a dozen of my books on every trip to the USA...

Pat Duffy, who caught over 1,000 salmon off the Drowes...

John Doherty, who made up his differences with John Hanna, and who became a great friend of Anthony O'Malley Daly...

And many others who came off the Eske and Drowes and other favourite rivers and lakes, and it was for the last time...

And Paddy Conwall, a native of Killybegs who was in Australia with me, was drowned off Teelin. Paddy was a small man in stature but tall in his heart. He would start a row in a pub and involve many of his comrades. We had to fight our way out while Paddy would bow out, and many times I saw Paddy seeking refuge under a table.

At the inquest after Paddy was drowned, his skipper said that Paddy was stowing the gear as they were entering the breakwater. He was talking with Paddy from the bridge. There was an unexpected swell. The skipper looked away for a moment, and when he looked back Paddy was gone.

The skipper told how Paddy loved fishing. Paddy Conwall is remembered on a memorial stone in Killybegs along with others who lost their lives at sea.

From 1985 to 1987, my wife Mary coached Paul Culkin of Ballyshannon as he swam in competitions leading up to the Special Olympics. Mary's tribute to him was published in The Donegal Democrat *on 18 September 1987:*

Paul Culkin: An Appreciation

By Mary O'Malley Daly

The theme song for the World Special Olympics 1987 was called "A Time For Heroes" and the opening lines say –

> *"We search for an answer,*
> *and when it appears*
> *we can challenge the world with*
> *our sweat and our tears".*

Paul Culkin, from Donegal Road, Ballyshannon, was born into this world 25 years ago, and was given a challenge that would daunt a lesser person. He had many interests, but it was at swimming – where our paths crossed – that he was to make his mark from Celbridge to South Bend.

Paul was a member of the Saimer Swimming Club. His first major competition was the European Special Olympics held in Dublin in 1985, where he won two gold medals for the front and back crawl. Paul Culkin and Seamus Cleary were honoured with a civic reception on their return to Ballyshannon. It was a joyous occasion. Paul made a great speech, and later sang many songs. He was a revelation. The following year he got silver and bronze at the All-Ireland Special Olympics held in Antrim.

Paul attended the Los Angeles Olympics Games in company with other members of his family, and that world sporting event sparked his ambition to be a competitor at the International Summer Special Olympics. Indeed, his determination to gain a place on the Olympic team was such that he successfully converted from freestyle to breaststroke.

His endeavours were rewarded with inclusion on the Irish squad to swim the 25M and 50M breaststroke and the freestyle relay team. Each month he travelled with his coach, to Dublin and Limerick for three hour training sessions. The way was hard, but Paul never faltered, or abandoned his quest. In competitions prior to setting out for America Paul was guest swimmer at the Leinster, Munster and Connacht Special Olympic Games, and he was presented with a special medal with the inscription "Good Luck In Indiana" by the Connacht Olympic Committee, the province he represented.

His endeavours were rewarded with inclusion on the Irish squad to swim the 25M and 50M breaststroke and the freestyle relay team. Each month he travelled with his coach, to Dublin and Limerick for three hour training sessions. The way was hard, but Paul never faltered, or abandoned his quest. In competitions prior to setting out for America Paul was guest swimmer at the Leinster, Munster and Connacht Special Olympic Games, and he was presented with a special medal with the inscription "Good Luck In Indiana" by the Connacht Olympic Committee, the province he represented.

Mary, Paul Culkin R.I.P., and John Hanna

On July 29th Paul as a member of the Irish team left for St. Mary's, Notre Dame University, South Bend, Indiana, to fulfil his ambition of swimming and winning gold for Ireland. On Friday 31st July he took ill. He died August 2nd at St. Joseph's Medical Centre, South Bend. Our American friends and hosts did everything possible and they were more than helpful and kind, and they will not be forgotten.

The American Olympic Committee granted Paul Culkin the first posthumous gold medal of the games, and a special commemorative Mass was said for him. The remaining Irish swimmers went out and swam for Paul, and won many medals. Crowds escorted his remains into Ballyshannon, but without the speeches and singing, and his family and friends mourned his passing. The words carved on his gold medal reflect his short life – "Skill, Courage, Sharing, Joy".

Injun Jo

Paul Culkin in his living and dying reminds us to have no regrets – for he was surely a revelation. And the final two lines from "A Time For Heroes" says:

> *"It's a time for heroes.*
> *When our backs to the wall,*
> *It's a time for the hero... in us all".*

When Paul Culkin showed his love for Ballyshannon, he was taken to our hearts. Some of the stories about Paul are singular. Like the time he was working in the shoe shop. He was trying to fit shoes for a well-known lady who was hard to satisfy. Paul had offered her practically every shoe in the store without results. He was losing the plot. He got a shoebox and said to her, "Will this fit you?" and he walked out of the shop.

By the way, the box did not fit.

Epilogue

"I Have Parkinson's, But Parkinson's Does Not Have Me ®"

When I was diagnosed with Parkinson's Disease, I decided not to let it slow me down. In fact, I took it as a challenge.

I had some tee-shirts printed to list my fund-raising activities for Parkinson's and Asthma. I'm very proud of every single one. Each tee-shirt reads as follows:

I Have Parkinson's, But Parkinson's Does Not Have Me ®

Water Ski
Car Rally
Sky Dive
10K Walk
Micro Lite Flite
Bungee Jump
Creevy-Rossnowlagh 5K Swim
Abseiling
Solo Parachute Jump
Ski Dubai
Rehab Donegal "People of the Year Award" 2010

Over the years I have done many things to raise funds to fight this disease. Writing this book is one of them, and I thank you for buying it. All of the profits from the sale of this book will go to the North West Parkinson's Foundation and to the Asthma Society. (I also have asthma, and I haven't let that slow me down either.)

Epilogue

Here are some of the newspaper stories about my fund-raisers. They call them stunts. I call them unforgettable memories.

Anthony and Jim Take to the Water

The Donegal Democrat, 10 August 2006

71 year old Ballyshannon man Anthony O'Malley Daly and fellow neighbour Jim White were forced to abandon an attempt to water-ski around Inis Saimer island this week.

The pair entered the waters at the Mall Quay, Ballyshannon on Bank Holiday Monday to raise much needed funds for Parkinson's watched by hundreds of spectators.

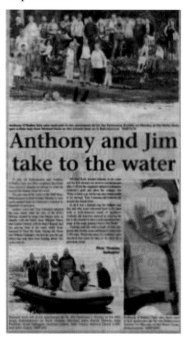

Andrew Lawn and Tony Cummins manned the man vessel while the crew of the RNLI lifeboat, headed by Hugh John Patton, were on standby with the Safety Boat. Michael Patton and Andrew Fenton, with his fiance Raquel, had the pick-up boat at the ready while boats manned by Noel Mc Grath, Declan Mc Gloin and William Gallagher checked the area for any debris that may have been floating about. The scene was set.

Michael Kane assisted Anthony in the water and the first attempt was about to unfold, but alas, after 4 efforts the organisers decided to abandon Anthony's goal and allow the younger Jim White to have a go, but he was also unsuccessful in his attempt. Tony Cummins did however ski around the island twice.

In all it was a fantastic day for Anthony and Jim and who were welcomed back to dry land with a well-deserved round of applause. Anthony did however, succeed in crossing the bar at the channel to have a well-earned hot beverage at the main sponsor Creevy Pier Hotel.

Anthony and Jim wish to thank all who supported this worthy cause and helped to raise over €2,000 euro. Watch this space for Anthony's next daredevil feat when he takes to the skies for a parachute jump!

Anto, 70, Jumps for Joy after Charity Tandem Skydive

Daily Mirror, August 28, 2006

Daredevil Granda Anthony O'Malley-Daly and his daughter Sarah had a day of adventure they'll never forget.

It started with 70-year-old Parkinson's sufferer Anthony completing his first parachute jump and finished with Sarah Meehan plunging into the sea to rescue an angler.

Anthony, from Ballyshannon, Co Donegal, said: "I'm still getting over it.

"The jump created enough excitement for one day, never mind Sarah risking her life like that."

Saturday's action started when Sarah and her mother Mary drove Anthony to the Irish Parachute Club at Clonbullogue, near Edenderry, Co Offaly, for his first ever free fall.

Anthony, who was taking on the challenge to raise money for Parkinson's Disease sufferers, refused to be talked out of the 10,000 ft jump by his family.

He added: "It was exhilarating. I was totally elated. I felt like I was falling on a soft cushion.

"But when I first looked out the open door of the aircraft I had a moment of fear. I said to myself, 'Oops, it seemed such a good idea at the time!' Then I just convinced myself to do it. I didn't want to let anybody down."

Several hours and 200km later, the family were back home and heading down to Creevy Pier for their regular evening swim.

As they got closer they saw a fully-clothed man leap from the pier into the sea. He had been fishing from the pier and was seen arguing on his mobile phone before throwing it into the sea and then appearing to dive in after it.

Sarah and passerby Philip McAvoy from Portadown, Co Armagh, leapt into the water and swam more than 50 metres through the heaving swell to the drowning man.

Mother-of-three Sarah said: "There was such a swell there were times when I lost sight of him.

"There was a very strong current. I couldn't believe how fast it was pulling the man out. It was the roughest sea I've been in for a long time.

"It took 20 minutes to pull him back to the pier."

The rescued man, in his 30s, was taken away by ambulance. He was later charged with a public order offence and released. The man will appear in Ballyshannon court on Friday.

Top Rescue Award for Brave Sarah

By Paddy Clancy, Donegal Post, 8 November 2006

A Ballyshannon community nurse and a visitor from Northern Ireland are to be awarded for a brave sea rescue off Creevy Pier last August.

Sarah Meehan, from Coolcholly, Ballyshannon, and Philip McAvoy, from Portadown, Co. Armagh, will be presented with the Irish Water Safety Association's "Just In Time Rescue Awards" at a glittering ceremony in Dublin Castle on November 21.The awards are presented to members of the public who voluntarily saved the life of another person from the water.

Sarah, 41-year-old mother of three, and Philip, a member of the Lough Neagh Lifeboat service, leaped into the sea to rescue a crazed fisherman when he jumped, fully clothed, off the pier as spray from huge waves crashed over it. The man had been fishing from the pier and was seen arguing on his mobile phone, then throwing it out to sea before jumping in after it. Sarah and Philip, who never met before that moment, swam more than 50 metres in a heaving swell to the man in difficulties.

Sarah, whose husband John is chairman of Ballyshannon Town Council, said at the time: "There was such a swell there were times when I lost sight of him. There was a very strong current. I couldn't believe how fast it was pulling the man out. It was the roughest sea I've been in for a long time."

A spokesman for the Irish Water Safety Association said: "These awards are not given out lightly. What Sarah and Philip did was very brave. They put their own lives at risk."

Anthony's Leap

What We Think
Donegal Democrat Tuesday, 29th August 2006

Courage is something we too often confine to the endeavours of our sporting heroes, and no doubt in Mayo it is a word that has been frequently heard since Sunday's memorable All-Ireland semi-final at Croke Park.

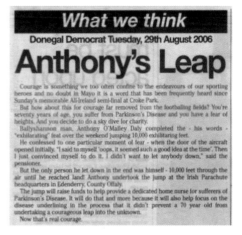

But how about this for courage far removed from the footballing fields? You're seventy years of age, you suffer from Parkinson's Disease and you have a fear of heights. And you decide to do a sky dive for charity.

Ballyshannon man, Anthony O'Malley Daly completed the – his words – "exhilarating" feat over the weekend jumping 10,000 exhilarating feet.

He confessed to one particular moment of fear - when the door of the aircraft opened initially. "I said to myself 'Oops, it seemed such a good idea at the time'. Then I just convinced myself to do it. 1 didn't want to let anybody down," said the pensioner.

But the only person he let down in the end was himself – 10,000 feet through the air until he reached land! Anthony undertook the jump at the Irish Parachute headquarters in Edenderry, County Offaly.

The jump will raise funds to help provide a dedicated home nurse for sufferers of Parkinson's Disease. It will do that and more because it will also help focus on the disease, underlining in the process that it didn't prevent a 70 year old from undertaking a courageous leap into the unknown.

Now that's real courage.

Ski Dubai

by Anthony O'Malley Daly

Dubai is a hot Middle Eastern country – near the Straits of Hormuz, which I mentioned before. They don't have any mountains, and they certainly don't have any natural snow, but they have lots of money, so they built themselves a snow-covered mountain to ski on. Which I did.

Also pictured here is Sean O'Mahoney, whose father has Parkinson's Disease. Those of us with Parkinson's can have trouble speaking clearly, because our vocal cords, like our limbs, sometimes seem to get stuck. Sean developed a simple chart called a SpeechAide with lines of the letter "X," and when we tap along those lines – X – X – X – it can help us get the words out.

Sean O'Mahoney is the General Manager of Ski Dubai.

Rally Day 2007

by Brian Crawford

Mary Morrow, my wife, came home from Ballyshannon and said that a friend of hers was very keen to take part in a "high speed" closed road car rally and asked would I help.

I had just won my respective class in the famous Circuit of Ireland Rally that year (2007), and I was a class winner in the Donegal International rally 2005 / 2006, so I suppose it was clear, that Mary considered me a safe pair of hands to look after Anthony

I had great respect for Anthony, and I considered it an honour that he would want to put himself in my car, so we went about getting an entry in a one-day event that would suit the purpose.

Because a competition licence was required for most "Speed Events," the licence became the first problem. The Rallysport Association January 2 event in Aghadowey, Co Derry was chosen as a temporary licence could be had on the day for this Christmas event

Anthony arrived in Raphoe "an hour" before we were ready to travel to Northern Ireland that day, had breakfast with us, and the day just got better and better after that.

Anthony was great fun and was very game for a laugh. We "knowingly" sent Anthony on his own to "sign-on" for the event that day, and he said he enjoyed explaining to the officials that he really was planning to compete in the rally that day, and he succeeded in getting signed up.

Motorsport is a very physical sport, and it takes its toll on very fit people, let alone anyone with Anthony's medical problems, but every one of the 104 competitors who entered that cold January day in 2007 applauded the efforts and clear enjoyment Anthony O Malley Daly took from the experience.

The "safe pair of hands" got carried away with encouragement from Anthony the navigator, and some big high-speed slides prevented us from wining any awards on the day.

It seemed that the adrenaline rush overcame everything and I was getting clear instruction over the intercom on the stages. Anthony had a rest and some sleep between runs to get ready for to go again, but we skipped the last stage to get ready for home.

On the way home, Anthony told us he had not travelled to that part of the north coast road through Limivady and Ballykelly for all the years of the troubles, and he marvelled at how things had changed and developed so much over the years.

The only help that Anthony needed that day was getting into the rally suit and helmet, and he managed every thing asked of him with a cheerful smile. This reminded me a lot of my late father Willie Crawford, and how much I would have loved that I could have done the same for him when he was alive, as he was a similar free spirit who never got old till the day he died.

Brian Crawford
Car: Talbot Sunbeam
Year – 1978
1600c – Class 10, 1600 modified,
and Class D3 Historic Class in recent International events 2012.

Anthony O'Malley-Daly is Ballyshannon Person of the Year

The Donegal Democrat, 10 April 2007

When Anthony O'Malley-Daly was named as the first ever Ballyshannon Person of the Year at a prestigious ceremony on Easter Sunday night, the crowd of local people joined with him in genuine and heartfelt jubilation.

The first Ballyshannon Person of the Year awards ceremony was the brainchild of the Ballyshannon Business Chamber sponsored by the Donegal Democrat / Donegal People's Press and Celtic Weave China. Hundreds of local people voted for 16 nominees in four categories of which Anthony O'Malley-Daly was the overall winner.

The winners were announced at a friendly and relaxed ceremony at Dorrian's Imperial Hotel, Ballyshannon, on Sunday night. The prizes, which were kindly sponsored by Tommy and Patricia Daly and family of Celtic Weave China, Clyhore, were presented by Editor-in-Chief of the Donegal Democrat / Donegal People's Press.

Well-known Ballyshannon bus driver Tony McGloin won in the Community Contribution category for his outstanding and tireless work with the elderly community in the area. Tony not only works as a bus driver bringing elderly people to and from the Shiel Hospital but would help in countless other ways from taking a friendly interest in the lives of his elderly neighbours and friends to collecting their groceries.

Brian Roper needs no introduction as the Ballyshannon man who has played centre 129 times for the County Donegal senior football team and who was awarded the Sports award on Sunday night.

Maura Logue received the Arts and Music award for her immeasurable contribution to arts, drama and entertainment in Ballyshannon. She will be known by parents, teachers and budding actors in the community for her work with the Abbey Centre, Tir Hugh Centre, Ballytours, Ballyshannon Town Carnival, in workshops and drama classes, and as an excellent actress in her own right.

Meanwhile, Jim Flynn, who is known to generations of Ballyshannon people as the Main Street shopkeeper who occupied the little shoe shop on the comer for almost half a century, was awarded the Trade and Enterprise title.

Anthony O'Malley-Daly fended off 16 nominees to become the Ballyshannon Person of the Year 2007 for his work as a community activist, campaigner for Parkinson's Disease sufferers and unique fundraising efforts in the past which have included sky-diving and water-skiing. Most people will know Anthony as a larger-than-life character with unstoppable energy and determination. Today, he is heavily involved in raising awareness about Parkinson's Disease and campaigning for a dedicated Parkinson's Disease nurse in the north west.

Over 200 people attended the ceremony on Easter Sunday night which was expertly compered by Cliondha Harney, PRO of Ballyshannon Business Chamber, and Sean Perry of Ocean FM.

"When Anthony O'Malley-Daly was finally announced the overall winner he jumped up from his seat and waved his hands in the air whooping as if he had just won the world cup," commented

Anthony O'Malley Daly winner of the overall Ballyshannon Person of the Year Awards in Dorrian's Imperial Hotel on Sunday night being presented with his award by Michael Daly, Editor in Chief Donegal Democrat/Peoples Press.

Michael Daly, editor-in-chief of the Donegal Democrat / Donegal People's Press.

"Everyone joined in with him because they were so pleased for him, his wife, Mary and family who were all there on the night."

3, 2, 1, JUMP!

The Donegal Post
30 January 2008

Intrepid pensioner Anthony O'Malley Daly added another death-defying stunt to a growing list of off-beat charity fundraisers last Saturday.

The 72-year-old, who suffers from Parkinson's disease, did a 300-ft bungee jump in Celbridge, Co Kildare.

He said afterwards, "There was a long queue, but I was at the front of it. I thought, 'Here goes.' I held on to the cage for dear life, and suddenly this guy said, '3,2,1, jump!' and I was on my way. It was exhilarating."

Anthony was raised in a cage by a crane to 300 ft over the grounds of the Setanta House Hotel.

Then, harnessed to his bungee rope, he stepped out of the cage and plunged toward the ground, being whipped skywards again by the elasticity of the special rope.

Anthony, of College Street, Ballyshannon, did it to raise funds for the Parkinson's Association and to raise public awareness of the disease and the continuing battle to find a remedy for it.

His previous fund-raisers included free-falling several thousand feet before opening his parachute, flying a micro-lite airplane, and attempting to water-ski up the Erne estuary.

PJ Branley, R.I.P., with Mary and me at another bungee jump event – this one in Bundoran

This article doesn't mention it, but I did two more bungee jumps. Sadly, it was PJ Branley who drove me to Bundoran for a bungee jump only a few days before he was killed in a road traffic accident.

Microlite Aircraft

For another fund-raising stunt I flew in an experimental "microlite" aircraft. I wish I had a good photo of that flimsy-looking aircraft with its skinny frame wrapped in plastic sheets.

The pilot Gary Snodden took me on a flight from Dundonald for two hours. We wend down the south side of Strangfort Lough and came back up the north side.

I sat straddled behind Gary in the plane. With no belt.

Five-Mile Road Race

A few years ago I ran in a Charity Five-Mile Road Race. I'm pictured here with Charlie McGloin, Foreman of the Donegal Democrat

5K Swim

In 2011 I participated in the 5K ocean swim from Creevy to Rossnowlagh. My team included Sonibhe Lally, her husband Patsy, her brother Maurice, and Andrew Lawn. It was the same day that the Marlins did the 5K swim under the coaching of Seamus O'Neill.

I had to be pulled out of the water after three hours. I was unconscious, and my teammates went around back of me lifted me out of the water. If not for them, and for the help of divers from Belfast, I would have been in serious trouble.

They gave me coffee and oxygen. I was unconscious and knew nothing for five or six hours.

Abseiling

Abseiling, or rappelling as it is called by many mountaineers, is sliding down a rope under controlled conditions. The term comes from the German word "abseilen," which translates as "top rope down." Sometimes they call it "rappelling."

I went abseiling down the tower in the Bundoran Adventure Centre. And I am the one who used to be too nervous to climb a six foot ladder!

The Wall of Death

I might take a motorcycle ride in the Wall of Death if another one is built in Ireland.

In the late 1970's two brothers-in-law built a Wall of Death in County Longford after they saw one in an Elvis Presley movie. It looks like a big barrel, and the idea is to ride around the inside on a motorcycle at high speed. Then someone made a movie about them called *Eat the Peach* back in 1986. At the end of the movie, their worried family members burned down the Wall.

I have heard that another Wall of Death may be under construction. John Mohon will keep me informed. His family is in the carnival ride business, with ramps and bumper cars. The Mohon family travels the country during the summers, and they spend the winter in South Armagh. His wife is Vera.

Thrillseeking Pensioner Leaps into Record Books

The Belfast Telegraph, 4 November 2008

Thrillseeking Ulster pensioner Anthony O'Malley-Daly, who suffers from Parkinson's disease, overcame his fear of heights when he made a record-breaking solo parachute jump.

Mr O'Malley-Daly jumped from 3,200 ft at the Irish Parachute Club headquarters at Clonbullogue, near Edenderry, Co Offaly, and into the record books as the oldest person to make a supervised solo jump at the club.

His first words after landing were: "It's the biggest thrill I've had apart from sex."

It was his second big drop – but two years ago he was strapped to a tandem jump partner when he free-fell for 5,000 ft before opening his parachute for the last 10,000 ft.

The daredevil grandfather from College St, Ballyshannon, Co Donegal, said he fears heights and won't climb up higher than a six-foot ladder.

But he was determined to make the solo jump as part of a continuing series of fund-raising stunts, including a bungee jump and an attempt to water-ski up the Erne estuary near his home, for the Parkinson's Association and to raise public awareness of the disease.

His instructor Caroline Cassidy said: "Anthony was amazing. He showed no fear."

He touched down and rolled over in a field by the Bog of Allen several hundred yards away from a marked landing target. Caroline added: "It was a good jump."

He plans a repeat in the spring.

Now I know what it's like to defy gravity. Caroline Cassidy was my coach.

To tell the full story of my solo parachute jump at Edenderry, I need to double back to the end of September. John Hanna and I were out fishing on the last day of the season. When we caught salmon, John and I would bargain over the catch, but with trout I usually got the catch for my daughter Sarah. She loves trout. On the last day of the season I got a catch of fine trout. I claimed them, saying, "This one is for Sarah," but John claimed the catch "for Bernadette."

Fast forward. It is now November, and I am going to do my parachute jump. My daughter Sarah is in the second car with her husband John Meehan and their children Patrick, Fiona, and Cillian. I am driving my car with my wife Mary and PJ Branley. Mary has been saying, "Anthony, there is a smell in the car" – which I can't smell because I have lost the ability to smell. PJ says he is smelling an "awful stink" too. I open a vent to satisfy them, and out fly five bluebottle flies. We all blame the smell on A.N. Other.

We land in Edenderry, the home of the Irish Parachute Club. I park my car and go to the hangar. I go about the parachute preparedness, and I actually perform the record solo parachute jump. The people who are waiting their turn are taking their lunches and coming and going.

At long last John Mehan comes to me and says, "Gaga! There is an awful smell! People are getting sick!" Now I take notice. I go to my car, open the boot, and realise that something is amiss. Although I have no sense of smell, I can "taste" a bad smell. Lo and behold, I remove my fishing gear and Barbour jacket. There before my eyes are a thousand, nay thousands, of white maggots. The spare wheel looks like it is moving.

John Meehan, PJ Branley, Mary, Sarah, Patrick, Fiona, and Cillian are puking. The trout have been in the boot for the entire month of October. I had to remove the spare wheel, and Mary would not get into my car until I removed the thousands of maggots and bluebottles. It seems that after John Hanna had claimed the catch "for Bernadette," he had changed his mind. Threw the trout into my boot. The rest is history.

Except there is a twist to the story. I found a container, filled it with maggots, and gave it to Charlie O'Doherty, who used them on the Eske to fish for charr. So Sarah got a dozen nice charr to eat.

Anto Meets Mary at the Aras

By Patrick Thomas, Donegal Post, 3 November 2008

President Mary McAleese and high-flying Parkinson's battler Anthony O'Malley-Daly discussed mutual friends when they met at Aras an Uachtarain.

Mrs McAleese was a childhood neighbour in Belfast of the Goan family which has strong links with Creevy.

And Anthony and the late Seamus Goan, who lived in retirement in Creevy, were close friends.

Anthony, from College St., Ballyshannon, was in the Aras last week as a member of a specially invited Parkinson's Association of Ireland group when the President hosted a reception for volunteers in charitable organisations of which she is Patron.

Anthony was chosen to go along because of his high-profile work in raising awareness of Parkinson's and of how sufferers can still have an active life.

He has sky-dived from 13,000 feet and attempted to water-ski in the Erne estuary as part of the campaign

Una Anderson Ryan of the Parkinson's Association said: "Anthony is an inspiration to all who are fortunate enough to meet him."

The 70-year-old is a champion for his own favourite charity. "We don't have a Parkinson's disease nurse in the North West, and in order to have one we need to raise €250K in order to train and pay for a nurse," he said.

We Knew You'd Do It!

*Congratulations on the
publication of <u>Trilogy</u>
from your friends
James and John at*

Sign & Print

Unit 1
Finner Business Park
Ballyshannon

071 9842957
<u>signprinting@eircom.net</u>

*signs
printing
picture framing
embroidery*

Besides fund-raising, I also spend my time visiting people and places where a smile, a laugh, or just simple companionship can mean a lot.

Smart Granny & Granddad Day Centre, College St., Ballyshannon

The Smart Granny and Granddad Day Centre in Ballyshannon is a Social club for pensioners that is funded by St Vincent de Paul and the HSE. It is organised mainly by Michael Tunney from SVP. It is currently operating every Tuesday, Wednesday and Thursday from 9am-3pm and is often the only contact that some of its clients have with the community and the 'outside world.'

For just €3 return, they are collected at their home (which can be anywhere from Kinlough to Rossnowlagh to Ballintra etc.) and dropped at the day centre at 9am. They are greeted by the Supervisor (and sole employee) Marion McGee, who will have Tea/Coffee and Breakfast for the 15 clients she entertains each day. After breakfast they fill their day with a variety of activities and games, knitting and crochet. They will have a Quiz followed by 'Spot the Ball.' They then sit for a Candle-lit dinner followed by the highlight of the day...Bingo! At 3pm they are collected by their friendly bus driver Tony McGloin and returned home.

The funding is minimal, and they try to be as self-sufficient as possible to provide any extras they require. They sell hand-knitted and crocheted socks/scarves in a bid to give them extra days out. For example, on St. Patrick's Day, Marion and volunteers bring some of the clients out to see the parades. They also try to raise the cash needed to provide the clients with a special Christmas party and dinner.

Marion McGee, Centre Director

The day centre is a life-line for the majority of clients that attend it. Shockingly, they can not get the funding to open on Mondays or Fridays. They currently have a waiting list of 20 people that have been on the list for quite a while now. Unfortunately, the only way to get a place in the day centre is when a place becomes available...which only really happens when a current client either passes away or becomes unable to attend any more...making the waiting list a very long wait indeed! The real shame about the situation is that the facilities are there, the staff and volunteers are there, but they can't get the go-ahead to open another day. With just 20 people currently on the waiting list, it would only take opening the centre one more day a week to give those people a new lease and quality of life .

Fortunately, I am lucky enough to be allowed to attend for the Bingo on Tuesday, Wednesday and Thursday between 2-3 pm.

I have made many friends here and have a lot of happy and fun times at the day centre. I would like to acknowledge and thank Michael, Tony, Marion and the other volunteers for all their help and support over the last few years.

If you would like to support the day centre, you can call in and purchase some of their hand knits, make a donation, supply some small prizes for their games or maybe just volunteer to help out for an hour or two. Who knows, you might enjoy it!

Tuesday at the Ballyshannon Smart Granny and Granddad Centre. From left to right: Kathleen Coughlin, Mary Clancy, Bridie Coughlin, Brid O'Sullivan, Maggie Regan, Mary McCauley, Ann McCafferty, Mary O'Rourke, Josie Gallagher, James Clancy, and staff member. It's hard to see in this photo, but there is an award for Josie Gallagher on the wall.

In the Wednesday Group, from left to right: Margaret Brown, Marion McGee, and me. Eileen Gavigan is sitting in front of me, and next to her are David Power, Joe McLoughlin, Bessie McHugh, Philomena Betute, Tony McGloin (bus driver), and Kathleen Coughlin. Bridie Coughlin is seated in the front on the right.

In the Thursday Group, from left to right in the back row: Marion McGee, Bernie Loughlin, Willie Donaldson, Mervyn Hassett, Eddie Meehan, Willie Anderson, Paddy Feely, and Barney Rafferty R.I.P. In the front row: Philomena Dorrian, Sarah McCullough, Lizzie Connolly, Mary Murphy, Teddy McSheen, Anne Connolly, Katy Connolly, and Bridie Coughlan.

I also visit people in the Ozanam House, and they give me a meal when I'm there. Ozanam House in Bundoran provides a low-cost holiday residence for people who need a break from the troubles in their lives. I've visited there over the last two Christmases, and I've joined in the Christmas parties in the restaurant.

I also visit people in the Rock Nursing Home. The Rock Nursing Unit is a unit that provides a nurse led residential service for older people, 24 hours a day, 7 days per week. I treasure the memories of people I've known there.

Ozanam House and the Rock are both valuable organisations that deserve your support.

Helping Hand

I must tell this story without naming any names, but I am very proud of what I was able to accomplish:

One Christmas, Mary and I went to the Carrigart Hotel to visit the owner, Dermot Walsh. The Carrigart Hotel is a long journey north of Letterkenny. Our son Patrick was going there to teach water safety in the hotel pool. And Dermot Walsh was a great friend.

While there, we saw a party that was "unusual." We were invited to join. It was a group from a regional mental hospital. At that time I was the Chair of the North Western Mental Health Association. Mary was also a member.

When the sing-song started, I was asked to sing a song, and when the piano player introduced me, he said that I was from Ballyshannon. A woman jumped up immediately and said, "I'm from Ballyshannon, and I never get a visitor!" I said, "Well, you will get visitors from now on."

As I got to know that woman, I learned that she had lived in care since she was very young. She had relatives overseas. From other sources, I learned that one of her brothers had died and left a small estate. Through a bit of detective work, I was able to help locate her birth certificate and establish that she had a claim to a small inheritance. Consequently she has been able to live much closer to her family home, enabling her to receive many more visitors over the years.

Injun Joe

Sometimes my ideas have met with resistance...

Comhairle Chontae Dhun na nGall
Donegal County Council
Corporate Health & Safety Advisor
FMS Building County House Lifford

07 April 2009

Mr. Anthony O'Malley Daly
College Street, Ballyshannon
Co. Donegal.

Re: Proposed charity jump off the Aodh Ruadh Bridge, Ballyshannon

Dear Mr. O'Malley Daly,

I am writing to you at the request of Ballyshannon Town Council to urge you to reconsider going ahead with the above event.

My main concern is not regarding the safety of a properly organised event, but that the charity jump could glamorise the notion of jumping among the youth of the area and spotlight the bridge as a venue.

Having spent a little time working with the Foyle Search & Rescue group I am all too aware of the unhappy outcome for many people who jump from bridges and for the families and friends they leave behind.

I would like to commend you for the considerable amount of money that you have raised for charity and I would be happy to discuss this project, or any other you might consider, further with you.

Seamus Hopkins
CHARTERED ENGINEER
CORPORATE HEALTH & SAFETY ADVISOR

I recently received this letter and a cheque made out to the North West Parkinson's Foundation:

Carrickboy,

Ballyshannon,

Co. Donegal

16th November 2012

Dear Anthony,

Find enclosed a draft for €300 which was collected for the Christmas day swim. My apologies for the delay in sorting this out. Overall there was €900 collected for the 3 charities and it is the sign of the times when 5 or 6 years ago we collected over €6000. I am sure every little bit helps no matter how small.

Kind Regards,

Seamus O'Neill

Seamus O' Neill

Other agencies who received cheques from the Christmas Day Swim were The Multiple Sclerosis Society of Ireland and the North West Hospice. The dwindling contributions are, sadly, a sign of the times.

Injun Joe

by Edward Hanna

He married my sister a long time ago
He called himself Anthony
I called him Injun Joe
The best of a friend you could not meet,
If you travelled from the west into the east.

A sailor by trade – fisherman by choice,
He taught me a lot when he lived in our house.
Old sailors never die – fishermen never lie.
No fishing rod in your hand
Unless you are fishing fly by hand,
These words he once said.
But we knew it was all in jest.
For a spinning rod in his hand,
He was the best in the land.

To come from Ballyshannon
And marry in Donegal,
He had to be accepted by one and all.
For if you knew this man,
It was not hard to understand
When Mary and Anthony got married
In the Townawillie townland.
He took me fishing on Lough Eske,
Saying, "Sit down and watch, Cub,
and learn from the best."

Those days of gold
Will never grow old,
And the memories of him
Are sealed within.
Injun Joe, John and Me,
We fished Lough Eske every Saturday
Up and down along the ridge.
Down to Corraber and back to the bridge.

Injun Joe

Heading for Callaghan's Point, we stop at Tommy Ned's.
Daly's confused, he's scratching his head.
Whiskey and beer, chicken and eggs.
Are all in the lunchbox beneath his legs.
"Give me an egg – Give me a beer,
But get me the hell away from here.
Come on John, Do your best!
Get me off number eight!"

The engine is running – Toby's are on
We're trolling along and singing a song
"Off Cape Horn on a winter's morning."
Eggs are all gone and the beer is all down.
Injun Joe gets hooked in a big brown.
"Bog her on!" is the cry.
The line goes out with a merciful roar.
John shouts, "Ed, you're on the oars!
Grab the net and get him in,
If we lose the fish he'll do us in."

Head for home, boys.
We've come to an end,
And all he can think of is fish number ten.
Fishermen come – Fishermen go
For I have fished with the best
Called Injun Joe

Afterword

It's hard to stop writing this book. There are more stories that I'd like to tell, more people that I'd like to remember, or thank, or reminisce with...

And I still have lots of photos. Some are old:

Me, playing cricket in Cyprus, in 1956

And some are new:

John and Mary Hanna, 2012

Maybe I'll write another book, or set up a website. But I'm going to finish this book here and now.

As promised, here are some blank pages for you to paste in the newspaper stories about my next fund-raising activities. But there's something else you could do. You could organise some fund-raisers of your own. They could be for Parkinson's, for asthma, for mental health – you'd have my support and gratitude for those. Or they could be for your own favourite charity.

Organise something! Raise money for a good cause! And paste the newspaper stories in here. You'll have my blessing, whatever it's for.

But whatever you do, don't waste a minute of your life.

Mi Amigo – My Friend – Mo Chara,

Injun Joe

FUND-RAISERS

Injun Joe

FUND-RAISERS

**Look Anthony, John and Edward, we are off to
Lough Eske to spawn.
See you there!**

Merry Christmas and a happy new year 2012

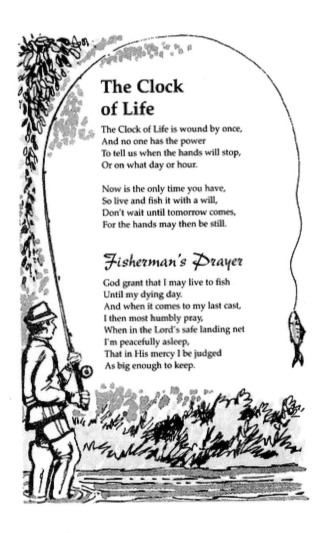

The Clock of Life

The Clock of Life is wound by once,
And no one has the power
To tell us when the hands will stop,
Or on what day or hour.

Now is the only time you have,
So live and fish it with a will,
Don't wait until tomorrow comes,
For the hands may then be still.

Fisherman's Prayer

God grant that I may live to fish
Until my dying day.
And when it comes to my last cast,
I then most humbly pray,
When in the Lord's safe landing net
I'm peacefully asleep,
That in His mercy I be judged
As big enough to keep.